GETTING
YOUR
BEARINGS

GETTING YOUR BEARINGS

Engaging with contemporary theologians

Edited by Philip Duce & Daniel Strange

APOLLOS

APOLLOS (an imprint of Inter-Varsity Press)
38 De Montfort Street, Leicester LE1 7GP, England
Email: ivp@uccf.org.uk
Website: www.ivpbooks.com

First published 2003

British Library Cataloguing in Publication Data
A catalogue record for this book is available from the British Library.

ISBN 0–85111–287–0

Set in Monotype Garamond 11/13pt
Typeset in Great Britain by CRB Associates, Reepham, Norfolk
Printed and bound in Great Britain by Creative Print and Design (Wales),
Ebbw Vale

CONTENTS

FOREWORD

Anyone approaching the study of modern religion and theology for the first time faces three daunting difficulties.

One is the sheer volume of output. The scholars covered in these monographs (John Hick, Wolfhart Pannenberg and Jürgen Moltmann) have all had long and distinguished careers, and all have been prolific authors. It would take many months of intense study to develop a first-hand acquaintance with the full range of their work: more time than any undergraduate can afford.

Allied with this is the difficulty of comprehension. The student is suddenly plunged into an alien new world. When she first pondered taking up the subject she probably imagined that discourse in the world of religion and theology would closely reflect that of the Bible. Instead she finds herself facing a whole new vocabulary and a thought-world much more akin to German idealism than to Christian thought and practice. She finds, too, that these authors often assume an extensive hinterland in history and philosophy. In the case of continental theologians, there is the further hermeneutical barrier that they are being read, for the most part, in translation; and translation involves not only the relatively simple task of finding an equivalent English word for the original German one, but also the much more daunting task of lifting

Moltmann and Pannenberg out of one religious and academic culture into another. The linguistic, conceptual and spiritual distance between an eighteen-year old British student and a sixty-year old German polymath is enormous.

Then there is the difficulty of evaluation. Are these views, so eruditely presented and so lauded by every expert in the field, true? How do they relate to Scripture? Are they consistent with the great doctrines of Christianity? Have they something to teach us, or are they merely to be endured as the latest ravings of modernists and liberals?

There is no substitute for first-hand acquaintance with the work of historic, seminal thinkers. *Ad fontes* ('To the sources!') must remain the motto of all serious students. But unless we are ardent deconstructionists we shall find the introductory studies gathered together in this volume invaluable. They provide indispensable biographical background, point the student to a wide range of secondary literature (much of it in obscure locations), identify the key themes, offer clear exposition and (in varying degrees) guide us in the task of critical evaluation. The selection of authors and topics is close to spot-on. Postmodernism is the matrix within which all of us, from architects to pop-stars, have to develop in the twenty-first century. Jürgen Moltmann and Wolfhart Pannenberg remain the two most influential contemporary continental theologians. John Hick, since the early days of his involvement with *The Myth of God Incarnate*, has been Britain's most provocative religious thinker: the closest we have to a campaigning theologian.

But why should evangelicals read the work of scholars whose thought-world, at first glance, is so distant from our own: even, indeed, so dismissive of it? The question is certainly not super-fluous, if only because these scholars will not return the compliment by reading *our* work. John Hick in his younger days was thoroughly familiar with the world of UCCF, but it is hard to imagine Jürgen Moltmann or Wolfhart Pannenberg reading IVP publications.

For students of religion and theology, the most obvious reason for reading these modern theologians is, of course, utterly utilitarian: this is the syllabus, and if we want to pass exams we have to get through the course. But there is surely more to it than that. For one thing, there is a sound educational reason. No-one can claim to be theologically educated while remaining ignorant of Hick, Moltmann and Pannenberg. There is also the issue of academic integrity. Christian scholarship must be rigorous as well as reverent. That means that we have to engage with views opposed to our own, and if our critical evaluation of them is to have any validity we have to engage them as propounded by their ablest advocates. We cannot lay an honest claim to our own cherished dogmas if we hold them only by dint of never considering the alternatives.

Take, for example, the uniqueness of Christ. No evangelical can ever cease to insist that Christ is the only source of truth, the only fountain of spiritual life and the only way to God. However, we cannot honestly proclaim such a message without facing up to the challenges posed to it by John Hick. Nor can we continue to chant the litany of inerrancy while utterly disregarding the very different views of God's self-disclosure set forth by such scholars as Moltmann and Pannenberg. Even less can we ignore the challenge of postmodernism. We may have an instant sympathy with the view that it is a word in search of a concept, or even with the view that it is itself the very acme of modernism (on the ground that the essence of Cartesianism was not radical certainty but radical doubt): but even so, we cannot take the risk of simply assuming that the world's love-in with postmodernism is either a charming aberration or final, definitive proof of the darkness of the age and the total depravity of the race.

But all this seems very grudging and not very far removed from the idea that we read these moderns only to find antidotes and theological vaccines. There are enormous benefits in interacting with great minds in any field. Even when Hick, Moltmann and Pannenberg don't convince by their answers, they stimulate and enrich by the questions they throw into our intellectual treasury. The very fact that their standpoint differs so radically from our own is an advantage. Speaking a different language from the evangelical, working to different norms and looking over their shoulders to a different God (or at least a God differently conceived), they move theology into new areas of exploration and research. At first, everything in the forward movement is confused and tentative, but gradually new, secure conclusions emerge. Thanks to Moltmann, we now have a different perspective on the doctrine of divine passibility. Pannenberg has warranted a change in our view of history, arguing that rather than outlawing such singularities as the resurrection it is defined by them; and arguing, too, that we must understand past and present in the light of the fulfilled future. And for all that he infuriates by his almost single-issue approach to theology, John Hick has forced us to recognize the truth-content of other religions and to seek explanations for this in the facts of general revelation, shared scriptures (common to Jews, Christians and Muslims) and the presence of the Logos within every human being (John 1:4, 5, 9).

Over postmodernism one hesitates. Has it taught us anything? But no matter how confident we may be that there is Truth, that Truth is one and that Truth is incarnate in Jesus, it is salutary to be part of a generation immersed in the notion of the provisionality of its own thought. The paradox is that the age of postmodernism is also the age of demonic certainty, as represented by Ulster's paramilitaries and Jerusalem's suicide-bombers.

Two final words of caution. First, the student of religion and theology cannot afford to ignore the apostle Paul's warning, 'Be on your guard' (1 Corinthians 16:13). If we seek not only to swot up theology but to assimilate it for our own personal enrichment, we need lavish supplies of spiritual discernment. This is why all study (and not only of theology, of course!) must be a matter of constant prayer. If critical evaluation is our concern, then what matters supremely is the judgment of the greatest critic of all: the Holy Spirit. To know that, we must keep in step with him.

Lastly, it would be calamitous if our readings in religion and theology were limited to the moderns. One of the curses of current academic life is the preoccupation with the 'recent'. We need a much longer historical perspective than the last ten or twenty years. Hick, Moltmann and Pannenberg will not offer a complete theological education. To achieve that, we need to supplement them with large doses of the great doctors of the church: Athanasius, Augustine, Anselm, Luther and Calvin. We also need to immerse ourselves in the greatest of the evanglical moderns, B. B. Warfield.

I warmly commend this collection of introductory essays. May they indeed enable today's novices to find their bearings; and may these novices quickly become giants.

Donald Macleod
Edinburgh, July 2002

EDITORS' PREFACE

From our own experience of what might be called 'theology according to the academy', at both undergraduate and post-graduate levels, we can understand the sentiments of those who doubt that liberal theologians have given us any significant insights into the doctrinal teachings of Scripture that are not already to be found in the work of evangelicals.

We are also aware of Donald Macleod's uncomfortable and yet perceptive observation, from the perspective of the Reformed faith, that the tragedy of the last hundred years has been that the church has habitually entrusted theological education to those with no higher qualification than that of common grace, and that, despite the real benefits of such grace, there is, when everything is stripped away, the 'absurd situation in which the Seed of the Serpent purports to be feeding the Seed of the Woman, notwithstanding that there is a God-ordained enmity between the two' (*Behold Your God* [Fearn: Christian Focus, 1995], p. 166).

Why then are we presenting these essays, which engage with various theologians and philosophers who, from the perspective of evangelical orthodoxy, range from the ambiguously heterodox to the clearly heretical? Why bother? Why not just leave them to it and get on with positive theological construction built on orthodox presuppositions? We suggest three reasons.

First, theology, wherever it is done, and wherever we think it should be done, is not the privilege of heterodoxy, liberalism or heresy. Those who are orthodox need to reclaim the ground for biblical truth in the academy as well as in the church, and so we must carefully and courteously (but with determination) listen to, engage with, and if necessary refute, those who deviate from the 'pattern of sound teaching'. Some of the subjects of these essays are not known for their perspicuity, but this does not mean that we should just give up, and not bother to listen to what they have to say. Such a response would be in direct opposition to the rule of love, let alone a weak apologetic and evangelistic strategy. While we may disagree profoundly with their own conclusions, the subjects of these essays do ask profound questions about theological method, epistemology, revelation, God, humanity and redemption. These questions demand a proper response.

Second, whether we like it or not, there are many evangelical students in universities and colleges who often have to engage with the likes of Moltmann, Pannenberg, Hick and Cupitt. Discovering these thinkers for the first time can be a bewildering experience, and a real danger is loss of critical discernment. This can lead down three wrong paths: wholesale embrace, wholesale rejection or just plain ignorance ('we know these people are wrong, but we don't know why').

Third, while it is an admittedly ambitious aim, we should be keen to nurture and encourage the next generation of evangelical theologians. We would contend that far from being sealed in a theological ghetto, the greatest evangelical theologians have achieved 'greatness' under God not only because they have been saturated in the Bible and historic orthodoxy, but also because they have been well-versed in a wide range of theological discourse, along with insight into the various theological trends of their day.

Hence, the essays collected here deal with some important and influential contemporary figures. The discussion is difficult at times, and makes demands on the reader, but (we would argue) this reflects the subjects themselves.

John Hick's work on religious pluralism is widely known. Christopher Sinkinson's engagement with Hick's long and controversial career concludes with an exclusive: a transcription of a dialogue with Hick himself.

Jürgen Moltmann's influential contribution to theology began with *Theology of Hope* (1964), and has extended beyond Germany and the West to the developing world. Stephen Williams offers a critical introduction to Moltmann's earlier, and arguably most important, works.

Wolfhart Pannenberg's three-volume *Systematic Theology* has been hailed as a major synthesis, joining those of Barth, Tillich and Rahner. Pannenberg is difficult, and to engage with him, one needs first to understand him. Timothy Bradshaw expounds the main themes of Pannenberg's trinitarian theology.

In the final essay – a challenging *tour de force*, which goes where few evangelicals have gone before – Mark Elliott moves beyond a predictable 'primer on postmodernism' to survey a wide variety of contributions and responses, including the non-realism of Don Cupitt and the 'radical orthodoxy' of John Milbank.

All of these essays were originally published as monographs by the Religious and Theological Studies Fellowship (part of the Universities and Colleges Christian Fellowship and the International Fellowship of Evangelical Students). Through collaboration between the RTSF and Inter-Varsity Press we are now pleased to present the essays, suitably updated, revised and edited, in this new format. This is the second such collection: the first was *Keeping your Balance: Approaching religious and theological studies* (Apollos, 2001). Once again, we are grateful to Elizabeth Fraser and to the authors for revising their mongraphs and permission to include them. We thank Donald Macleod for writing the Foreword, and commend the collection to students in the hope that here they will find help in 'getting their bearings' on the wider theological landscape.

Philip Duce
Daniel Strange
Leicester, 2002

1. JOHN HICK: RELIGION FOR THE MODERN WORLD?

Christopher Sinkinson

Chris Sinkinson is *minister of an evangelical church near Salisbury. He has a PhD in theology from Bristol University and is the author of* The Universe of Faiths: a Critical Study of John Hick's Religious Pluralism *(Carlisle: Paternoster, 2001).*

Introduction

John Hick has written on many different subjects in philosophy and theology during the course of his long and controversial career. He has lectured around the world and appeared on television debates. His view of how the religions of the world relate to each other chimes in well with the popular notions of contemporary culture. This essay will provide an introduction to what I consider to be his most significant arguments and contributions to religious studies. My aim is to provide a starting point for further reading, reflection and consideration of the crucial issues Hick has placed firmly on the agenda of theology and religious studies.

In order to achieve this end, the essay focuses on John Hick's understanding of the relationship between Christianity and the world religions. After a brief outline of John Hick's career there will be a short description of four important themes: faith, evil, salvation and the incarnation. Only then will we engage in a sustained account of Hick's most influential suggestion concerning the relationship between religions. The essay has a historical flavour as we try to chart the various developments in his work over the years. This sense of history will help us understand why he came to adopt the position he did. Hick's personal journey makes interesting reading and I have supplemented this account with questions that I put to him shortly before his eightieth birthday in January 2002.

Biographical sketch

Early years (1922–1956)
John Harwood Hick was born on 20 January 1922 in Scarborough, Yorkshire. His childhood was not marked with any great interest in religion. Indeed, he found the parish church his family attended a matter of 'infinite boredom'.[1] However, as a child he did meet the founder of the Pentecostal Church, George Jeffreys, and attributes a significant spiritual experience to the meeting.[2] His only encounter with alternative religious beliefs prior to university was a brief attraction to theosophy.[3]

Hick initially read law at Hull University and during his first year 'underwent a spiritual conversion' and 'became a Christian of a strongly evangelical and indeed fundamentalist kind'.[4] This conversion experience involved his support of the Inter-Varsity Fellowship Christian Union and, through it, his identification with 'Calvinist orthodoxy of an extremely conservative kind'.[5] Hick had come to believe in the inerrancy of Scripture, the virgin birth and the literal incarnation of Christ.

Hick's interest in religious belief had now been awakened and, in 1940, he began to study philosophy at Edinburgh University. It was here that his disillusionment with evangelicalism began. The war interrupted his studies and, as a conscientious objector, Hick served with the Friends Ambulance Unit. Consequently, it was not until 1948 that he graduated from Edinburgh University with a First in philosophy.

He did not rejoin the CU after the war as he began to feel that it was too rigid and narrow-minded in outlook. As one example, he felt that some members were intellectually dishonest in their attempts to reconcile the opening chapters of Genesis with contemporary scientific thought.

Hick completed a doctorate at Oriel College, Oxford, under H. H. Price. The area of his research lay in the philosophy of religion and, in particular, the nature of religious faith. His thesis was later adapted and published as his first book. However, in the immediate future his career did not lie in academia. After the completion of his thesis, Hick trained for ordination into the English Presbyterian Church (URC). His first pastoral ministry was at Belford Presbyterian Church where he served from 1953 until 1956. During this time he married Hazel Bowers.

Before we consider the next stage in Hick's life we may highlight two notable aspects of this stage. First, Hick was frustrated by what he considered a lack of intellectual depth in many evangelical friends. They seemed unwilling to engage critically with difficult issues. Secondly, we may note that Hick's major strength and interest lay in philosophy rather than theology.[6] This explains why much of our study will involve a consideration of philosophical issues and the theoretical foundations of Christian belief.

The developing philosopher (1956–1967)

In 1956 Hick was appointed Assistant Professor at Cornell University and so began his academic career. During this time he developed his doctoral thesis and published it as the book *Faith and Knowledge*.[7] In this work Hick considered the problem of religious epistemology: how we come to know what we know.

He moved to Princeton Theological Seminary in 1959 and into a theological storm. He wished to transfer his ministerial credentials from the English Presbyterian Church to the American Church and this provoked a serious dispute within the Presbyterian Church. Technically, Hick's position at Princeton and in the Presbyterian Church assumed adherence to the 1647 Westminster Confession of Faith. When questioned about his position on the Confession he expressed his doubts concerning 'the six-day creation of the world, the predestination of many to eternal hell, the verbal inspiration of the Bible, and the virgin birth of Jesus'.[8] His liberal stance, particularly on the virgin birth, led to a number of the ministers and elders preventing transferral of his ministerial membership. The dispute was finally settled at a national level with the Synod ruling in his favour. Clearly, Hick had departed from evangelicalism but was not yet the radical he was to become. While he did question the historicity of the virgin birth, he held an orthodox view of the incarnation.[9]

Hick returned to England in 1963 and lectured at Cambridge University. During this time he published his second major work, *Evil and the God of Love*.[10] This book involves a sustained treatment of various Christian attempts to reconcile the existence of a good God with the reality of evil and suffering in the world.

During this stage Hick was concerned with the defence of Christianity from various critiques levelled against it. He defended the rationality of religious faith as a form of knowledge. In particular, he responded to charges levelled at Christianity from the Positivist movement which denied the meaningfulness of religious language. Hick also reflected on the perplexing problem of evil in the world. In answer to this, he reinstated an ancient and unorthodox theodicy which included the universalist affirmation that God will eventually bring all people into eternal life.

Encountering pluralism (1967–1972)

In 1967 Hick took up the H. G. Wood Professorship at Birmingham University and began a phase that would lead to a revolution in his thinking. The most powerful challenge to his theology came not from academic circles but from the City of Birmingham itself. Birmingham had a large, multi-faith community, including substantial numbers of Muslims, Sikhs and Hindus, along with the more well-established Jewish community. Hick became aware of the other major world religions in a way he had never done before. This awareness came largely as a result of his involvement with an inter-religious movement set up in Birmingham to combat racism and in particular the ugly prejudice of the National Front. Hick worked alongside those of other faiths and in so doing was challenged by the faith that they embodied. He writes: 'Thus it was not so much new thoughts as new experiences that drew me, as a philosopher, into the issues of religious pluralism, and as a Christian into inter-faith dialogue.'[11] These new experiences led to a significant shift in his thinking. Hick had already come to believe in universalism and had felt that adherents of other religions had qualities sometimes missing in fellow Christians. The question then arose: how can only one religion be true?

In 1970 Hick began work on a major book that would mark a departure from his previous studies. This would be an attempt to explore conceptions of the future and the afterlife with reference to Hinduism, Buddhism and Humanism along with Christianity. No longer would his philosophy be pursued in isolation from the thinking of the various world religions. Furthermore, he wrote a number of shorter pieces designed to explore the possibility that Christianity was not the one true religion, nor even necessarily a religion superior to any others.

The theological revolution (1973 onwards)

Hick's shorter works on Christianity and other religions were compiled in the 1973 publication *God and the Universe of Faiths*.[12] For reasons already outlined, Hick had come to believe that Christianity was not the one true religion to the exclusion of all others. In this book Hick argued that Christianity needed to undergo a revolution in both its self-understanding and its understanding of other religions. According to this revolution, Christianity should regard itself not as the one true way to God but as one option among many available in the world today.

Contributing to this goal, Hick continued research on his next major work, published in 1976 as *Death and Eternal Life*.[13] His research required extensive trips to the East including India (1970–71, 1974, 1975–76) and Sri Lanka (1974) during which he developed his understanding of Eastern religions.

Perhaps the most controversial book with which Hick's name has ever been associated is one that he did not actually write. In 1977 Hick contributed to and edited *The Myth of God Incarnate*.[14] This symposium brought together a collection of radical biblical, historical and philosophical studies. Essentially, the contributors argued that historical studies do not substantiate the claim that Jesus was or even considered himself to be the second person of the Trinity, God the Son incarnate. Furthermore, the source of this belief is derived more from Near Eastern mythology and Greek philosophy than from biblical traditions. Hick's contribution to the collection used the critical work of other contributors to dismiss the orthodox view of the incarnation. He then used this work as a basis on which to substantiate his claim that Christianity had no absolute or superior status among the world religions.

In 1982 Hick moved to Claremont Graduate School in California as Danforth Professor of the Philosophy of Religion, and he remained there until his retirement in 1993. During this period Hick refined and developed his thesis on the world religions, culminating in his presentation of the Gifford Lectures in 1986. These were published as his major work on the theology of religions: *An Interpretation of Religion*.[15] The essential point of Hick's thesis is that all the major world religions represent diverse human responses to the same ultimate, transcendent reality. He has continued to develop this argument and respond to its critiques. Since his retirement, Hick has remained a vigorous defender and promoter of this pluralist position in writings and lectures throughout the world.

Philosophy of religion

What is faith?

In order to understand and respond to Hick's pluralist proposal, we must first understand his theory of religious knowledge. It is important to realize that John Hick is primarily a philosopher rather than a theologian and this has an important bearing on his method. His first published book discussed the nature of knowledge and how we come to have religious belief. While his position on many things has developed greatly, there is a stable core running through his work.

According to Hick, all knowledge involves interpretation.[16] Faith is not some kind of special knowledge. In order to understand this we may consider the use he makes of the work of the Austrian philosopher Ludwig Wittgenstein (1889–1951). Wittgenstein's work drew Hick's attention to the way in which we interpret pictures. You may know of the duck–rabbit picture in which the same line drawing when looked at in one way can be seen as a duck but when looked at in another way can be seen as a rabbit. Wittgenstein describes this experience 'seeing-as'. We see the picture as a duck or as a rabbit. In itself, the picture is ambiguous, being open to either interpretation. Similarly, suggests Hick, two people may see the same thing in very different ways. A geologist may see an unusual rock formation where an Aborigine sees a sacred place. Hick describes this activity of the human mind 'experiencing-as'.

Consequently, there are different ways in which we may experience the world around us. It all depends on the interpretation we bring to bear upon it. Of course, not just any interpretation will do. Parameters exist for the breadth of possible interpretations. This is particularly obvious at the level of our knowledge of the world. You may wish to interpret the lamp-post in the pavement as a large, soft marshmallow, but if you walk into it, then reality will have a habit of modifying your interpretation. Regarding natural knowledge, there is the least degree of ambiguity and, correspondingly, the greatest extent of agreement among people about how we should interpret the world.

However, there are other levels of knowledge that involve greater ambiguity. In the area of moral judgment and matters of taste there is still some agreement but there is also considerable diversity.

The ambiguity is at its greatest when we turn to religious knowledge. Religious faith involves a total interpretation of the universe. Hick argues that the universe, in itself, is ambiguous. Atheists may be rational people who justify their beliefs by pointing out that they cannot see God, that the existence of evil in the world suggests that there probably is no God and that there are alternative explanations of the universe that do not require belief in the existence of God. Yet convinced believers point to the apparent order of the universe, our recognition of evil in the world and the historical evidences for God's intervention in the world as justification for a religious interpretation of the universe. The universe remains ambiguous in this respect because no final, decisive proof may be produced one way or the other.

An important aspect of this conception of faith is its emphasis on human free-will. The theological reason why God allows the universe to be ambiguous is because he wishes to safeguard the freedom of human beings to believe or not believe in him. To give absolute proofs or demonstration of his existence would coerce people to believe in him and compromise their freedom to decide. Hick describes God as 'hiding' himself from humanity, 'leaving us the freedom to recognize or fail to recognize his dealings with us'.[17]

So why is one rational person a Christian and another rational person an atheist? According to Hick, the determining factor is personal experience. Recalling the duck–rabbit picture, some people see the universe one way, others see it differently.

In recent work Hick develops his theory of knowledge through the work of the famous German thinker Immanuel Kant (1724–1804).[18] Hick borrows one major insight from Kant's thought and uses it to develop his own model of religious faith. The insight is Kant's distinction between the world as we know it and the world as it really is. We cannot know directly the world as it really is (the noumenal world). Our experience of the world is conditioned by the structures of our mind that order the world in a particular way (the phenomenal world). The result is that we must be careful to distinguish between things as we know them and things as they really are in themselves. Hick applies this distinction to religion. God is beyond our immediate knowledge. All we can know are the influences of this divine reality as we interpret them. According to Kant, the structures of our mind are like a pair of spectacles through which we view the world. The spectacles do distort the real world so that we can make sense of it, but without the spectacles we can make no sense of the world at all. For Hick, faith functions in a similar way: through faith we interpret the otherwise unknowable divine reality, shaping it into a form we can at least begin to understand.

Hick's description of faith has much to commend it. It emphasizes the personal nature of faith as a subjective response to the world. Those who have faith are not required to provide lengthy philosophical reasons for their beliefs. They are justified in having faith through personal experience. This account of faith also raises a number of important questions. One problem lies in the apparent arbitrary nature of religious belief. How can one decide which beliefs are true and which are false? Personal, subjective experience can be so unreliable in other spheres that one has reason to be sceptical of beliefs based solely on such experience. Hick suggests a test for the truth of religious beliefs. We may remember that in the case of natural knowledge it is not possible to believe as we choose. If we interpret the lamp-post as a marshmallow and walk into it, then we will stand (or fall!) corrected by the experience. One cannot believe anything and everything about the natural order of the world. Analogously, religious beliefs may be tested by their practical fruits in helping us to order our lives. This is a pragmatic test. Beliefs lead to behaviour and disastrous behaviour probably signifies false beliefs. By this standard, some religious beliefs may be dismissed as false.

The problem of evil

It is often argued that the perfect design, order, purpose and beauty of the world provide grounds for belief in a good creator God. However, the argument has another side. The imperfection, disorder, extent of purposeless suffering, evil, cruelty and pain provide grounds for disbelief that such a God could exist. The force of the charge is felt particularly in Christian theology because of the kind of God he is understood to be. If God is both omnipotent, able to do anything, and all loving, willing the best for everyone, then the existence of evil discredits either God's power to remove the evil or God's love towards his creatures.

Evil and the God of Love is Hick's attempt to outline how Christian belief in God may remain rational in the face of evil. First published in 1966, the basic thesis of the book remains a part of Hick's theology to this day. He describes the work as a 'critical study of the two responses to the problem of evil that have been developed within Christian thought, and an attempt to formulate a theodicy for today'.[19] The first response is the classical theodicy that has been dominant in the history of Christian theology. The second response has been somewhat marginal in the West until recent times, but Hick seeks to build his own theodicy upon it.

The classical theodicy finds its roots in the sophisticated thought of St Augustine and is also developed by the reformer

John Calvin. According to Augustine, God made all things good. Therefore, evil was not created by God and cannot exist in its own right at all. Hence, evil is 'the corruption of a good substance'.[20] Evil describes something good that has gone wrong. As evil does not originate in God, it must originate in the free-will of his creatures. Augustine describes some angels as the first to use their free-will to oppose God and, consequently, to 'fall' from heaven. This fall is then paralleled in the choice of the first humans to disobey God. So evil originated in free choice, both angelic and human. Hick describes this 'creation-fall-redemption' narrative as a mythology. According to the mythology evil exists in the world today as humans are 'participating in the effects of their first parents' rebellion against their Maker'.[21] However, God has taken the initiative in repairing the damage by sending his son to make atonement for sinful humanity on the cross. As a result, it is possible for God to rescue some from the consequences of the fall through the work of Christ on their behalf. The classical account declares God innocent as regards the cause of evil, while placing full responsibility on the shoulders of angels and humans. The problem of evil in the world is the result of God permitting humanity (and angels) the exercise of their weak will.

Hick argues that this account is incoherent in two ways. Firstly, he questions how a perfect creation could include beings who choose to sin. Hick distinguishes between the freedom to choose to sin and the actual choice to sin: 'If the angels are finitely perfect, then even though they are in some important sense free to sin, they will never in fact do so.'[22] Only a flawed created being would make the seriously unwise and immoral choice to sin. Therefore, God remains culpable for a flawed creation and the existence of sin. The second incoherence that Hick points out concerns a further feature of Augustinian and Calvinist theology. According to the classical picture, nothing occurs outside of God's power. Human beings remain unable to believe in God without him enabling them to do so. The doctrine that flows from this logic (as well as from certain passages in the Bible and from Christian experience) is that of predestination. God must predestine in advance all that will occur and in particular who will come to repentance and faith and who will be eternally lost. Furthermore,

God must have predestined the initial fall of both angels and humans. Hick finds this notion objectionable. The picture of salvation and damnation as the result of divine decree represents 'a failure to think of God and of his attitudes to mankind in fully personal and agapeistic terms'.[23]

Irenaeus (130–202 AD) pursued a different approach to the problem of evil. He distinguished between humanity being created in the 'image' of God and humanity in the 'likeness' of God.[24] Because we are made in the image of God, we have a special status and potential in God's creation. However, we are called to become like God. Through our struggle against sin and evil we are involved in a gradual movement toward the likeness of God. Adam and Eve were not made perfect in their creation. Irenaeus described Adam and Eve as being made like children in the Garden of Eden. There was no 'fall' from initial perfection. Rather sin involved the recognition of weakness, finitude and imperfection. From this state of infancy Adam and Eve were called to grow into the likeness of God. According to this picture, the 'fall' is a necessary step towards God rather than a catastrophic falling out of favour with God.

Evil and suffering are understood very differently in the light of this theology. Rather than being punishments, the evils of the world become the means by which God enables us to grow and overcome sin. Rather than representing separation from God, Irenaeus sees the evils of the world as 'a divinely appointed environment for man's development towards the perfection that represents the fulfilment of God's good purpose for him'.[25]

This form of theodicy had been used by the German theologian Friedrich Schleiermacher (1768–1834)[26] and Hick develops it further still. According to Hick's version of this 'soul-making' theodicy, 'man, created as a personal being in the image of God, is only the raw material for a further and more difficult stage of God's creative work'.[27] God's creative work involves the permission of evil and suffering in order to prompt growth toward the likeness of God. The Augustinian theodicy 'looks back' to a fall from grace in order to explain the existence of evil. The Irenean theodicy 'looks ahead' to a time when humanity will, through suffering and partly because of suffering, reach perfection.

There is an obvious objection to this kind of theodicy. The apparent excessive quantity of evil in the world and its indiscriminate infliction on people does not fit well with its supposed function. There simply seems to be too much evil for it to be understood in this way and it is inflicted on good and bad alike. The teacher of Ecclesiastes notes how he has seen 'a righteous man perishing in his righteousness,/and a wicked man living long in his wickedness' (Ecclesiastes 7:15). One would think that the wicked people of the world are more in need of the corrective qualities of suffering than the many innocent people who suffer so much. It is at this point in the argument that Hick is willing to appeal to mystery. This is the point at which speculations must end. The rational mind cannot penetrate the profound mystery of awful human suffering. This may remind us of a key theme in Hick's epistemology: the ambiguity of the universe. No explanation can be entirely water-tight and everyone remains intellectually free to make up their own minds about the plausibility of this explanation.

The attraction of this theodicy lies in the rejection of what might be seen as a vindictive image of God central to the classical position. Evil in the world does not imply that God either punishes people through suffering or abandons them to suffering. According to this model, suffering is not a form of punishment but serves an ultimately good purpose in human development. Furthermore, the position does not depend on the complex notions of predestination and a historical fall. According to Hick, God does not overrule human freedom but respects it as the means through which human beings make genuine choices in the face of suffering.

Salvation and the afterlife
Hick's 1976 *Death and Eternal Life* marks a departure from his earlier major works. His work on faith and evil embodied a distinctively Christian approach to the problems. In this volume, Hick puts into practice conclusions reached in *God and the Universe of Faiths* and sets out to produce a 'global' theology of death. His attempt to explore the nature of death in global perspective involves a survey and assimilation of insights from existentialist

philosophy, parapsychology, humanism and some of the major world religions.

The questions of what death is and what happens after we die are not often the subject of discussion, but Hick tackles them in a characteristically straightforward way. First, as regards the general question of what happens after we die, Hick shows that no philosophical arguments can be formulated that categorically deny the possibility of continued existence. Furthermore, the insights of certain, admittedly fringe, studies in medicine and human physiology provide positive evidence in favour of the possibility (for example, there are many accounts of experiences from those who have reawakened after being pronounced clinically dead). Not only are there no findings that rule out the possibility, but the religious faith of the vast majority of humanity depends on the truth of a belief in some form of continued existence after death. Hick disputes the idea that belief in an afterlife may be dispensed with while leaving the core of religious beliefs intact. Most religious belief-systems are rendered incoherent without this truth claim.

We have already seen that Hick believes in a universal salvation of humanity. To justify this claim Hick makes some use of evidence from the New Testament and the work of the Swiss theologian Karl Barth (1886–1968).[28] Hick rejects the notion of hell as a 'morally intolerable' doctrine.[29] The primary truth claim of Christianity concerning the afterlife is the optimism that the self will eventually achieve a state of eternal bliss called heaven. Hick believes that the idea of a punishment or hell is a much less significant image and outweighed by the positive vision of a heavenly bliss. The resurrection of the body is the mythological picture given of this in Christian thought.

The worldviews of Eastern religions can cast further light on these conclusions. According to Hick, reincarnation, while not a Christian belief, is compatible with Christianity.[30] The core thought underlying the pictures of death in both Eastern and Western religions is that existence will be continued after death. The matter of dispute lies not in whether this will occur but where it will happen.[31] Hick finds an answer to this question in an image that draws upon both streams of religious thought. Essentially,

Hick's description of the process that occurs after death is a progression of the person through further worlds in which he or she will have continued opportunity to achieve the goal of moral and spiritual perfection. Reincarnation and resurrection are both compatible mythological ways of describing this future process. This hypothesis then lends substance to his theodicy and helps him answer the objection we have already noted. If suffering is the means by which God enables us to develop, then what of the many who meet with premature death? Consider children who died at Auschwitz with little or no opportunity to develop in this way. Death does not come to all at equal stages of development. Perhaps no-one dies in a fit state to enter God's presence. The postulation of further worlds provides the basis for believing that post-mortem development is possible.

Hick makes two important qualifications to this integration of resurrection and reincarnation. First, he distinguishes between the ultimate state, or last things, to which we are headed (eschatology) and the penultimate state between death and this fulfilment (pareschatology). Both of these states are pictured in various mythological ways by the different world religions. However, according to Hick it is only the second that is an appropriate subject of speculation. This is because the penultimate state is more proximate to our current experience. Being closer to us chronologically, it may bear more relation to existence as we know it. However, the final state lies far beyond our rational grasp and, though pictured in various ways by the world religions, is not open to philosophical analysis. This is an important qualification because it allows that while religions may have absolutely different pictures of what the ultimate destiny of humanity is, these images cannot be held to contradict the conceptions of other religions because they are not susceptible to that kind of rational analysis.

The second qualification to this integration of resurrection and reincarnation has since been dispensed with by Hick. This is the claim he makes in *Death and Eternal Life* that the self really does exist. Some forms of Buddhist and Hindu thinking deny that there is a true self and, furthermore, perceive the concept of being an individual as one of the very notions that prevents our release from suffering in the process of reincarnation. According to these ways of thinking, the ultimate state is not a matter of individuals enjoying the company of a God distinct from them. Instead, the final state lies in the individual being absorbed into the ultimate reality. Consequently, at this stage in his writing Hick sides with one tradition of Hindu thought against another in retaining belief in the ultimate reality of the self and distinction from the personal God.[32] In his later statement of the pluralist hypothesis this divisive point is dropped.

Hick's theology of death is a genuine example of an attempt at theology in inter-religious perspective. Rather than pursuing his theme in the context of one religion alone, as is most often done, and relying on certain principles of authority provided within that tradition alone (for the Christian that is the authority of the church, councils, leaders or the Bible), Hick takes up the challenge to produce a truly pluralist theology. Hence, underlying this work and all Hick's later work is a basic assumption about the nature of religion. Hick specifies this assumption at the outset of *Death and Eternal Life*:

> It is even possible ... to see the major world religions as pointing convergingly towards a common conception of the eschaton, the final and eternal state, although with partly different expectations concerning the pareschaton ...[33]

The philosophical basis for this assumption will be outlined later but we will now turn to another major theme in Hick's philosophy of religion.

Who was Jesus?

One of Hick's first published articles was a critique of the Christology that had been put forward by D. M. Baillie in a 1948 publication. The thrust of Hick's criticism was that Baillie had failed to provide a Christology that fully reflected the historic position of the church represented in the creeds. Less than twenty years later, Hick came to believe that Baillie had been right all along.

The shift in Hick's position occurred during his first real exposure to the diversity of the world's religions. This encounter

raised the profound question: how are these religions related to
God and to Christianity? If Jesus is the unique incarnation of God
on earth, then, at best, this relegates other religions to being
temporary movements awaiting fulfilment in Christ or, at worst,
human perversions blinding people to the truth of Christ as God's
sole means of salvation. Either way, Hick felt that the incarnation
created a sense of Christian superiority over other religions. The
dilemma of inter-faith relations provided the impetus in Hick's
search for a new Christology.

Along with the challenge of other religions, Hick also recognized that some biblical studies, in particular higher criticism, were
casting doubt on the possibility of deriving the incarnation from
the New Testament. Hick's attraction to these developments
eventually led to his editing the collection of essays published in
1977, *The Myth of God Incarnate*. While the essays represented a
diversity of opinions, the common theme of the collection cast
doubt on the possibility that Jesus was God incarnate in any literal
sense. The consensus seemed to be that Jesus did not understand
himself in that way and that the source of the doctrine lay more in
Near Eastern mythologies and Greek philosophy than in the
Bible.

Hick's basic problem with the incarnation was that it attempted
to describe the identity of Jesus as of one substance with God.
This notion of 'substance' was tied to a particular Greek thought-
world and meaningless in both the worldview of the Bible and of
today. In particular, Hick doubted whether the doctrine could ever
be stated in a way that would stand up to philosophical analysis.
He questioned how it could be possible that one, historical,
particular, limited, fallible human can also be the transcendent,
universal, infinite, perfect, divine being. For example, if one
affirms that Jesus was limited in knowledge or power (as the
Gospels might suggest at certain points), then it seems to follow
that he cannot be the same individual as the all-knowing
(omniscient) and all-powerful (omnipotent) God. Or, if one
affirms that Jesus was omniscient and omnipotent, then it seems
questionable that Jesus was ever truly human. According to Hick,
affirming the identity of God and Christ is like affirming the
existence of a square circle. It is a meaningless description.

Hick sought to describe Christology in terms of relationship rather than substance. His first attempt to do this is to be found in *God and the Universe of Faiths*.[34] Here Hick described the traditional view of Jesus being God incarnate as a 'static' concept: an identification of a particular person with a particular divine being. In contrast, he argued for a 'dynamic' description of the incarnation.[35] The incarnation is not a fact about Jesus and God but a description of an activity in which both Jesus and God were engaged. Jesus incarnated the love of God in his activity. His will was so perfectly matched to that of God that he made it possible to affirm that what Jesus willed, God willed. When his disciples were in his presence they felt as if in the very presence of God.

Hick's Christology developed further still in the course of his encounter with the world religions. Even the modest description of the incarnation in *God and the Universe of Faiths* is in danger of absolutizing the status of the historical Jesus to the detriment of other religions. Consequently, Hick's contemporary Christology must be understood in the context of his attempt to do theology in the light of the teachings of the world religions. Jesus is not to be understood in a unique way, but as one of a number of special people who have appeared in the history of religions. Such 'saints' include the Buddha, Zarathustra, Isaiah, Jesus, Mohammed and Guru Nanak. Had Jesus gone East, Hick contends that he would have been understood as an avatar.

In order to answer the question 'Who was Jesus?', Hick urges us to strip away later accreations and developments to see once more the figure behind the myths. Here, Hick believes that we find someone 'intensely and overwhelmingly conscious of the reality of God. He was a man of God, living in the unseen presence of God. He was so powerfully God-conscious that his life vibrated, as it were, to the divine life; and as a result his hands could heal the sick ...'[36] According to Hick, Jesus was not the second person of the Trinity, God the Son incarnate, in any literal sense. The difference between Jesus and other people is the degree to which he incarnated a consciousness of God possible in us all.[37]

Hick has been concerned with two aspects of Christology. Firstly, he has reassessed the identity of Jesus in the light of the world religions. He claims that believing the historical Jesus to have an absolute or supreme status is necessarily to devalue other religions. Secondly, he has attempted to produce an account of Jesus that is acceptable and meaningful in terms of contemporary thought. To do this he has responded to certain strands of biblical criticism and philosophical thought. Consequently, Hick is genuinely concerned to produce a defence of Christian belief in the light of these major issues. However, one may argue that this defence so distorts the content of that belief that it is no longer clearly Christian.

Religious pluralism

The world's religions
The expression 'religious pluralism' may refer to two different things. On the one hand, it may simply be a description of an observed state of affairs. In this sense, contemporary British society is marked by pluralism simply by virtue of the plurality of religious traditions, beliefs and values held by its population. On the other hand, it may refer to a specific philosophical position, such as that of John Hick. Hick's encounter with pluralism led him to question fundamental Christian convictions. We have seen how, by the 1960s, Hick had become doubtful about a number of Christian beliefs, such as the virgin birth, but none the less believed that Christianity held the normative, highest form of God's revelation to humanity. Pluralism challenged that conviction: 'If what Christianity says is true, must not what all other world religions say be in varying degrees false?'[38] Hick has never doubted that the exclusivist position can be a logical one to hold, but it did seem to him the height of arrogance. The primary problem for him arose through his experience of other religions. This led him to believe that adherents were being transformed for the better through their own belief-systems and that the great variety of religious practices conducted in these religions seemed to share a common structure. Through inter-religious relationships, activities and worship Hick came to be convinced that religions were not to be understood as mutually exclusive entities or as in permanent tension with each other. The major shift in his

position came with his reappraisal of the incarnation and subsequent Copernican revolution in his theology.

The Copernican revolution

Hick's new understanding of the relationship between Christianity and the world religions was put forward in *God and the Universe of Faiths*. He argued that a 'Copernican' revolution was required in Christian self-understanding.

Before Copernicus (a scientist of the sixteenth century), the dominant model for describing the universe pictured the earth at the centre, with the sun, planets and stars revolving around it. This became increasingly difficult to maintain in the light of later discoveries in astronomy. In order to maintain the Ptolemaic picture of the universe, 'epicycles' were introduced to explain the odd behaviour in the observed movement of the planets. Copernicus disputed this model entirely and instead described the sun as the centre of the universe with the earth, along with the other planets, revolving around it. When initially suggested, this caused a great controversy in the church as the new theory seemed to have implications for religious belief. The church had conceived the earth and humanity to have been central in God's creation, and so to displace the position of the earth somehow seemed to displace humanity from its important place in the creation.[39]

Hick uses this historic event as a picture of another, at least as important, controversy in the life of the church. In the later stages of the early church until modern times, Hick suggests, Christians had believed that outside of Christianity there was no salvation and only a dim knowledge of God. This belief had existed largely without challenge in a part of the world dominated by Christianity. However, the modern period has been marked by a new awareness of the global community in which we exist and the variety of religious beliefs held by human beings. The awareness that the great majority of humanity believe in something other than Christ and show little sign of changing their minds presents a challenge to the belief that Christianity is the exclusively true religion. The older, exclusivist, position is analogous to the Ptolemaic view of the universe with the earth at the centre. In recent times, a number of theologians and councils have suggested that while Christ is the means of salvation, this salvation may be mediated to non-Christians through their own religions. In keeping with the Copernican model, Hick describes these inclusivists strategies as theological 'epicycles' being added to the Ptolemaic model.

Instead of abandoning the old view of Christianity, these theologians try to tinker with the system by providing more generous ways to account for the world religions. Rather than modifying this model of Christianity, Hick calls for a revolution in the theology of religions. This revolution will no longer see Christ and Christianity as the centre of the religious universe, with other religions revolving around them, but will see God as being at the centre with all the world religions revolving around God. We will evaluate this proposal a little later, but at this point it is worth noting serious problems in the analogy. Copernicus proposed that the sun was at the centre of the universe, with the planets and stars in orbit around it. This was a step forward in our understanding of the solar system but mistaken as a view of the universe. Later astronomers recognized that the solar system is itself at the margins of a larger galactic system, which in turn is part of a universe of galaxies. The idea that the sun is at the centre of the system is grossly parochial. The same progress of modification must affect Hick's proposal. How can 'God' be at the centre of faiths that include non-theistic schools of Buddhism and atheistic Zen Buddhism or Shinto? The Copernican revolution in theology still privileged monotheism. However, Hick's reasoning was leading away from any personal God being at the centre of faiths.

An interpretation of religion

Hick's major work, *An Interpretation of Religion*, is the most comprehensive statement of his pluralist hypothesis. It is offered as an interpretation of all the major world religions in terms of certain unifying themes. In this work Hick also develops more fully the implications of his use of Kant's philosophy.

Hick describes each of the world religions as human responses to the same ultimate divine reality. He does not intend to devalue the diversity of the different religions. On the contrary, he hopes the rich diversity of beliefs will remain.[40] His own work is offered as an interpretation of those varied responses. However, his interpretation certainly gives the impression of seeking a lowest common denominator among religions and then dismissing distinctive beliefs as secondary or of little consequence. Matters which give religion their diversity may still have value but they are not treated as important. Hick reasons that the diversity of beliefs arises from the different ways human beings experience reality. Each religion exists as a cultural whole which influences the way participants experience and understand the world around them. On this assumption, it is not entirely impossible to reconcile even the apparently radical differences between a Buddhist conception of the world as illusion with nirvana the reality beyond and the Christian conception of the world as God's good creation with heaven ahead. The Buddhist and Christian worldviews represent different ways in which human beings can respond to the same ultimate reality.

Using Kant's model, Hick draws a sharp distinction between the way we know things and the way things really are. On the one hand, there is the Ultimate Reality beyond all possible human experience and rational thought and, on the other hand, human descriptions of that Real as God or Nirvana or Allah. These pictures function as symbols to help us understand the reality about which we could never otherwise speak. The radical difference between believing in a personal God or in an impersonal force behind the universe may then be understood as different symbols used by humans to live their lives in the light of the same higher reality.

In a previous work, God was at the centre of the universe of faiths. Now Hick recognizes the implicit imperialism in importing the word 'God' into the model. Such a word implies a whole Judaeo-Christian tradition of the personal God. Hick now prefers the 'Real' as a formal description for that ultimate reality about which we can never speak directly.[41] Furthermore, because of the nature of the Real, he/she/it can never be experienced as an object among objects but rather only as a human image of the Real. Therefore, we cannot know the Real directly. Its existence is something we must assume (postulate) in order to make sense of religious experience. Atheists may be content to conclude that religious experience is illusory, but Hick does not do so. He believes that his personal religious feelings and the fact that those feelings are shared so widely is reason enough to postulate the existence of an Ultimate Real.

An Interpretation of Religion also includes a treatment of the history of religions. This is important because one can point to all sorts of dangerous and sometimes short-lived religious phenomena that do not appear to support the idea that all religions are responses to the same reality. One might consider certain ancient religions that involved ritual child-abuse or human sacrifice. Or one might consider recent movements that have been exposed for sexual or financial scandals. It seems hard to recognize all of these religions as responding to the same reality. In order to deal with these anomalies Hick must establish that there is some basic thread of consistent religious thought running through history.

According to Hick, following the work of Karl Jaspers,[42] there was a great period of transition in human consciousness between approximately 800 BC and 200 BC. Religion prior to this time was a matter of humanity trying to preserve social cohesion in the face of the forces of chaos ranged against it. It did not primarily address issues of ultimate concern or direct itself to the welfare and fulfilment of individuals. Rather, religion provided justification for the existence of society and the laws necessary to preserve order. As such, religion was rather a gloomy affair in which an attempt was made to placate the mysterious spirits inhabiting the world.

The period of transition is known as the axial age, for during it human consciousness turned on its axis. Several significant figures developed a profound awareness of the divine centre of the universe. They became aware of the love and justice of the divinity which could even bring prophetic judgment on society itself. The earlier pessimism concerning the future was replaced by a cosmic optimism. These saintly people came to believe in an ultimate good destiny lying in the future, waiting for the fulfilment of all humanity. The great 'saints' of the axial age include the Buddha, Isaiah and Confucius. During this period all the major world religions were given birth.

Since the axial age, the new-found cosmic optimism spread and developed in the consciousness of humanity. More recently formed religions – Christianity, Islam, Sikhism and so on – are natural progressions from the insights discerned in the axial age. All the major world religions represent valid options for human religious experience as they have sprung from the deep roots of the axial age and have had their validity proven during the centuries of human experience that have tested them.

This historical account enables Hick to exclude certain belief-systems from his treatment and explain certain developments otherwise incongruous with his interpretation. Hick does not need to take seriously bizarre modern religious movements and cults, as they do not form part of the mainstream history of religions. Furthermore, Hick is able to explain why some religions have been successful in missionary work. The missionary successes of Christianity in Europe, the Mediterranean, central Africa and the Americas and the success of Islam in the Middle East and North Africa represent the transition from the pre-axial religion of those areas to the axial age. It is as if the era of cosmic optimism occurred late in certain parts of the world. This cosmic optimism is essentially the common thread of true religious thinking running through all the major world religions.

Conflicting truth claims

One of the most frequent challenges made against the pluralist hypothesis concerns the truth claims made by religious believers. The range of contradictory claims about reality in the world religions present *prima facie* evidence against the pluralist case. The pluralist hypothesis must maintain that religions are to do with the same ultimate reality despite making wildly different and some-times contradictory claims about the nature of that reality. Some claim that there is a personal creator God, while others, such as Zen Buddhism and Marxism, deny that there is such a being. Christianity claims that an atonement is required for forgiveness, whereas others dismiss this as unnecessary. Some claim that one set of writings are the only scriptures revealed by God, whereas others make the same claim for a different set of scriptures. The problem of conflicting truth claims is a very real one.

One way in which some theologians deal with this problem is to deny that religious beliefs are attempts to describe reality but affirm that they serve useful symbolic functions. According to these thinkers, to believe that God exists involves behaving in a certain way and having certain attitudes to life but it does not involve believing that a God really exists in the way, by analogy, that other people exist. This position is called non-realism. Hick has contested the claims of non-realists on the grounds that they fail to do justice to genuine religious beliefs. When religious people describe their faith in God or hope in eternal life they are doing more than using symbols to guide their behaviour.

In contrast, Hick has always maintained that his position is realist. He has defended the meaningfulness of religious language from the attacks of logical positivists. At least some religious language describes objective reality. For example, descriptions of heaven or reincarnation do point to a continued existence beyond death. Hick defines his own position as critical realism because, while affirming that the objects we speak of exist independently of our conceptions of them (realism), he also takes into account the contribution that the critical faculties of the mind make to our experience; hence, critical realism. We experience things in a particular way through the interpretation we bring to bear upon them. Hick further develops this point in terms of the distinction between how things appear to us (phenomenon) and what reality is like 'in itself' (noumenon). Using this distinction, no religious truth claim should be understood as an absolute, exclusively true description of ultimate reality. Each must be understood as an image produced in part by the cultural and intellectual influences on our thinking. If religious claims are not absolute, then one cannot take conflicting truth claims at face value. They must first be analysed in terms of the cultural context in which the claims are made. Through this kind of analysis Hick believes he can neuter the significance of any contradiction.

We already have an example of this with Hick's interpretation of the historical Jesus. To declare him to be the Christ, the second person of the Trinity, is not, according to Hick, to make a purely factual claim about the historical Jesus. Instead, it is a mythological claim providing some information about the historical Jesus but more information about Christian experience. It is a poetic expression of the believer's devotion to a particular way of life and attitude toward ultimate reality as it is glimpsed in the life of Jesus. Many religious truth claims can be understood in these mythological terms. This applies to all kinds of religious ideas. Having expressed a detailed philosophical treatment of theodicy, Hick has, more recently, described the various theodicies as essentially mythological.[43]

Hick defines 'myth' carefully in order to avoid the charge that to describe something as a myth is a polite way of describing it as false. He defines the meaning of myth in the following way:

> For the conformity of myth to reality does not consist in a literal conformity of what is said to the facts but in the appropriateness to the myth's referent of the behavioural dispositions that it tends to evoke in the hearer.[44]

A myth is not true because it correctly describes reality, but is true because for those who believe in a myth it produces a particular kind of good behaviour. Hence, the mythology of the Third Reich is a false mythology. A true myth would produce good behaviour and most of the mythologies of the world religions are 'true' in this sense.

In the light of this analysis, some truth claims that had been thought to be in conflict may be understood as compatible if they all evoke similar, appropriate behaviour in those who adhere to those claims. At the level of literal truth they remain contradictory, but this is not of ultimate consequence because they do not primarily serve such literal functions. Hick does consider certain difficult contradictions, such as the historical claim of Christians that Jesus died on the cross and the Islamic denial that this was what really happened. However, he considers these kind of claims as unsettleable in practice[45] and, more importantly, not of the essence of religious belief which is primarily a matter of conforming one's attitude to that which is appropriate in relation to the ultimate reality. In other words, if a religion is a context in which people grow in kindness, then it may be considered 'true' and any contentious factual claims dismissed as unimportant. This pragmatic approach to truth may ensure inter-religious tolerance, but there is a high price to pay.

Critical evaluation

Universalism

Hick's career has spanned many years and we have seen a number of changes in his own theological position. In particular, his thinking has changed regarding the meaning of the incarnation and the world religions. In many ways it is to be respected and admired when someone's thought develops and changes rather than stagnates. However, radical changes in belief can give rise to fundamental inconsistencies within a position. Hick's work has developed from within a mainstream Christian position. It may be the case that the pluralist hypothesis undercuts the very foundations of his theology. We shall examine this possibility with regard to his case for universalism, but the criticism applies more widely.

The pluralist position does not require that all people are finally saved, but only that the saved are not a group of people restricted to one particular religion. However, Hick's own attraction to pluralism stems in part from his prior commitment to universalism. If God loves all people and saves all people, then it is problematic to maintain that Christianity is the only valid religion. The universal saving will of God lends substance to the case for pluralism. We have seen that the main line of defence for his universalism lies in the character of God: an all-loving and all-powerful God would not allow countless numbers of people to perish in eternity. However, Hick has since suggested that the Christian conception of God should be relativized as one human construction among many that function as responses to the Ultimate Reality. The Ultimate Reality remains beyond human comprehension and characterization. Hence, to speak of an all-loving, omnipotent God is to use mythological language. According to Hick, mythology describes and evokes the proper orientation towards reality but does not describe Ultimate Reality itself (an impossible thing to do). However, the basis for a literal universal salvation lay in a literal description of what God is like.

Therefore, the justification for universalism no longer remains. As Gavin D'Costa expresses it:

> I believe that Hick severs the ground from under his Copernican feet. This is so because in arguing for the Copernican revolution on the premise of a God of universal love, such a position entails precisely that one form of revelation of God is definitive and normative compared to others.[46]

The range of teachings in the world religions provide very different accounts of the nature of ultimate reality. Certainly, not all believe that there is a supreme being who is omnipotent in the classical Christian sense. Furthermore, not all even affirm the existence of a personal supreme being. Yet to describe God as 'all loving' requires, at least, a personal God capable of love and relationship. Hick's case for universalism depends upon the truth of the Christian conception of God as personal, all powerful and all loving. The position to which his universalism leads him requires that he remain uncertain about the ultimate validity of universalism.

Another example of the crucial nature of this change of position may be found at the end of *Death and Eternal Life*.[47] At this stage Hick was willing to confess that certain schools of Eastern thought must be wrong if his own hypothesis was right. He no longer makes such statements. All major religious traditions have equal insights into the nature of Ultimate Reality. Consequently, while Hick affirms that the Christian God is a personal manifestation of the Ultimate Reality, that ultimate being cannot truly be understood as either personal or non-personal. However, the basis of at least his Christian case for universalism and his proposed answer to the problem of suffering depends upon the notion of a personal, purposeful, loving God. His description of Ultimate Reality cannot sustain the notion.

Universalism remains an attractive position. However, it must be asked how far it provides an adequate interpretation of the New Testament. Clearly, we are not free to create reality the way we wish it to be but must have some source of information about the way things really are. If one accepts that Scripture provides this source of information, then the proper interpretation of the New Testament will remain the deciding factor on this issue.[48]

The uniqueness of Christ

It is belief in the uniqueness of Jesus as God incarnate that prevents many Christians from following Hick along the pluralist road. If Jesus is the Christ, the Son of God, then he is God's self-revelation to humanity. Such a self-revelation is necessarily unique and superior to any other ways of understanding God. Furthermore, according to the traditional Christian position, part of the uniqueness of Christ lies in the atonement. The work that Christ came to do on the cross was a unique act of atonement: reconciling a guilty world to himself. Consequently, the person and work of Christ are absolutely crucial, normative and central tenets of the Christian faith and prevent any attempt to relativize Christianity as one religious option among many.

It is important in responding to Hick's work to stress that the doctrine of the incarnation does not depend on the early church creeds of Chalcedon and Nicea but is firmly rooted in the New Testament. Hick is quite right to point out that the ways in which these councils sought to express their understanding of Christ were not ways in which Jesus or the Gospel writers would have expressed themselves in their own time. However, it does not follow that the later creeds diverge from and are incompatible with the faith of the New Testament church and the teachings of Jesus himself.

Hick subscribes to an evolutionary model of Christology. According to this model, the way Jesus was understood by the later church had evolved from a much simpler belief held by the early church. He describes the historical Jesus as an ordinary human being, profoundly aware of the divine reality as only a few other figures in history have been. Subsequent reflection by the early church on their experience of the impact he had made led to poetic attempts to describe him. These are embedded in the New Testament. Much later philosophical thought at the Councils of Nicea and Chalcedon misunderstood the nature of such language and mistakenly attempted to state an ontological Christology. The identification of Jesus with God had poetic and metaphorical value, but the councils misinterpreted this language as literal.

A very useful analysis of the relevant data is provided by C. F. D. Moule, latterly Professor of Divinity at Cambridge University, in his work *The Origin of Christology*.[49] Moule presents a sustained critique of the evolutionary model and suggests a 'developmental' analogy as being a more accurate reflection of the evidence. According to this analogy, the way that the later church described Jesus was a legitimate development from descriptions of him in the New Testament. The beliefs of the later church were already present in the gospels though in an undeveloped form. We shall isolate a few strands from Moule's work in order to demonstrate that the doctrine of the incarnation is to be found in the New Testament.

Moule assesses the various titles that are used in the New Testament to describe Jesus and denies that these are the product of much later reflection or pagan thinking. A title of particular significance in this respect is the word 'Lord' (Greek *Kyrios*) that is often applied to Jesus. This word was used in Greek translations of the Old Testament to represent the sacred name of God: 'Yahweh'. Moule notes a lesser sense in which 'Lord' need only mean a term of respect, but these are only occasionally used of Jesus.[50] Hence, *Kyrios* was used to signify divinity. As further evidence of this point, Moule cites Josephus, the Jewish historian, who referred to the refusal of Jews to declare the Roman Emperor 'Lord' (*Kyrios*) because this expression was reserved for divinity. Yet it is this title that is used of Jesus in the very early strands of the New Testament. Philippians 2:6–11 provides a clear example of this. This is an early letter in itself but many scholars regard this section as a pre-Pauline hymn, dating it earlier still. The hymn contains the confession that Jesus is Lord (vv. 9–11) and this is a direct parallel to an Old Testament passage concerning Yahweh (Isaiah 45:23). The significance of attributing the title 'Lord' to the historical Jesus is a daring pronouncement of his divine status.

Another early indication of how Jesus was regarded is found in the worship given to Jesus. Moule points out that worship is offered to Jesus in the New Testament that should be reserved for God alone. The Greek word for 'worship' (*proskunein*) can mean either worship to God or respectful homage paid to a person. However, in the New Testament the word is reserved primarily for worship of God (Matthew 4:9–10; Luke 4:7–8; Acts 10:25; Revelation 19:10; 22:9). This same worship is offered to Jesus. Furthermore, Moule provides a number of examples where Jesus is described as far more than a man. His significance is taken to be of cosmic, corporate proportions. A useful line of evidence lies in the resurrection accounts that point to both the divinity and humanity of Christ. The resurrection event dominates the New Testament witness to Christ and any attempt to understand him without accounting for the resurrection is suspect. Klaas Runia, a Professor of Theology in the Netherlands, notes that in the contributions to the *Myth of God Incarnate* it 'is striking that the resurrection of Christ plays hardly any role at all'.[51] This is certainly true of Hick's account in that volume.[52]

Whoever the disciples understood him to be, he was clearly much more than a man. According to Moule, the disciples:

> ... attribute to him a unique closeness to God and a divine, creative initiative, which marks him off from their conception of what each believer – precisely because of him and through him – may become.[53]

The evolutionary model portrays Jesus as a man so open to the divine reality that others who met him found in him an example for their own lives and chose to follow him. The deification of Jesus was a later subsequent step in Christian thought. Moule challenges such a picture with the evidence. The reason why Jesus was seen to be a model for the believer was the result of, not the cause of, Jesus being understood as God incarnate. Colin Gunton, Professor of Christian Doctrine at London University, criticizes the notion that Jesus was later understood as God incarnate because he was first seen as a great moral example: 'Jesus is an example because he and he alone is the incarnate Son who by the enabling of the Holy Spirit remained unfallen where we universally fall.'[54]

While Hick has dealt directly with some issues in New Testament studies,[55] his major objection to the incarnation is derived from philosophical considerations rather than biblical studies. The reason why the doctrine of the incarnation cannot be accepted at face value lies in the incoherence of the concept. According to Hick, any attempt to express the meaning of the incarnation is either treated as heretical by the church or fails to convey anything intelligible. The Council of Chalcedon expressed the identity of Jesus in the following way:

> ... our Lord Jesus Christ ... truly God and truly man ... of one substance with the Father as regards his Godhead, and at the same time of one substance with us as regards his manhood ...[56]

Hick suggests that 'the council in effect merely asserted that Jesus was "truly God and truly man" without attempting to say how such a paradox is possible'.[57] In other words, the dogmatic assertion does not specify the meaning of the incarnation. Hick has criticized various attempts to spell out the doctrine as either unintelligible or incompatible with Chalcedon.

Hick's objection is to the apparent difficulty of describing a historic human being as both the individual human being, Jesus, and the individual divine being, God. This objection has two elements. Firstly, there is the impossibility of describing one person as two distinct people. I cannot be both Matthew and Robert. I could be a hybrid human or either person but I cannot be both simultaneously. Secondly, there is the specific problem of the compatibility of humanity and divinity. If part of the necessary definition of God is that he is all-knowing and all-powerful and part of the necessary definition of being a human is to be limited in knowledge and power (i.e. necessarily something less than God), then it is impossible for someone to be both human and God. Hick describes such a claim as logically similar to the claim that there could be a square circle.

The assumption underlying this claim is that we know that the incarnation is impossible factually because impossible concept-ually. We cannot believe the event to have occurred in history unless we can provide a conceptual account of the event. Interestingly, Hick does not deny that the Council of Chalcedon might have been right in its description of Jesus, he only argues that we have no right to believe that it has happened unless we can state exactly what it is we are talking about in modern conceptual terms.

This requirement is highly unreasonable. There are many things that we are entitled to believe even though we cannot give a full and convincing explanation to others. This is particularly important with eyewitness claims. Someone visiting from a developing country without knowledge of contemporary science might not understand some of the technology they encounter. Upon returning to their homeland they would certainly not be able to explain to their contemporaries how what they saw was possible. The evidence of eyesight or testimony would not be credible unless the processes and mechanisms involved could be spelled out in contextually meaningful terms. The attempts of the disciples, New Testament writers and the early church to give some propositional statement of their experience of Christ were clearly not attempts to give complete, philosophical accounts of the incarnation. The doctrine of the incarnation, as stated by the later church councils, is an attempt to do two things. Firstly, the statements reflect what Christians found to be true of the Scriptures and their experience. To be true to these sources, Christians confessed that Jesus was indeed God and was also human. The second objective of such statements was the identification and exclusion of heresy. Even while the New Testament was being written, false views of who Jesus was were creeping into the church. Some parts of the New Testament are written to combat such views (such as 1 John). The later creeds were formulated in such a way as to exclude certain erroneous ideas. The meaning of the incarnation was made better known by excluding certain false views, such as the belief that Jesus only resembled a human being. It is unfair to empty the doctrine of the incarnation of meaning on the grounds that it cannot be stated in terms of one particular philosophical tradition. The truth of the incarnation is no less literal for being made known to us in the Gospels through narrative.

Hick's attempt to exclude the possibility of the incarnation also involves an assumption that one knows what it means to be fully God or even to be fully human in order to exclude categorically the possibility of these ever being in harmony in one person. For many Christians, their reading of Scripture, understanding of history and personal experience provide the grounds for their belief in a truth that may not be stated in the terms required by Hick. Runia, having attempted to state the incarnation in modern terminology, admits that,

> ... the incarnation remains a mystery that can never be 'explained'. All we can do is to 'describe' it by listening carefully to the witness of Scripture and expounding what this witness ... communicates to us. But even in this exposition the mystery itself remains fully inexplicable ...[58]

Mythology and truth

We have already seen that Hick draws a distinction between the form in which we know God and what God is really like. This distinction holds true for all things that are beyond the natural order. Heaven, hell, angels and demons are also human ways of understanding supernatural reality rather than facts about the supernatural. This distinction leads him to make a linguistic observation that there are primarily two forms of language use: the literal and the mythological. Literal language assumes a direct relation between a description of an object and the object described. Mythological language has no such direct relation. According to Hick, metaphor and myth function by evoking human experience and inspiring a particular kind of behaviour. Hence, the incarnation was not a literal event in history (describing the identity of Jesus) but a metaphor or myth (evoking appropriate attitudes in those who use that language). The truth test for mythological language does not lie in assessing how far that language accurately represents its objects but in observing what kind of behaviour it evokes.

The myth/literal distinction is deeply unsatisfactory when applied to religious language. To attempt to categorize all truth claims as either mythological or literal suggests an unwillingness to engage with the sensitivity of language in general and religious language in particular. Some recent writers[59] have pointed out the difficulty of substantiating the claim that all language with clear

ontological import can be expressed in non-metaphorical terms.
On the contrary, even in ordinary discourse we must rely a great
deal on the metaphorical use of language. How much more, then,
must we rely upon it when attempting to describe aspects of
reality that are beyond sense experience. Even in scientific
discourse much use is made of metaphorical language. Obvious
examples would include descriptions of light and radio 'waves'.
None the less, the metaphors imply literal meanings.

This problem becomes most acute with the incarnation debate.
Hick understands the incarnation as a mythological picture
designed to evoke an appropriate dispositional response in the
believer. It is quite true that metaphor must be used in describing
the incarnation. Jesus is not the 'Son of God' in the same way that
men are sons of their parents. Nor is God the 'Father' in the same
way that men can be fathers. However, the use of metaphorical
language need not imply that the incarnation is a myth any more
than describing light as 'waves' implies that light waves are
mythological. According to Hick, the incarnation cannot be understood in literal terms because it fails to mean anything literally: it
cannot be stated without, at some point, recourse to metaphor,
narrative, paradox and mystery. Hick excludes the doctrine of the
incarnation from the status of literal truth because it cannot be
stated in the way required by Hick's theory of language.

The cash value of a mythological interpretation of the exclusive
statements in religious belief is a basis for what is called relativism.
According to relativism, truth claims are only valid within the
limitations of a cultural and intellectual context. They have no
absolute or ultimate status. Every major religion has made unique,
absolute or exclusive claims for the status of beliefs regarding
saviours, revelation, scriptures or moral codes. When understood
in terms of Hick's epistemology they cannot convey facts about
ultimate reality. As mythological statements they are interpreted as
a type of language designed to evoke certain patterns of behaviour
rather than attempting to provide literal descriptions of reality. In
accordance with this new understanding of language, religious
truth claims are not in conflict because of differences in meaning
(that is, one claiming that God is personal and one claiming that
God is impersonal), but only if the behaviour they evoke is at odds.

However, Hick points out that the moral codes and lifestyles of the major world religions have enough in common and so little in conflict that one can assume all their major myths have equal validity. Hence, particular claims about the character of God, the location of revelation and so on have only relative truth value.

The price of this relativism undercuts Hick's entire project. We have seen that Hick has wanted to maintain the realist claim that the core of religious belief is literally true. Hick would not want all religious language to be reduced to the status of myth. If it were, then religion would be no more than a helpful set of images with an important function but no bearing on reality. In particular, descriptions of the afterlife were understood by Hick to refer to a real event beyond death. However, if all the major world religions have equally valid insights regarding ultimate reality, then the bulk of religious truth claims must be interpreted as myths. The remaining number of literal truth claims would be alarmingly small. The core literal beliefs that would remain after such a reductionist account would probably be the existence of a Higher reality and that life will be extended beyond death.[60] There is nothing specifically Christian about these remaining claims and that is, of course, the point. These are the residual truth claims of the major world religions when their various optional, mythological packagings are stripped away.

This programme of reductionism raises two serious objections. Firstly, is there enough basis even to protect these truth claims from being reinterpreted along mythological lines? After all, some humanist, atheist and Marxist worldviews have a somewhat religious dimension too. Pluralism is obliged to credit such non-supernatural worldviews with equal validity insofar as they inculcate a pattern of high moral behaviour. If an entire religious belief-system is reduced to its mythological function, it can still be valued for the behaviour it produces without needing to have any bearing on objective reality. This final step of reductionism may become necessary as one realizes that even talk about 'Ultimate Reality' or 'life after death' involves metaphor, paradox and mystery. The core of religious belief follows the export of the incarnation from the realm of literal truth to that of mythological truth. If this happens, then pluralism is self-defeating as it ends up denying that there is any ultimate reality informing the plurality of world religions.[61]

The second objection concerns whether many religious believers could accept such a minimalist account of their own religion, be they Buddhist, Muslim, Christian or of any other religion. For Christians, Hick's account lacks the distinctive historical nature of religious truth claims. Christianity is not a religion of an abstract, moral philosophy. It is a religion rooted in claims about particular historical events. As Lesslie Newbigin, missionary and theologian, writes: 'The Christian faith is a particular way of understanding history as a whole which finds in the story about Jesus its decisive clue.'[62] Does the pluralist reductionist account offer an adequate description of any given religious worldview? If not, then Hick's work fails as an interpretation of religion and must, instead, be understood as a radical reinterpretation of religions and a manifesto for a new development in religious self-consciousness, albeit one which may be more attractive to those of an agnostic persuasion. Harold Netland, a critic of Hick, points this out:

> Hick, of course, is free to reinterpret such doctrines in mythological terms, but it must be recognised that in so doing he is parting company with the vast majority of religious believers in the major traditions.[63]

The pluralist reinterpretation of religions is methodologically agnostic. This means that while Hick may remain a theist in his personal beliefs, he must acknowledge when in dialogue with those of other religions that these beliefs are only one set of images among many, including the non-theistic, that help people orient themselves to the Real. Such a procedure is alien to the thought-world of most religions. Consequently, one may doubt whether the pluralist hypothesis could ever facilitate greater understanding among followers of different religions. Rather, it may lead to a mutual reinterpretation and misunderstanding.

Christianity and other religions
The traditional ways in which Christians have understood other religions tend to fall into two positions.[64] Exclusivism is often

understood as the mainstream position of the historic church. According to this position, salvation and revelation are known exclusively through Christ. Some special knowledge of Christ is necessary in order for anyone to share in that salvation. The inclusivist position has become particularly prominent in the last two hundred years. This position maintains that salvation remains the work of Christ but understands that salvation to be mediated through the saving structures of the world religions which bear an implicit witness to Christ. Adherents of other religions may then be included in Christ's work. Different thinkers tend to be classified in one of these two positions, but there is a great deal of overlap between the two.

Hick does not deny that such positions could be true. He admits that no irrefutable evidence can be produced to prove that they are false. None the less, he argues that they are not very plausible positions to take in the light of the world religions. The wisdom and culture they have engendered, the moral fruits they have produced and the 'saints' that have appeared in the course of their histories all suggest that other religions have their own unique place and value as products of the influence of the ultimate divine reality. Hence, the most plausible account of the world religions pictures them all as various pathways up the same mountain, all eventually reaching the same summit. This image points to another internal inconsistency in the pluralist account. Pluralism denies the possibility or desirability of having an absolute, cosmic vantage-point from which to assess all other religions. Such vantage-points are the products of exclusivist religions isolated from the realities of religious pluralism. However, it is just such a vantage-point that pluralism claims for itself.[65]

Hick denies this latter point, claiming that 'the pluralist hypothesis is not an a priori dogma, presupposing a cosmic standpoint, but a hypothesis built up from the ground level'.[66] Essentially, his response is that religious pluralism is an inductive hypothesis to which he is led by the evidence. This response misses the point entirely. Christian exclusivism may be reached inductively by a consideration of the evidence, but once the position is established it then becomes a framework from which

to judge all other ideas. Hick is no less an exclusivist than the
evangelical Christian in his commitment to a basic vantage-point
from which to interpret other religious ideas.[67]

Hick's theology of religions interprets the central teachings and
beliefs of all the world religions in terms of a supposed ethical
core. In so doing, all points of disagreement are relativized in
importance, while a common moral code is isolated as the
underlying truth of all religions. The fundamental question that
needs to be addressed is whether one can isolate the 'moral code'
of a religion apart from the doctrinal framework or belief-system
in which a religion finds its meaning. Beliefs and 'pictures' of God
or Nirvana are not optional, mythological packagings distinct
from the ethical core. They are the underlying truth that provides
the meaning of the ethical codes and motivation to pursue them.
Religious beliefs, however theoretical they may seem, are bound
up with the rituals, practices and lifestyles they produce. If this is
true, then there are no easy answers to the problem of conflicting
truth claims. They represent sincere points of difference between
religions, demanding that we respect those differences and even
debate their validity.

As an example of the former point we may consider the
Christian understanding of morality and belief. According to Hick,
the Christian moral code is summed up by Jesus in the so-called
'golden rule' that we should love our neighbours as ourselves.
Furthermore, similar golden rules are to be found in all the major
traditions. Hick interprets the purpose of Christian life (and all
religious life) as the pursuit of human transformation from self-
centredness to reality-centredness. Netland criticizes this reductionist presentation of the goal of the religious life: '... as it stands
this is largely a formal formula lacking specific content, and each
religious tradition would contribute strikingly different content to
the formula'.[68] For example, the Buddhist concept of the ego and
the Christian concept of sin are not two ways of talking about
'self-centredness': they represent distinct beliefs informed by
distinct contexts.

What is missing from Hick's account is mention of a central
feature in the New Testament account of salvation and ethics;
namely, a theology of grace. The New Testament writers are

agreed that in Christ there is a new means of human transformation that is not a matter of pursuing a particular ethical code in order to transform oneself. The theology of grace speaks of the initial transformation as the gift of God (Ephesians 2:10–11). Transformation begins with the gift of God in Christ and, through this gift, one finds the resources to pursue the Christian ethic. So clear is this teaching in the New Testament that there are even passages written in response to the misuse of grace as a principle of licence (Romans 6:1; James 2:14). Furthermore, for Christians the 'golden rule' cannot be divorced from its context of the demand that we love God with all our heart, mind and will; a demand that would be counter-productive if required of the Buddhist towards Nirvana.

As distinct from certain schools of Eastern thought, Christianity and Judaism are religions rooted in history. The exodus from Egypt is the constant refrain of the Old Testament. In the New Testament the various teachings, no matter how abstract, are all founded on the historical claims concerning the life, death and resurrection of Jesus. The revelation that is central to Christian belief is located in history rather than in human subjectivity. Hence, Christians are not free to alter doctrine to suit contemporary thinking but must continually reappraise themselves in the light of God's revelation through Christ in Scripture.

We have had reason to dispute the pluralist account of the world religions. However, this is only half of the story. Hick's provocative work in the theology of religions has been presented as the most plausible explanation of religious phenomena. It is not enough to refute his analysis: one also needs to present a better alternative. There is not, of course, space here to argue in favour of an orthodox account of Christianity, but we shall finish by briefly considering evangelical interpretations of other religions.

We have seen that there is a degree of overlap between exclusivist and inclusivist positions. However, most evangelicals would be exclusivist in their interpretation of other religions. This does not mean that they consider all non-Christians eternally lost. In fact, most choose to remain agnostic about God's work among the unevangelized.[69] Some, like Norman Anderson,[70] offer suggestions as to how some non-Christians may realize their own sin and need of grace and cast themselves on God's mercy. There is reason to hope that in doing so God will reach out to them in their need. Paul Helm gives further philosophical justification for how this could be so.[71] All these writers agree that salvation is through Christ alone and not through the structures of any religion (including Christianity when understood as a religious institution). However, they do not restrict God's saving activity to those who explicitly confess Christ. God's judgment on sin is a righteous judgment and the emphasis on grace reminds us that no-one deserves to be saved. Rather than speculate on the details of who will or will not be finally saved outside of the Christian community, these evangelicals ask with Abraham, 'Will not the Judge of all the earth do right?' (Genesis 18:25).

The insistence on the exclusiveness of salvation through Christ alone (texts commonly understood to imply this include John 14:6 and Acts 4:12) contradicts the possibility that salvation can be gained through other religions. If they are saved, then adherents of other religions are saved in spite of their religions rather than through their religions.[72] One might think this would lead only to a negative evaluation of other religions as demonic, idolatrous or human perversions. This need not be the case.

To affirm that salvation is through Christ alone and that this salvation is not mediated through the world religions allows for an interpretation of other religions on their own terms. Rather than interpreting other religions as implicitly witnessing to Christ (and facing the danger of entirely misinterpreting them), the exclusivist can consider other religions as genuinely 'other' and allow them to speak for themselves as to what they believe and teach. Some religions may have goals that are entirely unrelated to salvation as understood by Christians.

The question remains: Of what value are non-Christian religions? This cannot be answered in any general sense because they are such diverse movements. However, no-one need deny *a priori* that they may offer and promote much that a Christian values. Some evangelicals have used the category of general revelation to discern truth within other religions.[73] A strong doctrine of creation suggests that there is much that may be known about God apart from Scripture. Alister McGrath writes:

Calvin would have had no problem in allowing that both Jews and Muslims have access to a knowledge of God as Creator; while the particular and distinctive aspect of a Christian understanding of God related to knowing him as Redeemer rather than as Creator alone.[74]

The Evangelical Alliance statement on other faiths affirms that:

> There is much in other faiths which is in harmony with the Christian faith, e.g. the sense of the tremendous majesty of God, so clearly proclaimed by Islam ... and the love and adoration of a personal God, found in Sikhism and the bhakti movements in Hinduism.[75]

Exclusivists rarely 'write off' all other religions as if they were of no value. None the less, they have no desire to compromise the belief that salvation and a relationship with the God of Abraham, Isaac and Jacob has been made possible through the atoning work of the Son, Jesus Christ. It is this message of reconciliation that exclusivists believe is of universal validity and significance and thus they make every effort to proclaim this 'gospel' throughout the world.

Conclusion

During the course of his academic career, John Hick has sustained a prestigious literary output and become known as a leading radical theologian of the twentieth century. He has never shied away from some of the most perplexing and pressing problems facing Christians in the modern world. We have noted the trajectory of his career from 'fundamentalist' to 'radical' as he has pursued this range of questions. The pluralist hypothesis, with which we have been primarily concerned, is not some ill-thought out, *ad hoc* argument. Hick has been a passionate defender and promoter of his conclusions in debate, dialogue and publishing throughout the world.

However, we have also had reason to note deeply unsatis-factory aspects of his thought. There is a problem of consistency regarding the assumption in favour of universalism. We have mentioned scholarly work in biblical studies that has given cause to doubt the sceptical and radical conclusions drawn from the New Testament. There are growing numbers of biblical and systematic theologians who are finding the kind of arguments put forward by the contributors to *The Myth of God Incarnate* less and less convincing. Hick's treatment of religious language and his philosophical assessment of central orthodox beliefs rest on a particular Western stream of 'empiricist' thought that is coming under increasing criticism from various, particularly continental, schools of thought. Finally, we have noted some difficulties in the pluralist hypothesis itself that make it unsatisfactory, not only for Christians, but for mainstream believers in many of the major world religions. For evangelicals, Hick's work remains unacceptable in its description of a Christianity without incarnation, atonement, resurrection, Trinity, special grace or verbal revelation. Hick presents very clearly what is at stake for those who adopt the pluralist hypothesis.

Supplement: an interview

I visited John Hick at his Birmingham home in January 2002 in order to put a few questions to him that arise in this essay. I started by asking some biographical questions to clarify a little further his own experience of Christianity.

CS: In your writings you describe a number of spiritual experiences including an early encounter with Evangelicalism and your conversion to Christianity on a bus.

JH: No, the experience on the bus, an intense awareness of the love of God, was not the conversion itself but an incident afterwards. I was converted when studying law at Hull, age 18. The conversion experience lasted two or three days. I had been deeply impressed by the New Testament figure of Jesus. I was aware of an alien reality pressing in upon me, namely Christian faith – in its evangelical form because I was amongst friends who were in the IVF (now UCCF). At first this new reality was threatening because it involved a complete transformation of identity, but then at a certain point it became not threatening but inviting and was something to be embraced wholeheartedly. And I did embrace it wholeheartedly and with great happiness.

CS: So your conversion experience wasn't through something that you heard at a meeting, it was more from your relationship with individual people and reading the New Testament.

JH: Particularly reading the New Testament, yes. But I don't think you can disentangle that from the fact that I was among IVF evangelical students.

CS: And something struck you about the character of those students?

JH: Not their character, no, but the character of Jesus. But because I was among them rather than among, say, High Anglicans, I took on board, quite uncritically, the entire IVF package including the verbal inerrancy of Scripture and other fundamental beliefs including Jesus' deity, his virgin birth and bodily resurrection and ascension, his death as atonement for the sins of the world, and heaven and hell.

The war interrupted Hick's studies and he served in the Quaker Friends Ambulance Service. He returned to study philosophy and then go on to ordination in the Presbyterian Church. I asked him when it was that he no longer considered himself evangelical.

JH: When I came back from the war I completed the last 3 years of a philosophy degree at Edinburgh University. I joined the EU (Evangelical Union) there but found it unsatisfactory because of the questions I was raising. For example the sun standing still as recounted in the book of Joshua would require the earth stopping its rotation. That idea is mind-boggling. Back then within the EU raising such questions was seen as backsliding. So I detached myself from the EU but remained conservative, believing in the incarnation, Trinity and atonement but no longer in the verbal inspiration of the Scriptures.

CS: When you went to America to take up a teaching post, wasn't it your questioning of the virgin birth that brought criticism?

JH: Yes. I was first in the philosophy department at Cornell and then moved to Princeton Theological Seminary, which was pretty conservative. As part of this move I sought, as a Presbyterian minister, to join the local Presbytery. The man who reviewed my application was Clyde Henry, a disciple of Machen, who asked me, rather tactlessly I would think for the mid-twentieth century, whether there was anything I took exception to in the Westminster Confession of 1646. I had read it and knew the confession. It started with the creation in six days and was incompatible with biological evolution. But it was the virgin birth that caused the trouble. I didn't deny the virgin birth, but I held that it was not an essential and not to be confused with the doctrine of the incarnation. So I was received into the Presbytery but then a complaint was made and later upheld by the Synod, which removed my ministerial licence until the decision was reversed a year later by the General Assembly. I thought the whole episode somewhat absurd. In 1850 it would have been understandable but now it seemed totally anachronistic. Most of my mail was supportive but I also had plenty of hate mail telling me I was one heartbeat away from hell, etc. I have had a lot of that kind of mail since, too!

CS: I know that you have written a great deal on the subject of suffering and evil. However, you have also had a great deal of personal tragedy too, particularly the death of a young son, Mike. How has that experience shaped your thinking?

JH: Well, it was of course a colossal blow because he was twenty-four years old, visiting a friend in the Swiss Alps, and one evening, when it was getting dark, he slipped down a crevasse he didn't know was there. It was a great tragedy because it was so sudden and he was a very fine person and a promising artist. But when we are trying to think theologically about suffering it is important not to concentrate on personal circumstances too much because we must remember we are thinking about the entire human race, and tragedies of this kind happen all the time. So though it brings the reality home, it does not affect the problem itself. But I do have the conviction that through the entirety of life, with all its both glorious and terrible moments, a creative process is going on. Now in the case of Mike this process would be set back in so far as it had been going on in this world. But of course I don't think this world is all that there is.

CS: Would you say that your faith helped you in this experience?

JH: Yes, I would say so. But, in those circumstances, one doesn't get out a book on theodicy and think in theological or philosophical terms. If you are with someone in great distress, you don't start talking theodicy to them. What they need is sympathy, understanding and practical help. However, it does make a difference in the long term whether one believes that the material universe is all that there is, with human life simply a fleeting thing, or whether at the back of your mind is belief in a non-sensory realm in relation to which our lives have meaning. This is a background belief which provides the climate, as opposed to the weather, of one's day-to-day life.

We moved on to discussing the coherence of his work. There are various arguments about the extent to which Hick's writing can be treated as a consistent whole. I asked him how consistent he thought his ideas had been.

JH: They have changed a lot. I was fundamentalist at one point and pluralist at a later point, and there has been a good deal of development in between. But why not? I like very much the saying of the economist John Maynard Keynes who, when someone complained to him that he had done a U-turn on some issue, said 'When I find I've been mistaken I change my mind, what do you do?'

CS: Critics of your consistency are not concerned with whether you are permitted to change your mind but with whether you can still treat your work as a unified whole. Let me give you an example of what could count as an inconsistency. In your earlier work you were led to a universalist position on the basis of a Christian argument from the God of love. The universalist position can then lead to the pluralist case, not only for universal salvation, but for universal revelation. However, when one has reached the pluralist hypothesis, the idea of a God of love is only one image of God among many, including non-personal images of God. The original impetus for the pluralist hypothesis is no longer there.

JH: I didn't reach the pluralist hypothesis from the idea of a God of love, although that is a very good way of presenting it to

Christians, but from the ground up by starting with observable human life. It wasn't an *a priori* approach. I observed the lives of people with different belief-systems and concluded that if by salvation you mean something concrete, transformation from self-centredness to a new orientation centred in the divine, then this is not confined to Christians. An *a priori* position starts with a dogmatic belief and deduces what the facts must be, whereas my approach has been to start out with the observable facts and form a theory to account for them.

CS: In affirming universalism, you reject the Christian doctrine of hell. You have famously suggested the possibility of many possible worlds beyond this one in which the transformation of human nature from self-centredness to reality-centredness may continue. In a sense this helps respond to the intuitive problem with universalism – that Adolf Hitler and Mother Teresa would otherwise be treated as the same. However, given that this may require many possible worlds and given that human nature must always have the freedom to reject grace, doesn't this give rise to an alternative doctrine of hell. If someone lived through infinite possible worlds beyond this, rejecting love and embracing evil, wouldn't that amount to an eternal hell?

JH: It depends, I think, on our conception of human nature. If there is no religious element in our nature, then what you say would hold. But if we are basically religious beings, then sooner or later, over however long a time, we will freely fulfil that nature in response to the divine. St Augustine put the point perfectly, in theistic terms, when he said, 'Thou hast made us for Thyself, and our hearts are restless until they find their rest in Thee.'

It remained questionable just how free anyone actually is to reject God in this system.

CS: Your treatment of language is that, ultimately, language is either literal or mythological. Let's begin with the most significant example. A Christian wants to speak of Jesus being both God and man. You describe this way of speaking, if intended literally, as on the level of describing a square circle.

JH: To be God is to be omnipotent, omniscient, omnipresent and the creator of everything other than oneself. Strictly speaking, our use of language is either literal or tropic, the main trope being the metaphor, and myths being expanded metaphors. On the face of it, the idea of a person who is both fully God and fully man appears to be a contradiction. But a being who is fully human is not omnipotent but limited in power, not omniscient but with a finite brain and finite knowledge, not omnipresent but only locally present, and not the creator of everything but oneself. How can the same being have, at the same time, these mutually exclusive properties? But the square circle reference, which is often put to me, is actually a misquotation – what I said in that essay is that this idea of Jesus having all the attributes that anything must have in order to be human and all the attributes necessary in order to be God is logically self-contradictory unless it can be satisfactorily explained. Doctrines of the two natures are attempts to explain it but in my view they are just as much in need of explanation as the original claim. Nor, in my view, will the kenotic theories help. As you know, I have argued this more fully in *The Metaphor of God Incarnate*.

CS: You don't seem to be any better off in this kind of discussion when we talk about the nature of Ultimate Reality. You speak of something that is able to be both, because beyond, personal and non-personal. This would also seem to be very difficult to explain. How can a Buddhist's response to Nirvana and a theistic Hindu's response to a personal God both be responses to the same Ultimate Reality?

JH: This is where Kant's critical realism provides a brilliant basic epistemological clue. It is also found in Thomas Aquinas' famous saying, 'Things known are in the knower according to the mode of the knower.' It is the distinction between anything as it is in itself and as it appears to observers with their particular conceptual apparatus. The pluralistic hypothesis is that the different images of the personal gods and the non-personal absolutes are all phenomenal manifestations of the same Ultimate Reality. But that reality in itself, independently of all human awarenesses of it, is ineffable, or transcategorial. It is not both personal and impersonal, but neither personal nor impersonal – it is beyond the scope of our human categories of thought. But because it is within us as well as above, below and around us, we have a capacity to respond to it, though always in the particular ways made possible by our varying human conceptualities.

CS: You use 'noumenon' in a distinct way to Kant – using it to describe Ultimate Reality rather than reality as a whole. So I suppose, in a similar way, I could say that the identity of Jesus is beyond our limited conceptual apparatus ... He is beyond all our categories and so I feel permitted to use language appropriate to a reality that goes beyond our limited ideas.

JH: Yes, but there is no analogy of that with the pluralist hypothesis because the different manifestations do not contradict one another since they are formed in different terms and held by different observers. The same observer can not affirm two incompatible realities. If they did, then that would be an analogy with the incarnation.

CS: Your commitment to a Kantian epistemology gives rise to the charge that you should be seen more properly as an agnostic. You may have assurance that your experience corresponds to something distinct from yourself, which you posit as the Real. But given that we have no experience of the Real-in-itself, why do you not simply admit that there may well be nothing extra that corresponds to what would still be a profound human experience common around the world?

JH: Our experience is not of the Real-in-itself but always of one of its manifestations within human consciousness, let us say the Heavenly Father of Jesus' teaching. Now certainly a sceptic can – and there are many sceptics who do – hold that our Christian experience of the Heavenly Father, typically of being in God's presence and aware of the divine love, is delusory. This is equally the case whether one is a pluralist, an exclusivist, or an inclusivist. All religious people face this same challenge. But beyond that, the reason for postulating the transcategorial Real as well as its phenomenal manifestations is to make sense, from a religious point of view, of the varieties of apparently equally valid – because equally fruitful within human life – forms of religious experience within the different great traditions.

Clearly his answer showed that he does not want to be an atheist –

there really is something out there that correlates with religious experience, but I was unconvinced that he had really made any distinction between his own position and agnosticism. However, we went on to discuss how Jesus fitted with the pluralist interpretation.

CS: One of the most striking accounts of the life of Jesus is his arrival at the funeral of Lazarus in the Gospel of John. John seems to be at pains to stress that Jesus was sad, weeping and, the literal Greek word suggests, angry. Regarding his own death, the Gospel writers all describe Jesus as painfully regretting that this would be the path he must follow. Yet it seems to me hard to imagine a less Buddhist response to death and, thus, from within the Buddhist system Jesus would have to be regarded as much less than a Buddha.

JH: Let me say first that I would not want to base Christian doctrine on the Fourth Gospel, because of its generally acknowledged largely (though not entirely) non-historical character. But I would certainly assume that Jesus felt the full range of human emotions, including fear of death. Masao Abe, a leading exponent of Zen and a former colleague at Claremont, regarded Jesus as an Enlightened One. Now if you had pointed out to him Jesus' fear and resentment at facing death, I think he would have said that Jesus was part of the Jewish community and held Jewish presuppositions in his thinking, as the Buddha had Indian presuppositions. But I suppose that he would also say that ultimately, beyond this life, Jesus would have attained a total trust in the universal cosmic process – in Christian terms a total trust in the Heavenly Father, as distinguished from 'My God, my God, why hast thou forsaken me?'

CS: Non-attachment doesn't seem to be a doctrine that would follow from any consideration of the life of Jesus.

JH: Non-attachment means non-attachment to things that one desires for self. In other words, it's the opposite of being selfish – and Jesus was a supreme example of that. And it is a strong part of our Christian tradition that we should turn from self to God, become empty of self in order to be filled by the Spirit. 'It is not I who live, but Christ who lives in me' – this is non-attachment to the concerns of the ego in order to be open to the divine reality.

CS: Wasn't the Buddha's view of death wrapped up in his

understanding of non-attachment? From the very beginning the Gautama, who would become the Buddha, was moved by death itself. Non-attachment to desire and death were connected together.

JH: Yes, it's true that after his enlightenment death was not a big deal for him. After all, this is only one life among many.

CS: The fact that death is really somewhat trivial in the Buddhist view is exactly why Jesus would seem to be a bad example of someone approaching Buddhist enlightenment.

JH: Jesus was living in relation to a very different manifestation of the Real. (So was Mohammed.) In relation to a different manifestation of the Real one thinks differently and engages in a different form of life. The world religions are different, sometimes very different, totalities, but in my view they are different, equally valid, responses to the ultimately Real. I would, however, add that Christian theologians should pay more attention to Buddhism than most of them do, because in Buddhism we face the extraordinary paradox that metaphysically Buddhism could not be more different from Christianity, and yet ethically it could not be more similar. Central to Buddhism are the concepts (and practice) of *karuna*, 'compassion', and *metta*, 'loving-kindness'.

I have often been asked what Hick makes of the basic evidential argument for Christianity from the historical resurrection, so I pursued this line of enquiry with him.

CS: I know that you would prefer to speak in terms of a resurrection experience, but something more happened. The Jewish theologian, Geza Vermes, claims that whatever else happened there must at least have been an empty tomb. How do you deal with the resurrection facts that we can establish?

JH: To be quite precise, Vermes regards as one of 'two reasonably convincing points' that 'the women belonging to the entourage of Jesus discovered an empty tomb and were definite that it was the tomb' (*Jesus the Jew*, p. 40). But one has to say that for any interpretation of the New Testament you can line up scholars who agree with it and another group of scholars who don't. It is all highly debated. I think that Vermes has done a superb job of showing the Jewishness of Jesus. But (following many leading New Testament scholars) I regard the resurrection stories as a later creation. I think the best clue we have to the original experience of the disciples is the experience of St Paul on the Damascus road. There was no body there. There was a blinding light and a voice. I think the original experience was probably like that. It involved light, a sense of the presence of Jesus and possibly a voice. And note that this was accepted as Paul's encounter with the risen Christ.

CS: An audible voice?

JH: More likely not. More likely in Paul's mind: according to one of the accounts, 'Now those who were with him saw the light but did not hear the voice of the one who was speaking to him' (Acts 9:7 RSV).

CS: What would distinguish this experience from an illusion?

JH: That's a question that can be asked of all religious experience, and the criterion of authenticity, in my view, is always the long-term effects in the individual's life. In Paul's case these were immense and profound. But much less tremendous experiences, sometimes auditory and sometimes visual, of the presence of a recently deceased person are not uncommon. After my wife Hazel died I had a fleeting experience of this kind. And after Mike's death I had a fleeting vision of him there, beside a door of some kind through which he then went away. The experience carried a positive rather than a negative feeling. That kind of thing, taking various forms, is fairly common. In the case of Jesus, he was obviously a tremendously charismatic figure and I don't find it in the least surprising that his disciples may very well have had experiences of that kind.

CS: If the type of experience is so common, why did the first-century Christians make such a big deal of the resurrection – wouldn't they have been aware of this common pattern?

JH: They may have been, but those who have this kind of experience usually react to it as it has affected themselves. Later, the disciples' reports that they had seen, or heard, the Lord grew into the pattern of a bodily resurrection, which – though usually expected in the distant future – was common currency in first-century Judaism. By the time that Matthew's Gospel was written, around AD 80, some fifty years after the event, his readers were evidently expected to have no difficulty in believing that at the time of Jesus' resurrection 'the tombs also were opened, and many bodies of the saints who had fallen asleep [i.e. had died] were raised, and coming out of the tombs after his resurrection they went into the holy city [Jerusalem] and appeared to many' (Matthew 27:52–53 RSV). This shows the readiness of people to believe physical resurrection stories.

CS: If the resurrection were really a special case of vision, then wouldn't the first preaching in Jerusalem have been unable to get off the ground as the disciples claimed that there was an empty tomb and that the physical body of Jesus had been resurrected?

JH: The Catholic New Testament scholar Dominic Crosson, along with others, holds that quite possibly what happened to the body of Jesus is just what happened to the bodies of others who had been crucified by the Romans. They were buried with lime and simply dissolved.

CS: You do agree that in the New Testament accounts they are trying to portray a bodily resurrection rather than a visionary experience?

JH: Yes, but in my view a clue as to what actually happened is the first-hand account, given second-hand in Acts, of Paul on the road to Damascus.

CS: Yet Paul in 1 Corinthians 15 labours the point about a bodily resurrection – if there is still a body of Jesus, then his preaching is in vain, and so on. It was seen by many different people, 500 at one time, and Paul describes his own experience as one 'abnormally born' – which seems to admit that his experience was a little different from the other disciples.

JH: No, surely Paul was just saying that his experience was late. Other than that he described it as a genuine meeting with the risen Christ. As for the 500, that's something we can't check up on. It sounds a rather precise figure. It may mean that the visions were shared by quite a lot. We just don't know. Would you say that if the bodily resurrection were disproved it would destroy your Christian faith?

CS: It would, I'd probably end up a pluralist! Which I would understand as destroying my Christian faith. I believe partly because of certain historical evidences. Perhaps we could turn that answer around and ask what would count as evidence against the pluralist hypothesis, in this present life?

JH: Anything that could establish the unique superiority of any one of the world religions, as the one and only true faith, would refute the pluralistic hypothesis. Thus if it could be established that Jesus was God incarnate, it would follow that Christianity alone among the religions of the world was founded by God in person and must therefore be uniquely superior. This is the faith of orthodox Christians, not an objectively established fact acknowledged by all. In the world as a whole it is a minority belief. But beyond this life it could, if true, become universally evident. And the same is true of any other faith. But my own expectation is that what happens beyond this life will not fit into the expectations of any one religion.

This answer showed that Hick continues to believe in the basic evidentialist form of argument – if it can be shown that Jesus was God incarnate then pluralism is refuted. However, given all that Hick says about language, history, metaphysics and the meaning of the incarnation it is very hard to see quite what for him would count as evidence for the incarnation.

Bibliography of works by John Hick

(These works are listed in chronological order.)

Faith and Knowledge (Basingstoke: Macmillan, 1957).
Evil and the God of Love (Basingstoke: Macmillan, 1966).
God and the Universe of Faiths (Basingstoke: Macmillan, 1973).
Death and Eternal Life (London: Collins, 1976).
The Myth of God Incarnate, Hick (ed.) (London: SCM, 1977).
God Has Many Names (Basingstoke: Macmillan, 1980).
Problems in Religious Pluralism (Basingstoke: Macmillan, 1985).
Encountering Jesus (Philadelphia: John Knox Press, 1988).
An Interpretation of Religion (Basingstoke: Macmillan, 1989).
'Straightening the Record: Some Responses to Critics', in *Modern Theology* 6 (1990), no. 2.
Disputed Questions (Basingstoke: Macmillan, 1992).

The Metaphor of God Incarnate (London: SCM, 1993).
The Rainbow of Faiths (London: SCM, 1995).
The Fifth Dimension (Oxford: Oneworld, 1999).

Further reading

Professor Hick has had an enormous literary output during the course of his career. However, there are some helpful shorter books that provide an overview of his ideas. Paul Badham has compiled a number of Hick's own essays in *A John Hick Reader* (Basingstoke: Macmillan, 1990). John Hick's *Philosophy of Religion* (4th edn., Hemel Hempstead: Prentice Hall, 1990) provides not only a useful introduction to philosophy but also brief essays describing his own position on epistemology, theodicy and the world religions.

John Hick's *God and the Universe of Faiths* provides a basic statement of the pluralist position, while *An Interpretation of Religion* is the most comprehensive statement of and defence for his position to date.

There is a great deal of critical material on Hick. One of the best single-volume collections of this material is *Problems in the Philosophy of Religion* (Basingstoke: Macmillan, 1991), edited by H. Hewitt Jr. This includes chapters by various writers on the most important themes in Hick's work. There are also responses to each writer by Hick himself. The first part provides a particularly useful discussion of *An Interpretation of Religion*. Paul Helm's *The Varieties of Belief* (London: George Allen & Unwin, 1973) includes an incisive critique of Hick's epistemology (ch. 8). There is a helpful treatment of evil and universalism in a collection of papers edited by Nigel M. de S. Cameron, *Universalism and the Doctrine of Hell* (Carlisle: Paternoster, 1992). On the incarnation debate, C. Moule's *The Origin of Christology* (Cambridge: Cambridge University Press, 1977) is a modern classic. N. T. Wright in *Who was Jesus?* (London: SPCK, 1992) responds to a number of radical writers (though not Hick) and provides much useful material.

The most comprehensive treatment of Hick's pluralism is provided by Gavin D'Costa's *John Hick's Theology of Religions* (London: University Press of America, 1987). D'Costa also includes a comprehensive bibliography of Hick's published writings up to 1987. Chester Gillis has written a wide ranging response to Hick in *A Question of Final Belief* (Basingstoke: Macmillan, 1989). Harold Netland surveys the wider problems of Christianity and other religions in *Dissonant Voices* (Leicester: Apollos, 1991) which includes a fine summary of Hick's pluralism and some excellent critical material. There is also my own *The Universe of Faiths* (Carlisle: Paternoster, 2001) which is based upon my doctoral thesis.

Of course, pluralism is only one attempt to understand the world religions. There are two useful introductions to various ways in which Christians have sought to respond to religious pluralism. These are Gavin D'Costa's *Theology and Religious Pluralism* (Oxford: Blackwell, 1986) and Alan Race's *Christians and Religious Pluralism* (London: SCM, 1983). Growing numbers of evangelicals are writing on these issues. One such response to pluralism is Norman Anderson's *Christianity and the World Religions* (Leicester: IVP, 1984). While written in a way that will be understood by those without an academic interest in the subject, Anderson includes discussion of major theological positions including John Hick, Hans Küng and Karl Rahner. He also provides a balanced assessment of the fate of the unevangelized. Of great help is Chris Wright's *The Uniqueness of Jesus* (London: Monarch, 1997). Moving beyond Hick's view, an engaging and significant treatment of Christian engagement with pluralim is found in Vinoth Ramachandra's *Faiths in Conflict* (Leicester: IVP, 1999). Finally, *The Gospel in a Pluralist Society* (London: SPCK, 1989) by Lesslie Newbigin is well worth careful consideration, as are most of the books that he wrote.

Notes

[1] *God Has Many Names*, p. 1.

[2] *The Rainbow of Faiths*, p. 161.

[3] The theosophical movement was a Western form of Hindu philosophy.

[4] *God Has Many Names*, p. 2.

[5] *Disputed Questions*, p. 139.

[6] Hick studied theology at Westminster College, Cambridge, as part of his Presbyterian training. His only formal qualification in theology is an honorary doctorate from Uppsala University in Sweden.

7   *Faith and Knowledge.*
8   *Problems in Religious Pluralism,* p. 2.
9   Ibid., p. 3.
10 *Evil and the God of Love.*
11 *Disputed Questions,* p. 141.
12 *God and the Universe of Faiths.*
13 *Death and Eternal Life.*
14 Hick (ed.), *The Myth of God Incarnate.*
15 *An Interpretation of Religion.*
16 *Faith and Knowledge,* p. 54.
17 Ibid., p. 135.
18 Especially Hick, *An Interpretation of Religion.* Also see D'Costa, Kellenberger
    and Hick in H. Hewitt Jr (ed.), *Problems in the Philosophy of Religion* (Basing-
    stoke: Macmillan, 1991), section 1. The theme is also taken further in
    C. Sinkinson, *The Universe of Faiths* (Carlisle: Paternoster, 2001), pp. 85–103.
19 *Evil and the God of Love,* p. 3.
20 Ibid., p. 59.
21 Ibid., p. 247.
22 Ibid., p. 63.
23 Ibid., p. 126.
24 Ibid., p. 211.
25 Ibid., p. 215.
26 See F. Schleiermacher, *The Christian Faith* (Edinburgh: T. & T. Clark, 1960),
    i.e. Part 2, section 2.
27 *Evil and the God of Love,* p. 254.
28 *Death and Eternal Life,* p. 259f. On Barth and universalism see his treatment
    of the doctrine of election in *Church Dogmatics* (Edinburgh: T. & T. Clark,
    1960), Vol. II, part 2. Whether Barth was in fact a universalist remains
    debatable; see John Colwell, 'The Contemporaneity of the Divine
    Decision: Reflections on Karl Barth's Denial of "Universalism"', in N. M.
    de S. Cameron (ed.), *Universalism and the Doctrine of Hell* (Carlisle:
    Paternoster, 1992), pp. 139–160.
29 *Death and Eternal Life,* p. 456.
30 Ibid., p. 366.
31 Ibid., p. 371.
32 Ibid., p. 464.
33 Ibid., p. 12.
34 *God and the Universe of Faiths,* ch. 11.

35 Ibid., p. 150.

36 Hick (ed.), *The Myth of God Incarnate*, p. 172.

37 This is a 'degree' Christology in the tradition of Schleiermacher.

38 *God Has Many Names*, p. 4.

39 Actually, the historical debate is much less clear-cut than this, but the outline serves Hick's purposes as an analogy. See Sinkinson, *The Universe of Faiths*, pp. 10–17.

40 *Encountering Jesus*, Epilogue.

41 Ibid., pp. 10–11.

42 See K. Jaspers, *The Origin and Goal of History* (New Haven: Yale University Press, 1953).

43 *Problems in Religious Pluralism*, p. 104.

44 *Encountering Jesus*, pp. 59ff.

45 Ibid., p. 348.

46 G. D'Costa, *John Hick's Theology of Religions* (London: University Press of America, 1987), p. 102. Cf. Hick's reply in Hick, 'Straightening the Record: Some Responses to Critics', *Modern Theology*, Vol. 6, no. 2.

47 *Death and Eternal Life*, p. 464.

48 See the useful discussion of universalism in Helm in Cameron (ed.), *Universalism and the Doctrine of Hell*.

49 C. Moule, *The Origin of Christology* (Cambridge: Cambridge University Press, 1978).

50 Ibid., p. 35.

51 K. Runia, *The Present-Day Christological Debate* (Leicester: IVP, 1984).

52 Hick gives a brief treatment of the resurrection in Hick (ed.), *The Myth of God Incarnate*, pp. 170–171. Other treatments include his contribution to *Encountering Jesus* and an inadequate account in *The Metaphor of God Incarnate*, pp. 15–26. See also the interview section at the close of this essay.

53 Moule, *The Origin of Christology*, p. 103.

54 C. Gunton, *The Actuality of Atonement* (Edinburgh: T. & T. Clark, 1988), p. 158.

55 I.e. *The Metaphor of God Incarnate*.

56 Ibid., p. 47.

57 Ibid., p. 48.

58 Runia, *The Present-Day Christological Debate*, p. 108.

59 I.e. Janet Martin Soskice, *Metaphor and Religious Language* (Oxford: Oxford University Press, 1985), and Chester Gillis, *A Question of Final Belief* (Basingstoke: Macmillan, 1989).

[60]   Brian Hebblethwaite suggests that three literal truth-claims remain in
       A. Sharma (ed.), *God, Truth and Reality: Essays in Honour of John Hick*
       (Basingstoke: Macmillan, 1993), p. 131.

[61]   Hick responds to this in a fictitious dialogue in *The Rainbow of Faiths*,
       pp. 67–69, but the argument is weak because it fails to justify theism.
       Essentially Hick argues that if you are already a theist (for other reasons),
       then the pluralist hypothesis is compatible with the assumption that there
       really is a God. The 'other reasons' are spelled out elsewhere in his
       treatment of faith as a basic religious perception. If you don't have this
       perception then there's nothing you can do about it.

[62]   In M. Goulder (ed.), *Incarnation and Myth* (London: SCM, 1979), p. 200.

[63]   H. Netland, *Dissonant Voices* (Leicester: Apollos, 1991), p. 232.

[64]   An excellent resource for understanding the historic variations is John
       Sanders, *No Other Name* (Grand Rapids, MI: Eerdmans, 1992), which
       provides detailed historical documentation of the various positions.

[65]   For a useful treatment of this theme see D'Costa, *John Hick's Theology of
       Religions*, pp. 141–142.

[66]   Hick, 'Response to Alister E. McGrath' in D. L. Okholm and T. R.
       Phillips (eds.), *Four Views of Salvation in a Pluarlistic World* (Grand Rapids,
       MI: Zondervan, 1996), p. 183.

[67]   This point is quite brilliantly applied to Tibetan Buddhist pluralism in
       G. D'Costa, *The Meeting of the Religions and the Trinity* (Edinburgh: T. & T.
       Clark, 2000), pp. 72ff.

[68]   Netland, *Dissonant Voices*, p. 225.

[69]   In D. Edwards and J. Stott, *Essentials* (London: Hodder & Stoughton,
       1988), p. 327.

[70]   N. Anderson, *Christianity and the World Religions* (Leicester: IVP, 1984).

[71]   P. Helm in Cameron (ed.), *Universalism and the Doctrine of Hell*, p. 278.

[72]   For example, A. McGrath, 'A Particularist View: A Post-Enlightenment
       Approach', in Okholm and Phillips (eds.), *Four Views of Salvation*, p. 179.

[73]   For example, see G. R. McDermott, *Can Evangelicals Learn From the World
       Religions?* (Downers Grove: IVP, 2000).

[74]   McGrath in Okholm and Phillips (eds.), *Four Views of Salvation*, p. 164.

[75]   *Christianity and Other Faiths: An Evangelical contribution to our Multi-Faith Society*
       (Carlisle: Paternoster, 1983), p. 22.

2. JÜRGEN MOLTMANN: A CRITICAL INTRODUCTION

Stephen Williams

Stephen Williams is Professor of Systematic Theology at Union Theological College, Belfast. He is the author of Revelation and Reconciliation: a Window on Modernity *(Cambridge: Cambridge University Press, 1995).*

Preface

The following account of Moltmann's thought was first published in 1987. It ended with an appendix on what was then Moltmann's latest major work, *God In Creation* (1985), the second of a series of volumes making up his studies in dogmatics. That work was succeeded by *The Way of Jesus Christ* (1989) and then *The Spirit of Life* (1992). At the time, I wrote brief reviews of these which are now reprinted here as part of the Appendix. Moltmann's series of studies in dogmatics began with *The Trinity and the Kingdom of God*, so we see how the subsequent three volumes followed a trinitarian sequence, dealing with God, Christ and the Spirit, respectively. Moltmann's doctrine of the Trinity made its appearance in his second major work prior to this particular series, namely *The Crucified God*.

His very first volume, which launched him on to the international scene, was *Theology of Hope: On the Grounds and Implications of Christian Eschatology*. So, fittingly enough, these later trinitarian studies were followed by a volume on eschatology, *The Coming*

God.[1] This is Moltmann's latest, perhaps last, contribution to the series. It has attracted enough attention for Richard Bauckham, the leading British commentator on Moltmann, to edit a volume devoted to it.[2] Bauckham has always been more partial to Moltmann's work than I have and has concentrated more on teasing out underlying insights where I have tended to highlight difficulties.[3]

When the present account first appeared, Moltmann was just over sixty years old, having enjoyed two decades of a reputation that had gradually established him as one of the most influential figures in contemporary theology. That influence extended beyond Germany and the West to the Third World, and beyond academic institutions into pulpits. Hence the potential helpfulness of this brief critical introduction to his thought for those unfamiliar with it. While it concentrates on his major works, it makes use of the range of his writings. Over the years, Richard Bauckham has offered both bibliographical surveys and full- length treatments of Moltmann's work, which are invariably helpful.[4]

One cannot appreciate properly the flavour of Moltmann's thought without some grasp of the continental philosophy of the last two hundred years and of modern theology. One obvious limitation of an essay such as this is that the author's thought must be presented shorn of the technical, but important, intra-disciplinary discussions with his protagonists, past and present. It may therefore be useful for the reader to consult such general works as Colin Brown's *Philosophy and the Christian Faith* (London: Tyndale Press, 1969) or its expanded first part, *Christianity and Western Thought* (Leicester: Apollos, 1990) and introductions to twentieth-century theology by S. Grenz and R. E. Olson, *Twentieth Century Theology: God and the World in a Transitional Age* (Carlisle: Paternoster, 1992) and by S. Grenz and E. Miller, *Introduction to Contemporary Theologies* (Minneapolis: Fortress, 1998). However, it is to Moltmann's credit that a presentation such as this essay can, in principle, be made without undue distortion of his thought, for he seeks in his work to recapture a biblical simplicity of thought, susceptible of relatively straightforward exposition where it is needed.

In his major works, Moltmann has concentrated on theological principles and I have attended to this in the expositions. He is repetitive and hammers home his convictions on key themes such as eschatology or the Trinity time after time; but eschatology (generally, 'the doctrine of the last things') and the Trinity are explored and explicated in order to teach us to bear the cross of the present in our discipleship and seek therein the liberation of humankind, which is the goal of God. Moltmann's thought is anything but abstract in its intention. If one reads, for example, *The Experiment Hope* or *On Human Dignity*, one finds him reflecting on a range of social issues and making specific proposals about them. His own religious experience and appreciation of religious experience in general is set out in *Experiences of God*,[5] and the importance of prayer and meditation conveyed in a generally illuminating essay in *Hope in the Church*.[6] He is deeply and practically concerned for the handicapped.[7] Even apparently technical philosophical distinctions, such as that between a 'dialectical' and 'analogical' principle of knowledge (into which I do not enter, despite its importance), are significantly earthed in Christian piety and outreach.[8] Finally, he tells us that 'according to my conviction, scholarly theology has for its target the sermon'.[9]

I have certainly been critical of Moltmann's work, letting the reader, perhaps, find his or her own way to areas of agreement. But obviously there is much to commend in his theology, especially the alliance between theological reflection and call to action, and the attempt to discern and delineate the stark contours of biblical theology. Moltmann has spoken of his own youthful war-time experience thus:

> As I continue to look back I see a young prisoner of war interned in an English camp. His horizon there is the barbed wire, even though the war has been over for some time. His path is one which curves in a circle around the edges of the barbed wire. Freedom lies beyond – out there where people live and laugh ... Hope rubbed itself raw on the barbed wire! A man cannot live without hope! ... The prisoner experienced an inner conversion when he gave up hope of getting home soon, and in his yearning he rediscovered that deeper 'hope against hope'.[10]

With that young man, his longings and his discovery, we can and
surely must identify.

A theology of hope

Ideas, unlike ordinary physical objects, are in the air before they
get off the ground, so to speak. In the 1960s revolution was in the
air and sometimes on the ground; indeed, one should speak of
revolutions, in the plural, when one takes into account student
protests in France or Japan, civil rights or hippies in America.
Moltmann proved sensitive to this feature of the contemporary
scene. The most dramatic of all revolutions, however, judged by
its slogan, occurred in the realm of religious ideas, for some
theologians were heard to say 'God is dead!' The drama is
lessened, though not lost, on recalling that what was broadly
meant by this was that the joint pressure of new perspectives on
Christianity from within and cultural changes without entailed, for
some, abandonment of the traditional notion of God and
associated norms of conduct. Moltmann himself took up the
theme of the death of God, albeit with reference to ideas from
early in the nineteenth century, and his own revision of traditional
notions of God has proved to be pivotal in his work. Yet, in the
1960s he celebrated not the death of God but the birth of hope.
His *Theology of Hope* did not spring out of nowhere, nor was it the
product of purely private, unparalleled theological reflection.[11]
However, it made its own peculiar impact and is one of the most
important works of contemporary theology.

'No matter what Jürgen Moltmann publishes, he will always be
remembered foremost for his *Theology of Hope*.'[12] The word 'hope'
is probably the most persistent in Moltmann's entire theological
vocabulary. It remains so in some of his most recent writings: *The
Power of the Powerless* is dedicated to friends in 'a common hope' and
the concluding essay of *On Human Dignity* refers to a 'common
way of hope'. The word 'common' here is significant, for it is of a
hope common to humanity that Moltmann has wanted to speak
from the beginning. More than this, to speak of it is not only
a theological responsibility, but the theological responsibility,

according to *Theology of Hope*. Years on, when other organizing principles of theological discourse have also been brought into play, one can still speak of eschatology, the doctrine of Christian hope, as 'the foundation and medium of Christian theology'.[13] An important early essay, in *The Future of Hope*, refers to 'Theology as Eschatology'. *Theology of Hope* has proved memorable not just because it set out the content of Christian hope but because it charged Christian theology with the task of conducting its entire reflection in the light of it and as an exploration of it. 'From Moltmann's standpoint, the distinctive contribution of Christian faith is the hope it engenders in the midst of the ambiguous and even hopeless circumstances that plague human existence.'[14] 'The Bible,' said Moltmann, 'is the textbook of hope, and the best presupposition for the theology and church of today to understand it correctly is this: every page and every word is concerned with the burning question, What may I hope?'[15]

The word 'hope' is familiar enough; but what exactly is 'eschatology'? The quick answer, mentioned earlier, is 'the doctrine of the last things'. There is a sense in which such a reply is acceptable to Moltmann. But the problem, as he sees it, is that eschatology has often been the last doctrine too. That is, it brings up the rear in books that offer general treatments of Christian doctrine. *Theology of Hope* expresses the conviction that, on the contrary, eschatology is pivotal. The key New Testament themes of the death and resurrection of Christ are really eschatological themes. In *Theology of Hope* it is the resurrection that is focal, and it is expounded in terms of the 'foreglow' of the end-time. The kind of hope set forth in the Bible is not an other-worldly hope, incapable of promoting this-worldly change. Authentic Christian eschatology presents us with a this-worldly eschatology, the driving force for this-worldly transformation. So Moltmann wants to establish the content of eschatology (this-worldly), its method (an exposition of Christology, set in the context of general biblical theology), its importance (the medium of Christian thinking) and its effect (world-transforming activity).

In taking up the question of eschatology and according it theological centrality, Moltmann was tackling a question that had surfaced with particular force at the turn of the century.[16] He felt,

however, that the question had not been given realistic, biblical
treatment in theology. For example, two mid-century theological
giants, Karl Barth and Rudolf Bultmann, emphasized in different
ways the finality of the revelation we receive through Christ in the
present and *Theology of Hope* is largely a running battle with these
two and others. The problem with this was that eschatology and
Christianity came to be robbed of their future orientation.
Moltmann, on the other hand, wants our gaze to be consistently
'forward, not upward', as it has been put. This he finds to be the
biblical perspective, and therefore major portions of his book are
given over to outlines of selected, but central, features of Old and
New Testament theology.

In the Old Testament we encounter the God of promise.
Moltmann plays this off against the idea of presence. If one asks
concerning the revelation of God and the content of his word in
the Old Testament, one is not directed to God's self-revelation
in the present and communication of something presently done.
Rather, one is directed to the promises that he will reveal himself
in the future and what will be done then. Those promises,
constantly renewed in the history of Israel, actually created history,
for they drew Israel on into the future, ever moving towards the
promised land of fulfilment. This perspective is by no means
abandoned in the New Testament. True, something absolutely
decisive has happened in Jesus Christ. By raising the crucified
Christ from the dead, God has opened out history for all mankind,
inaugurating some kind of trend that will culminate in the all-
embracing glorification of God. History is now what happens
between resurrection and eschaton (the end) according not to
some immanent progress but to the operation of the divine
promise. But this way of putting it shows that a future orientation
and activity based on promise is still valid. It is thus misleading to
think of the New Testament as related to the Old in terms of the
fulfilment of promise, as though the present, not the future, could
now be our chief interest.

Sustaining this thesis involved Moltmann in a number of
important proposals. One had to do with the nature of God, a
God with 'future as his essential nature', to quote the revisionist
Marxist, Bloch, who has had such a profound influence on

Moltmann and other continental theologians.[17] The importance of this conviction in *Theology of Hope* emerges in *The Experiment Hope*, chapter 4. Moltmann's doctrine of God here could be characterized in what will strike most of us as remarkable terms: '[Moltmann] will not say that God "is" or that "God is not", but he has no difficulty in saying that God is "still not yet".'[18] What Moltmann is trying to do is to apply the biblical emphasis on the future to the very being of God. An exegetical foundation for this could be Exodus 3:14, translated as 'I WILL BE WHAT I WILL BE',[19] where God discloses himself to Moses. Gerald O'Collins stated that Moltmann surprisingly did not refer to this passage in *Theology of Hope*,[20] but it is implicit in reference to discussion of Exodus 3[21] and later in his work explicitly cited.[22] Still, it is not on a particular text that Moltmann's argument turns. Throughout *Theology of Hope* Moltmann underlines the contrast between Greek and Hebrew thought in many ways, including the emphasis on eternity (which is timeless) in the former and futurity (which is temporal) in the latter. This kind of contrast received powerful rebuttal in the 1960s in the work of James Barr.[23] But Moltmann wanted to detach from God the idea of timeless, eternal presence in order to keep in line with the biblical narrative which seems to portray God as a dynamic being, coming to the fullness of glorious being only at the end-time. Moltmann's thought here has provoked dissatisfaction from the outset and, in fact, he does not seem to have persevered in the notions implicit in the doctrine of God's being as future. Yet he has persevered in ascribing to God experience of time, as we shall later see.

A second important proposal involved in arguing the claims of *Theology of Hope* had to do with the interpretation of history. Moltmann pointed out that to be conscious of history today is to be conscious of the way it is punctuated by revolution and its potential so that some sort of permanent crisis seems to mark the movements we make, manage or endure. History is dynamic passage. Several philosophies of history have been devised to plumb its deep currents and Moltmann offers a critique of these together with an alternative proposal. His proposal is that we think of history in terms of its promised future in God's hands and the present impact of that promise. The Christian hopes in the decisive, ultimate and universal manifestation of God in his righteousness. The gospel is a call to Jews and Gentiles to participate in the life and the coming glory of God; hence it is a missionary call, offering life for all and participation for all in missionary activity. 'Mission' was a key theme in Moltmann's work from the beginning[24] and received full-length treatment in *The Church in the Power of the Spirit*, as we shall see. Here, in *Theology of Hope*, it is emphasized that history is the arena for missionary work. In light of reconciliation begun and promised, the gospel calls for the emergence in man of the true humanity which is to be his. It calls for world transformation, activity which corresponds to the secret of history.

It is the resurrection of Jesus Christ that offers us a decisive perspective on all these things in *Theology of Hope*. If we are looking, in Moltmann, for a clear statement of belief in an empty tomb and corporeal resurrection, we will be disappointed.[25] But he certainly views the resurrection of Christ as an objective event forming and transforming history in its train. It instantiates and signals in the crucial way for Christianity the fact that God is the author of possibilities released into history, not derived from it. It inaugurates a trend that is not identical with the history of the world but yet is decisive in the purposes of God for history to bring it to its consummation. More exactly, it is the risen Lord himself, not some world process, that guides time to its goal. In this connection, Moltmann attends especially to Pauline theology and to 'apocalyptic', a complex theme which has nevertheless become important in biblical and doctrinal theology.[26] His discussion is ordered to show how the resurrection leads to the future which it anticipates, the future of the risen one, the future of life, righteousness and the kingdom of God. The heart of eschatology is thus manifested in the resurrection of the crucified one.

In the light and power of the resurrection, the church sets out not to achieve the kingdom of God itself but to achieve anticipations of it in history. It is an 'exodus church' aflame with the light of eschatological liberation. Christians are not to hang around and wait for the realization of the goal of history, for the 'hope of justice, the humanizing of man, the socializing of

humanity, peace for all creation'[27] are its passion and goal.
Moltmann expounded some of the implications of this in *Religion,
Revolution and the Future* where he expressed the conviction that
'unless it [truth] contains initiative for the transformation of the
world, it becomes myth for the existing world'.[28] It is the task
of hope to foster a Christian ethic, Christian ethics being 'the
forward-moving, evolutionary and revolutionary initiative for the
overcoming of man's bodily predicament and the plight of
injustice'.[29] The accent is on social transformation. Moltmann is
setting out, in accordance with needs that came to be felt in
ecumenical circles in the 1950s, a general 'ethical field theory' for
hope.[30] 'Field theory' recalls the quest in modern science for
unifying principles that will explain some of the awesome totalities
of the world, and readers with a background in modern physics
may wish to press a comparison between what Moltmann
(borrowing from Bloch) terms 'tendencies' and 'possibilities'
with uses those terms have, for example, in discussion of
quantum theory. But Moltmann's hope, while it unifies the
Christian perception of reality, is not meant to titillate the intellect
with its conceptual possibilities. It is meant to stimulate the
activity that must correspond to divine possibilities. This goal,
which comes to light in *Theology of Hope*, we must surely consider
salutary.

The God of the cross

Perhaps the word 'hope' brings with it a different set of
associations for different people. This is natural, as it bears varied
meanings. But it often has a poignant ring to it. Its gaze is towards
the future, towards the fulfilment of that wished or longed for, and
its atmosphere is captured by Moltmann in the autobiographical
fragment cited in the preface and sustained by him in his literature.
Its future reference, however, reminds us that it advertises some
sort of lack in the present, otherwise there would be no room for
hope. Indeed, one might even speak of 'contradiction' here, for
Moltmann's future hope is a hope of glory, whereas the present
state of the world appears as its diametrical opposite. Moltmann,

in fact, adopts the vocabulary of contradiction in this very context. And instead of diametrical opposites he speaks of dialectical opposites. The concept of dialectic in Moltmann's theology is central. This word has had a long and rich history, particularly, for modern theological purposes, in the last couple of centuries, and it embraces a wide range of meaning. 'Dialectic' broadly directs us to the interplay of two opposite things. In relating future to present, glory to suffering, life to death, Moltmann focuses methodically on cross and resurrection, for do we not see here the stark antitheses of godforsaken death and glorious victory taken up into a unity whose reality and truth inform and engulf the story of the world? So Moltmann believes. If *Theology of Hope* focused on the resurrection, though it emphasized the resurrection of the crucified one, so the second major work, *The Crucified God*, focused on the cross, though it emphasized the cross of the risen one.

If strong claims had previously been made about the eschatological key of all Christian thinking, equally strong ones are made on behalf of a *theologia crucis*, a theology of the cross. In fact, it is largely the angle of vision that has changed in this work, for Christian eschatology is an eschatology of the cross.[31] Moltmann tells us: 'I identify the Pauline theology of hope with his theology of the cross ... the theology of the cross is the theology of hope ...'[32] Indeed, he could say: 'Not the great historical acts of God as such interest me (including resurrection), but the suffering of God in the Passion Story of the world.'[33] These words indicate that Moltmann connects the suffering of the cross with the suffering of the world. They also indicate Moltmann's willingness to speak of 'the suffering of God'. Both these things invite comment.

Timely awareness of the fact of suffering occasioned *The Crucified God* as a counter-balance to, though by no means contradiction of, *Theology of Hope*. Suffering is fundamental to human existence: 'I suffer, therefore I am.'[34] Its existence is a governing factor in a form of profound and pervasive modern atheism: 'protest atheism'. Its protest against suffering is a protest against the traditional God of pure omnipotence who compounds his threat to the freedom and humanity of man by co-existing impassibly (that is, without suffering) and all-powerfully with suffering humanity. Under its aegis criticism of the status quo, as Horkheimer put it, became the substitute for faith in a heavenly judge. The problem of belief in God in the face of evil or of suffering is often termed the question of 'theodicy'. In *The Crucified God* Moltmann wants to take some steps towards resolving that question, convinced that a Christian view of God and the world that cannot take to its heart the truth in protest atheism is self-defeating and valueless. It is in a theology of the cross that we begin to find answers. Moltmann is not alone in forging a theology of the cross in some sort of dialogue with atheism; see the title of a work by his influential university colleague E. Jüngel, *God as the Mystery of the World: On the Foundation of the Theology of the Crucified One in the Dispute between Theism and Atheism.*

Talk of the 'suffering of God' becomes (literally) crucially important in this context. At the heart of the attempt to work out a theology of the cross there must be a revolution, as Moltmann terms it, in the concept of God. Protest atheism rightly sees that the true humanity of man, burdened by his suffering, cannot possibly be squared with the glorious omnipotence of God, incapable of suffering.[35] But it is wrong to abandon the notion of God, as in atheistic conclusions. It is our idea of God that must be refashioned. And surely, as Bonhoeffer put it, 'only the suffering God can help'. However, it is not a case of atheism dictating here to Christian theology. It is the cross itself that is the critique of alien ideas of God within our own (Christian) tradition. Moltmann's special target here is the doctrine that God does not and cannot suffer, the doctrine of impassibility. To all appearances this was axiomatic in the early church, profoundly affecting its Christologies.[36] Hence the 'revolutionary' nature of Moltmann's proposal.

The point of a theology of the cross, like a theology of hope, is to energize us in our witness. Luther had spoken of a *theologia crucis*, but for our day it must take the form of a social criticism. It must be unashamedly iconoclastic of all the idols of power and glory especially in the political realm that are foreign to the mission and spirit of the crucified God. It must be gladly willing to identify with the wretched and godforsaken in the social realm that are invited to share the company of the wretched and

godforsaken Christ of the cross. This practical note, then, in
Theology of Hope is also preserved. How does Moltmann execute his
programme?

In *The Crucified God* he begins by outlining the 'identity-
involvement' dilemma characterizing much contemporary Christianity.[37] Keeping one's Christian identity leads too easily to social
withdrawal; social involvement in the name of relevance leads too
easily to a forfeiture of distinctively Christian identity. Here the
cross must guide us. Christian identity is forged and found in
identification with the crucified Christ; the core of such identification lies less in mystical, passive suffering, ingredient though that
is in Christianity, than in active, imitative suffering. This suffering
arises from reaching out, as did Jesus, to the abandoned and
godforsaken in their misery. Such activity leads the Christian to
connect the cross of Jesus and the criticism of society. It leads
to what has been described as 'political theology'.

'Political theology', Moltmann tells us, emerged as far as he
was concerned, at the end of the 1960s (following the lead
of the Catholic theologian, J. B. Metz) in translating the hope of
faith into hope in action.[38] Broadly, it directs theology into the
social-political arena; the concept is developed and expounded in
several writings such as *On Human Dignity* (subtitled *On Political
Theology and Ethics*)[39] and *The Experiment Hope*.[40] Political theology,
as Moltmann describes it, denotes 'the field, the milieu, the realm,
and the stage on which Christian theology should be explicitly
carried on today. Political theology wants to awaken political
consciousness in every treatise of Christian theology ... The
church must develop a critical and self-conscious political theology'.[41] This is no crude despiritualizing politicization of Christian
religion. On the contrary it expresses authentic Christian spirituality – the spirituality of the crucified Christ. Did not his life,
ministry, teaching and, finally, death at the hands of the mighty
Roman Empire stand against the gods of power and self-
glorification which are idolatrously formative of our cultures?
And do not the biblical texts themselves unfold their meaning to
those who read them as a clarion call to suffer in the world in the
cause of God? Thus to a political theology Moltmann allies a
'political hermeneutics' of the gospel ('hermeneutics' being,

roughly, principles of interpretation). Here, then, a theology of hope is true to its missionary orientation when it becomes a political theology in the shadow of the cross.

Again, as in *Theology of Hope*, we note the Christological basis. Too often we approach Christ from a distorting perspective. The New Testament witnesses to him in the context of the eschatological future and redemption of the world. That future belongs to the one crucified – such is the nugget of promise set in the heart of the scandal of the cross. That scandal started with his ministry and life. For a long time biblical criticism has led us to ask how much we can know of the historical Jesus. He is sufficiently accessible to us, Moltmann insists, for the concrete reality of the cross, in its setting in the life and society of Jesus Christ, to manifest God and his truth to our understanding. As a matter of historical fact, Jesus, in God's name, proffered the kingdom of the Father to the outcasts – and blasphemed in the eyes of those who would be justified by the law. Further, he was a political rebel, for he substituted brotherhood with the poor for the kingship of political might. Yet, though he lived and acted in the name of God, his Father, at life's end, on the cross, the most bewildering thing of all occurred: he experienced forsakenness at the hands of the very God in whom he believed. In that desolate cry: 'My God, my God, why have you forsaken me?' (Mark 15:34) Moltmann discerns the answer to the riddle of God, suffering, righteousness and truth. How so?

We know that the one crucified was raised, and an eschatological Christology views this in the light of the world's future when divine righteousness and truth will be established. If that is the case, God, by the resurrection of Christ, has sealed the truth of Jesus' earthly witness to him. But if he identified with Jesus in his life, resurrection and eschatological lordship, does he not identify himself with him in the cross? How can such identification take place within the God-forsakenness experienced by Jesus? The answer gives us the clue to God's relation to the world. In that very God-forsakenness God comes to be present. The cross shows God taking into himself the burden of guilt, death, suffering and the misery of the world and humanity, for he identified himself, through Christ, with that humanity and takes up into his divine being the story of human sin and sorrow. Here, then, we find a suffering God.

In claiming this, Moltmann certainly wants to disclaim a substantial conviction of early church Christology. He found its central difficulty in its failure to account properly for the suffering of the cross.[42] In the classical Christological formula of the early church, Jesus Christ is spoken of as a single person but possessed of two natures: divine and human. Different properties may be ascribed to each nature: humanity suffers and dies, for example, but deity is immortal and impassible. To ascribe to God capacity for suffering would be to subject him to conditioning to that external to himself; that, in turn, would mean that he was changeable; that, in turn, would mean he was imperfect. So one could represent the broad logic of the patristic denial of impassibility in conceptually abstract terms. But, further, Chalcedonian Christology was set squarely within the frame of the doctrine of the Trinity. Is Moltmann then denying this doctrine?

On the contrary: the emergence of Moltmann's trinitarianism is a central feature of *The Crucified God*. He argues that only a trinitarian interpretation will do, confronted with the story of the cross. For here we have to do with the Son delivered up to death by the Father. The Father suffers the loss of the Son as the Son suffers death, but the Father himself does not die. These distinctions between Father and Son are inconceivable in the biblical perspective without thinking of God as two persons. Further, in their separation they are united, and out of the event of the cross comes the Spirit. Hence we have to do with a third person. When Moltmann later elaborates his trinitarian theology, he finds evidence of trinitarian activity, of course, in the creation of the world and the sending of the Son, but what the cross distinctively reveals and achieves is the way the Trinity opens itself out in time to embrace the extremities of God-forsakenness. Hence we learn too at the cross that God is not timeless, for he experiences time as well as suffering. God has a history – a trinitarian history. These are themes Moltmann will take up in his next major works.

Meanwhile, if we understand God thus, we are liberated. We are freed psychologically because the cross 'leads man into the history of God' and this 'frees him for an acceptance of human life which is capable of suffering and capable of love'.[43] And political liberation comes in train of the recognition that God is no God of Caesarian power but God of the poor and abandoned, who can create anticipations in time of the liberation of the future. The God of hope is the God of the cross and the cross lifts up the head of the suffering that they might look forward to God. Present and future, suffering and hope are thus established by the event of divine trinitarian love in the death of Christ which led to a resurrection unto life.

Church and Spirit

Easter looks back to Good Friday and forward to Pentecost. As *Theology of Hope* had concentrated on resurrection and *The Crucified God* on the cross, so does *The Church in the Power of the Spirit* concentrate on the Spirit. The three works between them make up a trilogical series of attempts to take in the main elements in theology each time from a special perspective. Moltmann's next work, *The Trinity and the Kingdom of God*, began a series of explorations of particular themes built on principles established in the earlier works. The explorations starting with *The Trinity and the Kingdom of God* form units of a 'messianic theology' or 'messianic dogmatics'; *The Church in the Power of the Spirit* is described as 'a contribution to messianic ecclesiology' in the preface and note the title of Richard Bauckham's forthcoming work which includes the phrase 'messianic theology'. The Messiah is the expected deliverer. First he must suffer before entering into his glory. The creation also groans in travail on the way to its own liberation. All theology is messianically oriented in its expectant suffering and hope, and the 'church in the power of the Spirit' must show forth this truth. In this work we encounter themes with which we are already familiar in Moltmann, but new, perhaps startling, implications are brought to light. As in the path from *Theology of Hope* to *The Crucified God* one might detect changes in the doctrine of God, here in the doctrine of God as Trinity, we are encountering development in *The Church in the Power of the Spirit*.[44] But in accordance with the purpose of this

essay I am not pursuing the discontinuities or the puzzles amidst
the governing continuities and clarities, at least of intent.

The words 'church' and 'Spirit' in the title advertise that feature
of the theological tradition that Moltmann wishes to challenge in
this work. *Theology of Hope* had set out the universal eschatological
perspective from which we look at the whole. But the bounds of
the universe are wider than the bounds of the church. Hence,
argues Moltmann, we must locate our understanding of the church
and her mission within the wider context of the universal mission
of the Spirit. Consistent with his earlier convictions Moltmann
derives his view of the Spirit's mission from Christ's mission. In
giving primacy to the universal mission of Christ, and then Spirit,
in the context of universal eschatology, Moltmann is breaking with
the tradition which orientates the world to the church rather than
subordinating the church to the world, as Tripole puts it.[45] If
pneumatology (the doctrine of the Spirit) and ecclesiology (the
doctrine of the church) are established thus on the foundations of
eschatological Christology, how is the church to pursue her
mission in the power of the Spirit? For in accordance with his
emphasis on praxis (practice or activity), in this work Moltmann
keeps a constant eye on the mission of the church.

Moltmann holds that if our eschatological perspective informs
us of God's design for the future, this has some immediate
implications for the task of ecclesiology. It becomes wrong to
view the church according to a timeless nature, constant through
history. It becomes wrong to separate the church from the world
as though they are different unities with different destinies. It is in
the context of God's dealings with the world that we understand
his dealings with the church. 'Understanding' the church,
however, is ordered to the task of world transformation; a
doctrine of the church must be the point of departure for her
reformation in the light and service of world renewal. The church
is a channel for messianic mediation to the world. Protestantism
rightly has connected the mediator with ecclesiology traditionally,
by founding the church on the rock of justification in Christ. But
if Christology is adequately understood, it is eschatological, so that
there is a fuller perspective to be found for grasping the nature of
the church in the eschatological calling of Jew and Gentile.[46] It is

in this way that the story of Christ, who bore his cross in order to lead the world into eschatologically liberating lordship in a new creation, becomes the focus of the church's responsive attention.

Keeping in mind the Christological foundation of our thinking, Moltmann is able in *The Church in the Power of the Spirit* to expound what he terms the 'trinitarian history of God'. This way of speaking departs from traditional trinitarianism to the extent that the former ascribes timeless eternity to the trinitarian being of God, whereas Moltmann insists on the temporality of the Trinity, that is the inner reality of history for the being of God.[47] As trinitarian history, however, is exhibited and experienced in the event of the cross, it is seen to embrace world history, since the Spirit that flowed out of Calvary, in whose power Christ was sacrificed (Hebrews 9:14) unites the abyss of death and misery with the very being of God in himself. Moltmann thinks in what can be called dynamically panentheistic terms. God is dynamic, not static; there is a form of self-unfolding in his being. He is also not apart from the world (an idea which, in its extreme form, is often labelled deism) and yet he is not identical with the world (strictly, pantheism). He transcends the world by choosing freely a form of union with it, a union whereby he takes into his own being, voluntarily, the being of the world. This is the gist of Moltmann's panentheism. Its basis and distinctive slant is its trinitarian nature. A useful introduction to some concepts of God by a proponent of what is known as the 'classical' viewpoint in Christianity is Huw Parri Owen's *Concepts of Deity* which should help readers get acquainted with some of the options that have been exercised in traditional and modern doctrines of God.

It is because trinitarian history in its way comprehends world history that the church rightly allows the universal perspective to be her own. In the midst of the clamour to understand world history the great sign of the times, for the church, is constituted by the path of the liberating Spirit. That Spirit, binding Father and Son in dynamic love, flows out in mission to the world with that same love. The mission will be accomplished with the eventual glorification of the world. The trinity is the story of the eschatological unity of God with his creation to his glory. In this goal of the messianic mission of Christ and the creative mission of the Spirit – for the new creation is the substance of the eschaton – the church participates. Here she finds her identity.

All this means that the presence of Christ in the Spirit cannot be confined to the church. Christ's messianic mission on earth terminated in representative self-giving destined to herald a liberating lordship. In this the church participates by setting forth all kinds of liberation in sympathy and joy, thus living in the presence of Christ. But 'Christ is confessed in the Holy Spirit and by him ... where the power of the new creation is active. He is confessed where prisoners liberate themselves from oppression.'[48] The parable of the sheep and the goats in Matthew 25 is taken by Moltmann to teach the presence of Christ in the poor.[49] Christ is not present here in a Christian congregation, but his presence makes the poor fellow-members with the institutional church of the kingdom of God.[50] This is where eschatological Christology takes us in ecclesiology and missiology (understanding of mission).

What Moltmann is doing here is further exploring a theme, theologically prominent in our century, of the sacred and the secular, with a view to breaking down barriers in that realm that take the form of a church–world separation. Much of the inspiration for Moltmann's and others' way of thinking here came from Dietrich Bonhoeffer.[51] In the later stages of his short life Bonhoeffer referred to 'religionless Christianity', sometimes (but questionably) rendered 'unchurchly Christianity' to get its proper force. This was done in the service of a wider attempt to relate the presence of Christ to the world, not just to the church. Moltmann also wanted to relate 'church' to the substance of Christianity in a non-traditional fashion, even if there are dissimilarities with Bonhoeffer. The upshot, as far as Moltmann is concerned, is that 'Christ's presence in word and sacrament points beyond itself (by virtue of its indwelling logic of identification and his presence itself) to his identity in the world'.[52]

This has implications not only for relations between the church and the poor but also for relations with other religions. The church has her partners in the world 'who will never become the church',[53] but whose future is yet the universal lordship of God. A theology of hope knows no limits: 'It hopes for all, and it hopes for everything.'[54] Hence there is hope for Israel and hope for other religions. Israel has a special vocation in partnership with the church which must not be assimilated to the church's more specific vocation with respect to the gospel but which is nevertheless a true partnership, for the Messiah is the Messiah of Israel and of the church. They are united in a mission of hope: 'Let Christians and Jews turn to the world together, with the ardour of hope.'[55] Moltmann's treatment of Israel is important in his theology[56] and indeed the Christian attitudes to Israel and the Jews are exceedingly important in the modern world. What emerges in the context of his treatment here is that mission can be shared by Jews and Gentiles in some form and can thus take the form of promoting hope: 'mission is the infection with hope' (Hoekendijk) and 'Christianity is mission' says Moltmann.[57] The traditional missionary task of making disciples for Christ must be supplemented (not replaced) by the task of 'infecting' people, 'whatever their religion, with the spirit of hope, love and responsibility for the world'.[58] In adopting this attitude Moltmann, who is a Reformed theologian, partakes of convictions expressed within other confessions. The Lutheran George Lindbeck thus says that 'the missionary task of Christians may at times be to encourage Marxists to become better Marxists, Jews and Muslims to become better Jews and Muslims, and Buddhists to become better Buddhists'.[59] Lindbeck takes his own cue from attitudes that surfaced in Roman Catholicism in the 1960s, it would seem.[60]

Moltmann's incentive to think thus is consistently Christological and eschatological. In its light he discusses the concrete forms of hope – social, political, economic, racial, cultural. Liberating activity here must 'correspond to' and 'anticipate' the kingdom of God. 'The church in the power of the Spirit is not yet the kingdom of God, but it is its anticipation in history.'[61] New possibilities exist in the power of the coming new creation mediated by the Spirit. *The Church in the Power of the Spirit* makes concrete the implications of *Theology of Hope* with the aid of developed trinitarianism.

Has Moltmann abandoned traditional elements of the doctrine of the church? In his view, he has rather reinstated them in proper

context. Receiving the word means liberation for the future;
baptism is initiation into missionary participation in the trinitarian
history of God; the Lord's Supper is an inclusive, not exclusive,
feast of hopeful friendship; worship anticipates the eschatological
doxology of creation. The church is in fact distinguished by all
these things, but not immured in an ark of salvation with sealed
safety valves, cocooned from a damned world. As is the case with
'means of grace', so with ministries of the church the Spirit must
not be tied in exclusivistic fashion to ministry and sacrament. In
line with the liberating Spirit, we must not go in for hierarchies
which confer traditional 'monarchical' authority on individual
bishops or hierarchical theologies which locate apostolic succession in hierarchical representatives rather than in community
mission. It is the congregational community that serves to show
the reconciling, humble presence of Christ to the world and in
Hope in the Church, for example, Moltmann expounds the thesis
that the future of the church lies in the local congregation, a
prominent theme in his ecclesiological writings. Congregational
fellowship is best set forth under the rubric of 'friendship',
another concept used extensively by Moltmann, including in
his description of the relation between God and man.[62] Friendship is love in freedom which enables the truth of divine
friendship, which is itself love in freedom, to shine forth. In
this light, 'the goal of all strategies is the building up of
mature responsible congregationalism'[63] for the sake of an open
society.[64]

Moltmann winds up with his reinterpretation for our day of the
traditional marks of the church as set out in the Apostles' Creed.
They are to be interpreted in the light of Christ's activity and in
the service of hopeful living. They must confront the church with
the world. Thus emerges unity in free, suffering solidarity with the
oppressed; catholicity, which is relatedness to the whole world in
mission; holiness, a sanctified suffering and poverty in this world,
and apostolicity, which is 'a fellowship of poverty which becomes
a lived hope'.[65] So Moltmann ends an account dedicated to
ecumenicity and 'oppressed Christians throughout the world'. In
suffering and hope the church marches on to the universal future
in the power of the Spirit.

Trinity and kingdom

The doctrine of the Trinity is not one which, on the face of it, is likely to command detailed attention from the kind of theologian who wants theological thought geared to praxis. Many who believe in God as trinity and affirm the importance of such belief are likely, nevertheless, to feel that reflection soon comes up against the boundaries of what can and should be said on it. Presumably enough has been glimpsed of Moltmann's work up till now for us to see why he is unlikely to be disposed to share such a view. Reflection on the Trinity takes in reflection on the whole span of human history and our persistent missionary responsibility. In *The Trinity and the Kingdom of God* Moltmann certainly wants to break with any theology of the Trinity that would bring on suspicions of a speculative luxury. But such a break had been attempted already by the greatest Protestant theologian of his century, Karl Barth. Barth, in his monumental *Church Dogmatics*, had put the Trinity in the forefront of the dogmatic, theological picture. It gradually emerged that Moltmann, heavily influenced by Barth (as many continental Protestant theologians have been), though often not persuaded by him, also wished to accord the doctrine of the Trinity a central place in theology. Yet the theological scheme is not that of Barth.

The juxtaposition of 'trinity' and 'kingdom' in the title of this work, *The Trinity and the Kingdom of God*, is suggestive from the standpoint of New Testament theology. The 'kingdom of God' was apparently the dominant theme of Jesus' preaching but recedes in the preaching of the early church. To some extent it appears to have passed out of theological currency as time went on. On the other hand, it may be debated whether there is a doctrine of the Trinity at all in the New Testament. To be sure the answer to this depends in part on what one means by 'the doctrine of the Trinity', whether one means its classical form, attained in the fourth century (obviously that is not in the New Testament) or the elements of trinitarian doctrine (about whose presence or significance one might argue to a certain extent). At any rate, the doctrine of the Trinity looks from many angles like an understanding that emerged or developed late in or from the New

Testament writings in relation to the preaching of Jesus. Hence, while 'kingdom' is an early term with no obvious connotations of trinity, 'trinity' is a later one without any obvious connections with 'kingdom'. Moltmann, however, wants to wed the concepts. The goal of history is the kingdom of God; the unfolding of history is the trinitarian life of God. Such a connection can be established ultimately in sufficient detail to make proposals on its basis about the political structure of society.

If 'history' belongs to trinity, so 'freedom' belongs to kingdom. O'Donnell comments that in *The Trinity and the Kingdom of God* the main thing is that 'the path from history to freedom is opened up'[66] and that, indeed, Moltmann's 'entire theological enterprise is an effort to work out the theological implications of this vision'.[67] Yet again, the 'oppressed' are mentioned in the preface to *The Trinity and the Kingdom of God*[68] and the battle for their freedom is fought by reiterated polemic against 'monotheism' and 'monarchianism'. 'Monotheism' in theological writing usually means 'one God' but when Moltmann attacks it he means to attack a concept of God which is not properly trinitarian. That, however, may apply to some traditional and contemporary doctrines of the Trinity in the church for they may obscure the reality of three trinitarian persons by emphasizing the oneness of God and the primacy of the Father in the Trinity. 'Monarchianism' is used in theological literature to refer to a group of heresies in the early church which could, for example, collapse the three trinitarian 'persons' (as they came to be called definitively in the fourth century) into effectively one person. Moltmann often uses it in much the same sense as 'monotheism'. But it links up with the political idea of 'monarchy'. As Moltmann sees it, false ideas of God as an absolute world ruler (monotheistic, monarchian ideas), dwelling in patriarchal unity, spawn unchristian political ideologies with absolute kingship ruling the roost. Attention to trinitarian history, which presents us with a fellowship of persons united by mutually interpenetrating activity, not Fatherly domination, will lead us to see how a kind of democratic socialism in political structure corresponds to the trinitarian being of God. Thus the path from history (trinitarian history in its principle) to freedom (social freedom in the end) is carved out.

Moltmann aims so to present his doctrine of the Trinity that it achieves ecumenical ends. Most broadly, this means a doctrine that connects up with Jewish theology, and thus Moltmann latches on especially to those Jewish theologians who emphasize the passion, the suffering of God. More domestically, this means a doctrine that creates rapport between Eastern and Western Christianity, officially split over the doctrine of the Trinity in the eleventh century. In a discussion of the so-called 'filioque' controversy in this connection, Moltmann tries to promote some unity. But, as in the case of Judaism, the ecumenical objective is to be attempted mainly by presenting a genuinely Christian under-standing of the Trinity in general terms, which in its own right begins to heal some rifts.

As Moltmann expounds his position, several familiar themes receive renewed treatment. We read of participation in the history and experience of God; of ascribing suffering to God; of the passion and exaltation of the Son. The aim, however, is now to establish the distinction between persons to a large extent. Trinitarian theology has typically in the past walked the tight-rope between stressing the unity of God, thus obliterating the distinc-tion between persons, and stressing the distinction of persons, thus heading for tritheism. There is no doubt as to the side on which Moltmann falls. He emphasizes the three persons. But he does not wish to approach the question speculatively. We start with the suffering of God; we learn that this suffering is the function of freely acting love; we learn of God's inner compulsion to reach out to man, and come to see love as the self-communica-tion of the good, the opposite of solitude, the deep passion for friendship and self-disclosure. All this we learn, however, in the relations established in history between God and man through the relations played out in history between Father, Son and Spirit. The history of the Son, seen against the background of God's plan for the world, shows us the way to this understanding.

At least three sets of Moltmann's convictions in this context should be noticed. First, he is unwilling to separate the 'immanent' and 'economic' trinities. In theological literature the 'immanent' trinity is sometimes called the 'essential' or 'ontological' trinity and it refers to God as he is in himself, immanently. We learn to think of God this way because of divine activity in history, at least in part, and that activity can be termed the divine 'economy', hence, the 'economic' trinity is the Trinity in action, as it were, in time and history. For Moltmann, if one took the line taken in the tradition, that God is timelessly eternal ('timeless' here strictly means that all is, to God, an eternal present) or impassible, then the immanent trinity is other than the trinity economic and that would mean that we do not apprehend God himself in the economy. Giving it his own distinctive twist and interpretation, he accepts the maxim of Karl Rahner, a leading Catholic theologian of our century, that the economic trinity is the immanent trinity.

Secondly, Moltmann insists that what God does affects himself. Traditionally, it had been held that divine activity has effects, of course, *ad extra*, in relation to that external to God. Creation, redemption or glorification affected the world, not God. Moltmann, however, holds that God is in himself affected by this. Does he not suffer, respond, listen, decide – all in response to human agents? Here one must note that Moltmann's determination to ground the doctrine of God in trinitarian economy is associated with a theological principle scarcely discussed *qua* principle in his work, namely the place of the biblical narrative in the formation of theological concepts. 'Narrative theology' has become important over the last few years, apparently grounded in the work of Karl Barth.[69] 'The New Testament talks about God by proclaiming in narrative the relationships of the Father, the Son and the Spirit, which are relationships of fellowships and are open to the world.'[70] Indeed, were God not as he is presented to us in the narrative, capable of being affected in some way, Moltmann claims he would be impoverished, for the capacity to suffer and to respond is part of the richness of love.

Thirdly, Moltmann is concerned to show how the pattern of interaction between the different trinitarian persons in the economy varies with the activity under consideration. Hence he concludes sections on the sending, surrender, exaltation and future of the Son with summaries of trinitarian activity in each case which exhibit varying patterns. The thrust of this is to establish, as far as possible, trinitarian life as one of mutual fellowship, rather than domination by the Father, though there is room to make something of the traditional idea of the Father as *fons et origo divinitatis* ('fountainhead and origin in the deity'). Moltmann is anxious to stress how the nature of sonship and fatherhood displayed through Jesus Christ stamps itself on all other concepts, like lordship. The Spirit who is mediating to us the new creation of the future, mediates thus the filial lordship of Christ which creates patterns of sonship and relationship in the church corresponding to the non-monarchical trinity.

There is plenty here that has invited critical comment.[71] Moltmann discusses several of the detailed questions discussed in the tradition in relation to the Trinity. But he has set it all in a new context. Moltmann's story of the Trinity is the story of universal salvation where world history is a vast exodus from bondage in light of messianic hope in world transformation. The creation of the world, the incarnation of the Son, the transfigura-tion of the cosmos by the Spirit are the main elements in the story. It is learnt at the cross where we discover God as trinity in suffering love and in light of the resurrection where we see the pre-reflection of coming glory. God created the world as an efflux of love for the Son and seeks by the Spirit the communion of that which is unlike himself, man. When God saves, he deals with sin, but the goal is more than the overcoming of sin, for the Spirit sets in motion the future of the world whose grand destiny is to be the divine domicile. In the world, the Trinity moves out that humanity may come in: that is the story and song of salvation.

In *The Trinity and the Kingdom of God* a question which comes to light with regard to the Trinity concerns the ascription of 'personhood' to Father, Son and Spirit. It has often been pointed out that when the word 'person' was used in this connection in classical trinitarianism, it did not mean an independent entity which would turn the three persons of the Trinity into three gods. But does Moltmann use it tritheistically? He seems to take the risk, for he warns us not to fight shy of speaking of three centres of activity, three subjects in trinity. That, he says, is what the Bible does, after all. What is to be avoided is an extremely individualistic idea of 'person', as if one can be a person without being essentially related. Father, Son and Spirit are ever and always united in their

personal activities – that very unity in trinitarian fellowship
suffices to establish the oneness – there is no tritheism here.
Moltmann reminds us that as a matter of principle of course
concepts expressed in our ordinary language undergo transformation when applied to a theme such as God as trinity.

In a fairly brief but important final section Moltmann considers
the social implications of his doctrine of God as trinity. As human
liberty is thwarted in the religious sphere by the traditional all-
knowing, all-powerful God, so it is thwarted in the political sphere
by the omnipotent earthly monarch. A 'social' understanding of
the Trinity (as Moltmann's can be termed) entails political
socialism. But this is not the socialism of a static, timeless creed.[72]
Drawing on the work of the medieval thinker Joachim of Fiore,
Moltmann adumbrates a scheme for looking at world history in
terms of the kingdoms of Father, Son and Spirit, concurrent, not
consecutive kingdoms and in accordance with the economy laid
out in the Bible. How can such trinitarian history, culminating in
such a kingdom, do other than promote freedom for man? Is that
not the goal and method of God? Freedom in love; freedom for
the possibilities of the world; the freedom of servants, children
and especially friends – these are increasingly the privileges of man
in relation to God. No social system that fails to adopt such
principles into its political and ethical foundation can be worthy of
our acclaim. So much the doctrine of the Trinity establishes.

Critique 1: the eschatological perspective

There are several welcome features of Moltmann's work. He seeks
to be biblical and applied in his theology; intellectual and spiritual.
Karl Barth emphasized the spirituality of religious knowledge for
the Christian and Moltmann continues in that vein. There is plenty
that moves, convicts, humbles and challenges, especially when the
'underprivileged' are discussed in any way. Further, there is a
studied and sustained attempt to ground our theological statements faithfully in the promises and activity given to us and
undertaken for us by God in Christ.

Preliminarily to more specific discussion of the content of

Moltmann's thought, it is worth commenting on his style. In theological circles, corresponding to philosophical ones in this respect, one often comes across sharp differences between general ways of doing theology (or philosophy). One such difference is in mind here as far as theology is concerned: the difference between an analytical approach and a pervasively continental approach. The historical background and conceptual dimensions of this difference are not our concern. The analytical approach, often found in the English-speaking world, proceeds in practice much of the time by meticulous attention to the logic of concepts, the logical relations of concepts and the precise linguistic formulation of an argument. It would be wrong to deny that what I am labelling 'continental' approaches also often do this after a fashion. But if one cares to compare two of the books already mentioned, Kelsey's *The Uses of Scripture in Recent Theology* and Moltmann's own *Theology of Hope*, taking Moltmann, for our purposes, as typifying a continental attitude, one will detect a difference in approach. David Brown complains of Moltmann's indifference to appropriate conceptual, philosophical analysis. Without expressing preferences or value-judgments here, let it simply be said that one certainly struggles in vain to understand mighty and evocative ideas expressed in technical language unless one can depict the contours of an argument for a conclusion which our ordinary words 'therefore', 'and', 'but', 'consequently' or 'merely', 'partly', and so on, signify. But if one finds Moltmann typically continental in his broad approach and would like to see more of the logical attentiveness that scrupulous handling of the above little words would imply, it is nevertheless our Christian and intellectual responsibility to offer any position we eventually reject its best defence on its behalf first. Writers such as Moltmann often have reason for expounding things in the way they do and can provide insights missing from the works of the more logically sophisticated. If it is a weakness of Moltmann's basic approach that he sets forward his theological judgments in a logically vulnerable way, it is also a weakness in the approach of a protagonist if such a failure is deemed to rob the work of theological merit. I say this without any intention of disagreeing with Brown or defending Moltmann or of expressing preference

for the approach of the one over the other to the general doctrine
of the Trinity!

When Moltmann brought to the fore the eschatological
perspective in Christianity, in his own way he gave good account
both of its centrality and of its connection with cross and
resurrection. His eschatology was both 'universal' and 'this-
worldly' and it has persisted so since *Theology of Hope*. But there
are deep problems at the heart of this.

'Universalism' can mean different things in theology. One of its
most frequent meanings is the belief that all people, not some, will
eventually be saved. Discussion of this in recent theology is
usefully summed up in Stephen Travis's work.[73] When Moltmann,
as he persistently does, speaks of the universal eschatological
salvation of all humanity, he is seldom directly attending to the
question of whether all without exception will enter the kingdom.
Many people use the vocabulary of 'all' in a similar way, it would
seem, though they profess ignorance on the question of whether
any will finally, through constant rejection of God's love, forfeit
that life eternal. Yet many of Moltmann's statements seem to
point unavoidably to 'universalism' in the sense under consideration.[74] There are two problems with Moltmann on this count. The
first is that he never defends universalism in this sense – he merely
states it. In light of the traditional rejection of universalism in the
church, it is not good enough to assume that the broad gist of
one's theology of hope, eschatology or biblical theology constitutes an argument for universalism. Moltmann speaks of the
crucified Lord as constituting the deepest grounds for Christian
universalism,[75] though he seems to have in mind a perspective on
cosmic eschatology (the grand future of this world), as he so often
does, rather than a stricter view of the salvation of all individuals
at this point. Nevertheless, he never demonstrates this stricter
universalism on Christological premises in the way he tries to
demonstrate that God suffers, or that eschatology is the context of
Christology, for example.

It may be thought that criticism on this point is at best criticism
of one element in his thought and not of anything very important
in its general fabric. This brings us to the second problem. For
Moltmann, universal salvation is the basis for missionary activity.

Because God calls and includes all to and in his kingdom, we are motivated without reserve in infecting all with hope, suffering in solidarity with all, reaching out to all. According to Moltmann's implicit belief, it is not, as some have traditionally thought, that universalism robs one of missionary incentive; rather, it constitutes it. This can be amply documented from almost any of Moltmann's major or lesser works where the broad question of eschatological hope or missionary activity is broached. Those of us, therefore, who dispute dogmatic universalism cannot accept this view of the link between eschatological perspective and missionary activity in the broader sense of that term.

It might, however, be argued that what Moltmann says in general is compatible with an agnostic, rather than dogmatic attitude to universalism, whereby he refuses to pronounce on the question of whether any forfeit salvation.[76] This is a widespread attitude across the different confessions in modern theology. If this is Moltmann's position at least he is clear that we must hope for all. The force of this would be that we are bidden, with good reason but without dogmatic certainty, to hope for the salvation of all, for this is the desire and design of God, though for all we know persistent rejection of him leads of itself to exclusion from the eschatological kingdom. Surely we can hope for all in this sense and must do so if we are to reach out in love to all?

The answer to this is that we must beware of the different meanings of the word 'hope'. In our ordinary language it has a variety of nuances, but we normally contrast it with 'certainty' or with a well-grounded certainty. To hope for something is to be unsure of whether it will happen, or if we are sure, we have to admit that we can scarcely justify absolute confidence about anything in the future. Such, at any rate, is a typical way of seeing 'hope'. However, where 'hope' appears in the Bible and thence in theology, it has a distinctive meaning over against this. 'Hope' here can be subjective or objective. 'Subjective' hope refers to what I may hope for, and arguments have raged in the tradition over whether any is entitled to have assurance or certainty that 'I' will be saved. We do not enter into this discussion here. However, there is 'objective' hope which refers to that which is hoped for. This can be described in the Bible and theology in a variety of ways: for example, the reappearing of Christ or the consummation of the kingdom of God. These are taken, in the Bible, to be objective realities, albeit yet to come. Some today would protest against theology simply taking these over as 'objective realities', but that does not matter in our context, for Moltmann believes that such things are a matter of divine promise and that our hope is a certain one.[77]

What is the force of this discussion of 'hope'? My point is that if Moltmann holds that we must hope for all, in the sense compatible with nondogmatism on the question of universalism, he is not using 'hope' in this biblical sense or in its biblically based sense in the tradition which sees it as one of the three 'theological virtues' (together with 'faith' and 'love'). Of course, there may be no reason why Moltmann should not in general use the word 'hope' in a slightly different sense, a sense more akin in relevant ways to the ordinary-language use mentioned earlier. Indeed, he distinguishes frequently and explicitly between the kinds of hopes that may be disappointed and the certain expectancy of deeper Christian hope.[78] The problem is that when he speaks of hope for all it is usually of the kind of hope that does not disappoint – it is of eschatological hope. The vocabulary of hope seems therefore to be confused unless Moltmann is a dogmatic universalist.

It might be objected to our critical discussion so far that the point of Moltmann's expositions of hope has been missed. For he holds that emphasis on individual salvation and destiny is misplaced – we must think of the entire created order in and with which humanity is to be redeemed. Hence we are fastening on to questions which draw his words out of context or at least to questions preoccupation with which is in some ways deleterious. In response to this, however, it must be remembered that his avowed aim is to imbue all with hope, to implant hope as a living thing in the hearts of the hopeless. For what, then, are the hopeless to hope? If it has to do with the redemption of the cosmic order, it is natural and right to ask about their own participation therein, for while certainly preoccupation with personal salvation can lead to selfishness, the New Testament clearly wishes to communicate a hope that informs us of our destiny. Moltmann acknowledges that in time we can create only anticipations of the kingdom, not the kingdom itself and well knows that generations have died and will die, presumably, without even the realization of such anticipations in their particular society. Hope for earthly improvement in one's lot would thus be hope for possibilities, however greatly to be encouraged.

However, Moltmann's view of hope does contain hope for the individual's participation in the eschatological reign of God and, though he does not emphasize it, for life after death. It is true that doubt has been expressed about whether Moltmann holds such belief for the individual.[79] One could be excused for such doubt on the basis of the earlier major works, for Moltmann expresses the conviction that individual, other-worldly hope of personal survival hinders the task of world-transforming activity. Yet what he really has in mind seems to be a combination of certain types of belief in life after death and certain attitudes engendered by beliefs, for, despite omission of such reference when one might expect it,[80] resurrection seems to be unequivocally affirmed elsewhere.[81] It is indeed difficult to know what his universal, eschatological hope, with its heart-lifting impact on the individual, would amount to *if* this were not the case. However, it is true that Moltmann does not want us to fix our theological gaze on precisely this. There is certainly something to be said for this, though Sykes appropriately asks whether indeed Moltmann has got right the historical and theological connection between individual eschatology and failure to engage in world-transforming activity.

This leads us on to consider the 'this-worldly' as well as universal aspect of Moltmann's eschatological perspective. The term 'this-worldly hope' is often, in theological writing, opposed to 'other-worldly hope' and often the meanings of the terms are taken to be obvious. But are they? In a recent article Richard Bauckham has called on theologians to give proper theological attention to the nuclear threat, so that the meaning of providence, hope and redemption can be articulated with specific reference to that context.[82] He is clear that this threat conjures up the real prospect of extinction. The question that must arise for anyone who takes seriously such a prospect is the sense in which Christians may now speak of a this-worldly hope. If one believes in a new creation of new heavens and a new earth inhabited by the redeemed, a world that is tangible inhabited by beings that are embodied, it would still not normally be described as this world in its historical future, if holocaust has taken place. And if 'hope' is held to mean 'certain expectation' then one can scarcely say that one has this-worldly hope and that nuclear holocaust may come about.

Bauckham indicates his own dissatisfaction generally with theology of hope at this point, though he does not press the case in the fashion stated. As Moltmann appears to admit the prospect of annihilation, his vocabulary of this-worldly hope requires far more attention than he gives it.[83] Yet this is a matter of importance for Moltmann, for the kind of hope he proffers is meant to stimulate a kind of activity culpably avoided by those who speak in other-worldly terms. It may, indeed, be that Christian hope is misleadingly characterized as 'other-worldly' or, if it is so characterized, requires explanation which strips it of elements found in it as often understood by people. It may be that New Testament eschatology cannot be characterized straight-forwardly as either this-worldly or other-worldly. It may be that these forms of hope should be combined in some ways and that Moltmann, as seems to be the case very often, actually has that persistently in mind. Yet the meaning of this-worldly hope for one who admits the extreme nuclear prospect requires exposition. And that exposition would then have to demonstrate with more specificity than does Moltmann the relation of our ultimate eschatological hopes to the anticipatory activities of the kingdom promoted in history in its light.

I have laboured this theme because it is central in Moltmann's work. Clearly his analysis of eschatological hope or hope as a phenomenon in human existence is open to other kinds of response, for instance the relative importance that should be attached in theology to the sin of despair and the sin of pride and thus the hope that overcomes the former and the kind of humility that drives out the latter.[84] One major consequence, however, of denying universalism would have to do with the whole way in which Moltmann relates the church to the world. As far as he is concerned, church and world are set on the same course toward eschatological salvation. But his discussion ignores the types of connection often drawn in the New Testament between the eschatology, the church and salvation, for example, in Ephesians and Colossians. It might be denied that the visible church is the 'ark of salvation', it might be admitted that there may be salvation outside the visible church, but even if such were the case, Moltmann's analysis of church and world could be found unsatisfactory. The importance of attaining faith in Christ in this world, reiterated in the New Testament, is scarcely given its due place in Moltmann's theology.

Having said this, Moltmann has much to teach us. Many churches are more interested in guarding the truth suspiciously than in sharing it joyfully, in proclaiming a truth that is against the world rather than one that is for the world. Many who bear the name of Christ do not suffer with the oppressed when they could, nor even care for the poor when they should. Few of us will care to exculpate ourselves entirely or even largely in these or affiliated respects. In setting before our eyes the eschatological hope, Moltmann provides the stimulus for Christian life and suffering which is provided by the New Testament itself, whatever we may deem defective in his presentation. The eschaton is at once goal and spur for Christian living and the element in which it dwells. It is better to have as our focus the crucified Christ, risen and hoped for. Of that Moltmann clearly reminds us.

Critique 2: God as trinity

In some of the great credal formulations of the early church, such as Nicaea and Chalcedon, Christological dogmas were hammered out in the interests of stating or preserving Christian belief on the person of Christ in the church. Reflection on his relation to God the Father led to the trinitarian affirmation when supplemented by reflection on the relation of the Spirit to Father and Son: God is one in three persons. Reflection on the relation of Christ's deity to his humanity, whose results were credally formulated after the trinitarian decision and within a framework of trinitarian theology, led to the Christological affirmation that Jesus Christ was one person possessed of two natures (divine and human).[85] Prior to our century, however, these credal declarations were found, within the church, to be problematic for a number of reasons and today one can find them sustained, modified, reinterpreted or disavowed. Which of these procedures best fits Moltmann's enterprise is no doubt a moot point. Certainly he aims at doctrinal reconstruction. Its principal basis seems to be the biblical story about Jesus Christ.

The superficial difficulty of squaring features of the biblical account with the mainstream of Christian orthodoxy, as it came to be identified, in relation to Jesus Christ, is not difficult to see. If the cross of Christ in the context of his life and the prophecy of the Old Testament does not reveal to us a God who suffers, then surely what we can gather about God from the life of Christ seems exceedingly tentative, to say the least. Yet it is commonly said of the Church Fathers (and I do not wish to dispute it) that they denied God's capacity to suffer in a way that gave them enormous difficulty in accounting adequately for the sufferings of Christ. It could be and was said that those sufferings were sufferings of his humanity or that, paradoxically, the divine Word suffered impassibly in Christ. But this, in turn could accentuate doubt felt by people on the score of the doctrine of the two natures. Is the Christ of the Gospels really one of whom we can predicate two sets of characteristics, one human, the other divine? Does this mean that he was, for example, divinely omniscient and humanly limited in knowledge simultaneously? One can confess there is mystery in the deity of Christ, but is it this mystery, or is this a mystery of our devising? And what is the borderline between mystery and self-contradictory nonsense? All these questions have been given a thorough airing in contemporary theology.

Moltmann is determined to start with the biblical story about Jesus Christ and reject any subsequent view of the Trinity which cannot be squared with that story which forms part of a larger story constituting the very stuff of the biblical witness. Though in some contexts one might have to distinguish between them, Moltmann is happy to refer to this narrative story in terms of the history of Christ: the story is not like a fictitious account but it presents us with the real history of the Son. Subsequently we may speak of the history of God.

Whatever may be said about Moltmann's method of approach, however, it leads him to make a statement in *Theology of Hope* which throws into question his foundations for trinitarian thinking. He is developing a theme, given further treatment in *The Crucified God*, concerning the identity of Jesus Christ. The point is that the cross and resurrection constitute the identity of Jesus Christ. They are part of who he is; he is not a being whose identity is fixed, apart from any deed he accomplishes or events that befall him. In *The Crucified God* Moltmann protests that the separation of the two natures wrongly presents the biblical witness to God himself, identified with Christ. In the course of arguing this he makes a claim in *Theology of Hope*, the ramifications of which become obvious in *The Crucified God*. Jesus, he says, was 'wholly dead and wholly raised'.[86] In *The Crucified God* this leads to the claim that God thus embraced death in his own divine life: the reality of the death of Jesus Christ is indissolubly linked with the reality of God's appropriation of death, the most extreme of universal or human opposites, into his own history.

However, on the traditional trinitarian view, the claim that Jesus Christ wholly died would amount to the claim that the second person in the Trinity died. That would make deity, at least in the case of the second person, mortal. If Moltmann is really committed to saying this, he is in effect saying, at the very least, that God can exist as trinity or alternatively not exist as trinity, for one who is wholly dead cannot be part of trinitarian life. On the face of it, a response to this objection is that it presupposes the very understanding of the Trinity that Moltmann is concerned to challenge. That, of course, is true in a relevant way. The point is, however, that if a theology insists that Jesus Christ was wholly dead, then it cannot really count as a form of trinitarian theology. The question here concerns the limits of what may be called a 'reinterpretation' in new form of trinitarian theology. It is hard to see how Moltmann here avoids propounding a different, rather than legitimately reinterpretative doctrine, however one might conceive the latter.

It might, of course, be said that what matters for theology is whether a doctrine is right or wrong, not whether it should be called trinitarian or non-trinitarian. This raises many questions

outside our province. On the question of content, what grounds
have we for saying that Jesus Christ was wholly dead? That he was
biologically dead in the same way as all die, we must affirm. But
quite apart from the view countenanced by some that there is a
part of the self that cannot die in ordinary humanity, we must note
that no amount of scrutiny of the biblical narrative in the light of
those New Testament affirmations which some take to support
the pre-existence of the divine Son can convince us that Jesus
Christ was wholly dead. Nor, as I have indicated, is this an
incidental point in Moltmann's work, for he insists on the
importance of death in God so that in our suffering we might
know we suffer in the most intimate participation in him and gain
the victory of hope in the trinitarian life of God. Even if there is
plenty of room to quarrel with traditional trinitarianism even on
the points I have mentioned, Moltmann needs to demonstrate,
which he does not, the validity of his argument for the ascription
of death to God in this sense.

This discussion gives us an indication, too, of ways in which we
might relate the biblical narrative to the doctrine of God.
Moltmann is impressed by the reality of time in the divine
experience, for the divine economy reveals a God in motion, as
it were. In modern theology much has been made of Hegel, a
philosopher of the last century who sought to unify theological
and philosophical perspective in a grand, speculative scheme
whose lynch-pin was the idea of God as one who unfolds himself
in the processes of the world. Hegel's thought is patient of several
interpretations, but the general influence of his way of relating
God and history is marked on subsequent theology, including that
of Moltmann. It would be wrong just to label Moltmann as
Hegelian, for his frequent appeals to Hegel do not amount to an
endorsement of his general theistic metaphysics (that is, the view
of divine reality) and he takes issue with Hegel more than once.
However, he prefers to ascribe temporality to God than to take a
classical position on divine timeless eternity. And if we apprehend
God in the life, death, resurrection and coming of Christ, why
maintain that God himself does not experience time in the sense
of its inner reality for his own being?

I do not intend to embark on an assessment of the classical

doctrine of God's eternity here. What must be said, however, is that attention to the biblical narrative does not compel us to adopt Moltmann's conclusions. We apprehend Christ through his words in conjunction with his life. He spoke, for example, of divine forgiveness and extended it to people himself; it would be impossible to believe in Christ and yet maintain that God was unforgiving. But of God's relation to time in the sense under consideration we learn nothing from Jesus or other biblical writers that would enable us to endorse definitely Moltmann's conclusions. Experiencing God's appearance or activity in time does not either tell us of the inner relation of God to time for, on the face of it, we can account for this either on the assumption of divine temporality or on the assumption of divine timeless eternity capable of unity and identification with those who are in time. This question, if it can be settled at all, requires consideration of issues not treated by Moltmann in sufficient detail to warrant his conclusion. It may, however, be thought that at least on one point we must not deny the persuasiveness of Moltmann's doctrine of God, namely on the question of impassibility. It is noteworthy in this context that even a leading and stalwart defender of the 'classical' doctrine of God, H. P. Owen, has admitted that leeway should be given here and that the ascription of suffering to God at least should not be ruled out.[87] Moltmann may indeed be right both on the need to ascribe suffering to God and on the fact that this ultimately requires a trinitarian interpretation. But the kind of trinitarian interpretation he gives it is connected with his claim that there is death in God, a claim which, as we have seen, rests on doubtful premises. Moltmann does not wish to espouse a doctrine of passibility or temporality which is non-trinitarian, nor does he wish to adopt a doctrine of the Trinity which holds God to be eternally impassible. This is why the general considerations advanced in this critical section bear specifically on his trinitarian theology.

If it is meticulous adherence to the biblical narrative, albeit interpreted, of course, in the context of New Testament theology, that occasions Moltmann's doctrinal tenets, it also accounts for his strong insistence that God is three persons. That insistence in itself is not the occasion of criticism here more than Moltmann's

admirable attention to the biblical narrative in the adumbration of
theological concepts in principle. The difficulty can be expressed
in the words of George Hunsinger, written long before the
appearance of *The Trinity and the Kingdom of God* but still relevant
after it: 'The result seems to be three gods, separate in being yet
united in intention. The unity of the trinity seems to be volitional,
but not ontological.'[88] A 'volitional' unity is a unity of will; an
'ontological' unity is a unity of being. The Christological thought
of Nestorius in the early church (who lent his name, perhaps
improperly, to the heresy 'Nestorianism') was deemed inadequate
by his theological opponents because he did not give proper
account of the ground of union of the divine and human in Christ,
making it look somewhat like a union of will. That, of course,
tended to divide up Christ into two persons. A parallel criticism
might be brought against Moltmann, though with important
differences. Does he, like Nestorius, so fail to explain the ground
of the unity of God that he leaves us with three gods?

In traditional trinitarian thought a distinction is often drawn
between two different 'models', ways of conceiving the Trinity:
'analogies' as they can also be termed. According to the 'psychological' analogy, it is the human individual, looked at from a
psychological viewpoint, that is a model for the unity of God (for
example, the tripartite division of memory, will and understanding
in the context of an ancient psychology shows three constituents of
one being). According to the 'social' analogy it is three persons,
looked at from the social viewpoint, that are a model for the unity
of God; the unity of three apostles, for example, gives us an
example of a unity embracing three persons. Moltmann, within his
own revised framework, opts for the social analogy or model. But it
must be admitted that his trinitarianism does seem to take the
model to represent the reality far more strictly than it should. He
talks, as we have seen, of three 'centres of activity'. Such language
requires some elucidation at the best of times. When regeneration
takes place in the individual life, does one have now a new centre of
activity (the Spirit rather than the self)? How are self and Spirit
related? Does this help us to understand anything about the Trinity?
Given the unity of Father, Son and Spirit in the New Testament
account, it seems difficult to say without hesitation that we have

here three centres of activity, as we would, confronted with three
human persons. Moltmann does not distinguish sharply enough
between the kind of unity the divine persons have and the kind
human persons have, to avoid the charge of tritheism successfully.
Granted, we may be able to say little about the divine unity. But we
should avoid construing it along lines so similar to human unities.

Both in the expositions and in the criticism I have concentrated
on theological principles. But just as Moltmann deemed a right
eschatological perspective necessary for fruitful social activity, so
he deemed a correctly trinitarian understanding of God necessary
for worthy social witness. In terms of eschatological perspective,
one challenge we are offered in Moltmann's work is the challenge
of providing an adequate basis for mission and social action on
non-universalist principles.[89]

But what of the consequences of trinitarian theology? It is
worth referring to two of them here, from Moltmann's perspective. Firstly, he feels that proper trinitarianism enables a proper
ordering of the principles of political society along broadly
socialist lines. Secondly, he feels that as an exposition of the cross
(the Trinity is 'the theological short summary of the passion of
Christ'),[90] this doctrine of God takes the sting out of protest
atheism in the sense that it also protests against traditional theism,
but does so in the name of authentic Christianity. In conclusion, it
is as well to remark on these two consequences.

Clearly the way in which Moltmann draws consequences for
social and political theory from his trinitarian doctrine is not quite
open to those who question his particular trinitarianism. Yet a
conclusion arrived at along different lines, that God's inner
distinctions are real and worthy of the description 'personal', can
certainly have political consequences not unlike those sponsored by
Moltmann. Political theorists have often discussed 'individualism',
though it is a term that can bear varied meanings.[91] When the
church is understood as 'the body of Christ', as it is in the New
Testament, a certain kind of individualism is dismissed. The human
self comes to self-fulfilment, if one wants to use that term, in mutual
unity with others. The more one is integrated into the one body, the
more one becomes what one is meant to be. True 'personhood' and
'individualism' in this sense are antithetical. If the relation of the

individual to the church is at all grounded in the relation of
the divine persons to each other, one can see how the church,
because it sets forth something of the mystery of the Trinity, reveals
to the world that human society corresponds best to the trinitarian
relations that ground our existence. It does so by emphasizing not
the values of individual self-fulfilment but the unity of the 'body
politic' in mutual submission. Let me stress, however, that this has
been mentioned to draw attention to the possible fruitful lines to
follow if one wants to connect trinity and political society; anyone
who wants to establish such connections definitively has to take into
account a host of considerations and distinctions that would make
such a demonstration extremely demanding.

Finally, does a trinitarian theology of the cross affect 'protest
atheism' in the way Moltmann holds? Again one must say that to
the extent we have questioned his thought here it is not possible
to draw lines exactly as he does between Christianity and atheism;
and yet, to the extent that we have not challenged (or outrightly
endorsed!) Moltmann's ascription of suffering to God, the virtues
of this move on his part require comment. The whole question of
theodicy is obviously so big and so emotive that it is of little avail
to go into it here. Further, the whole question of the roots of
modern atheism is so important and complex that no justice can
be done to it here either. However, it is worth noting that
Moltmann scarcely seems to question the 'good faith' of 'protest
atheism' – that is, he seems to accept the translucent sincerity and
justice of its spirit. There is no need, indeed, to doubt that false
views of divine power have provoked resistance to Christianity or
that protest atheists often protest in sincere good faith. But
scrutiny of the historical development of modern atheism out of
its proximate source in Enlightenment thought will suggest that
any view of a transcendent God who at all legislates for man is
likely to be anathema to the atheist. And reflection on the spiritual
psychology of modern atheism in its Western form will likewise
suggest to many of us that it is largely to be read as a manifestation
of that rebellious self-will which is in all of us. If this is so, the
problem of theodicy begins to wear a different guise in its context
and the effectiveness of Moltmann's partial solution, in ascribing
suffering to God, becomes questionable.

But I do not, by these concluding comments, mean either to underplay the problem of suffering or to impugn the integrity of all protest. Such would be the height of arrogance in any of us who do not really suffer with those who suffer or act on their behalf. And which of us has no plank in our eye in that respect? Moltmann has directed us to our tasks of solidarity with those who suffer and grounded our activity in the outgoing love of God. One may not see things in all respects as he does; but if we see or do less than we find in his presentation, we are scarcely in a place to criticize.

Appendix

God in Creation: an Ecological Doctrine of Creation

Moltmann's work *God in Creation* (SCM, 1985), raises a number of issues rather different from the ones we have been considering, in the areas of evolutionary biology and theological concepts of space and time for example. I shall not pursue these critically here nor even give a full account of the argument of this work. Rather, some of the key themes will be indicated briefly. Here we find plenty of continuity with what has gone before. In *The Trinity and the Kingdom of God* Moltmann tells us that 'by taking up panentheistic ideas from the Jewish and the Christian traditions' he wants to 'try to think ecologically about God, man and the world in their relationships and indwellings' (p. 19). He makes good his intentions in *God in Creation* which is subtitled *an Ecological Doctrine of Creation*. His method is to complement a certain insight developed in Jewish theology with a trinitarian account of creation (see *God in Creation*, pp. 15ff., 87ff.) and to do so with the eschatological perspective governing all. The familiar scheme, then, seems fundamentally to be still in business.

An 'ecological' account might lead us to expect discussion of environmental ethics in light of environmental pollution. The last page of the main account (p. 296) closes with reference to that. But, according to Moltmann, the ecological crisis is much more than this: 'this is really a crisis of the whole life system of the modern industrial world' (p. 23). Moltmann is therefore concerned to explore the general question of the relation of man to the world in light of the doctrine of God, the Creator, and in order to integrate human social and natural life within the trinitarian vision.

Specifically, the doctrine of God as Creator must emphasize the Creator Spirit. Moltmann wants to draw attention to the divine immanence. Traditionally, God is conceived of as both transcendent (apart from his creation) and immanent (in some way present in his creation). Moltmann does not deny the divine transcendence: on the contrary, it is emphasized in the work and his defence of 'creation out of nothing', a test of Christian orthodoxy on the doctrine of creation, for many, apparently, seems to satisfy a condition for a view of divine transcendence that stands broadly in the tradition. Yet, says Moltmann, if such transcendence is domination, it leads to disastrous consequences, for then man takes to dominating his world, interpreting his creation orders in that light. However, the doctrine of the Trinity shows us that mutual indwelling is what we find in God and, moreover, an indwelling in his own creation and created humanity. The special agent of this indwelling is the Spirit. If we grasp that creativity comes from within the world by the agency of the Spirit apart from the primal act of God in creation, then our ecological doctrine of creation is on the right track for we live in a Spirit-filled environment.

Arguing this point leads Moltmann to the consideration of many themes. They include the question of our knowledge of God the Creator (where he maintains that the world is a kind of visual parable of future glory); the way in which creation occurred (by a process of divine withdrawal or contraction into himself thus allowing 'room' for the creation of the other); the nature of time (which is determined by the divine experience of time prior to, with and in the consummation of creation) and the nature of space (where he distinguishes between 'the essential omnipresence of God, of absolute space; second, the space of creation in the world-presence of God conceded to it; and third, relative places, relationships and movements in the created world' [p. 157]). Never, however, does he permit himself speculation that cannot be geared to practical ecological doctrine. Thus the doctrine of 'heaven and earth' that follows the discussion of space emphasizes heaven as a sphere of possibilities for the earth, though Moltmann distinguishes carefully between senses of 'heaven' in the tradition and in doctrinal theology. There then follow sections on evolution (deemed compatible with a non-pantheistic doctrine of creation when the world is seen as a vast system, anticipating glory); the image of God in man (to be seen in trinitarian and eschatological – future – light); the importance of embodiment (against separating soul and body so that the former is the reality of man and focus of divine activity) and the sabbath ('the feast of creation', the ordained destiny of creation).

An appendix on 'symbols of the world' closes with a plea to avoid patriarchal domination of the world in view of an equality of the sexes and an integration of man and environment amply suggested to us by many of those symbols.

Moltmann's work is a welcome balance to his earlier attempts to relate God to human history by this study of the 'history of nature'. It is open to scientific critique both on the question of total evolutionary systems and relativity theory as it has been developed in modern physics. Theologically one of the principal points at issue is the coherence or cogency of the account of God's relation to space, including, e.g. the question of divine 'withdrawal'. Whatever the strengths and weaknesses of this work, it is a thoroughly conscientious attempt to get to grips with a doctrine and its implications that are manifestly vital for our day.

The Way of Jesus Christ: Christology in Messianic dimensions[92]

A quarter of a century ago, *Theology of Hope* set the pace, though it was no pure, independent novelty. Now *The Way of Jesus Christ* stays the course, though it is not mere familiar repetition. The eschatological Christology of the former is still the lynch-pin of this third volume of Moltmann's 'Messianic dogmatics'. Here Christology is structured by the movement from Old Testament expectation to future parousia; it is answerable to the Bonhoefferian: *Who really is Christ for us today?*, and it is ordered to ethics. Moltmann examines the messianic mission, apocalyptic sufferings, eschatological resurrection, cosmic dimensions and parousia of Jesus Christ. This establishes an ethic wide enough to create solidarity with the poor and endure the whole span of sufferings, specific enough to treat the fertilized ovum as a person (p. 267) and call for punitive sanctions against exterminators of plant species (p. 311). All this is undertaken only after taking steps to avoid alienating Jews or feminists.

Moltmann's is a singular exercise in rhetorical, narrative biblical theology. It is problematic. As regards biblical theology he will dissatisfy some to the right (who find his use of biblical data too selective) and to the left (who dispute his use of the same data as theological normative). As regards narrative, he justifies much too abruptly his method of constructing the identity of Jesus Christ by attending (largely) to the contours of the storied life. But the crucial difficulty is the status of his theological language. Rhetoric can illuminate; but it can also obscure. Things come to a head in the chapter on 'the eschatological resurrection of Jesus Christ'. The rather opaque claim emerges that 'the symbol of "the raising of the dead" also excludes ideas about a "life after death" ...' (p. 222), compounding the difficulty with an earlier section on 'the community of the living and the dead' (pp. 189–192). By the time the statement just cited is re-expressed (p. 267), we have read that all life 'endures death with pain' (p. 253), that 'Christ's resurrection is bodily' (p. 256) and that resurrection has become the universal law of creation for stones (p. 258). There are too many switchbacks here.

Positively, one recognizes that Christology with an ethical orientation is a worthy objective and one salutes the author's persistent commitment to serious applied theology. Here theologians may certainly follow if they follow the way of Christ.

The Spirit of Life: A Universal Affirmation[93]

This is the fourth volume in a series that began with *The Trinity and the Kingdom of God*. Its thesis is: 'The Operations of God's life-giving and life-affirming Spirit are universal and can be recognised in everything which ministers to life and resists its destruction' (p. xi). This is developed by considering (a) biblical data, (b) the dogmatic *ordo salutis*, (c) the fellowship and Person of the Spirit. Moltmann picks up the threads of earlier works and ties them together as a theology of the Spirit and one is tempted to say that he is seeking to accomplish a dogmatics of the Holy Spirit where Barth did not. But 'trinitarian' is fairer than 'pneumatological'.

We have a typically Moltmannian contribution in two ways. First, one puzzles over whether the enterprise successfully embraces the biblical and contemporary worlds or whether it hovers between them. That way of putting it, of course, indicates that Moltmann is no post-modern. Secondly, the ethos is familiar to those who have followed Moltmann's scrutiny of the eschatological horizon and his affirmation of humanity over the years of his authorship. There is longing. But I confess I found the work very weary and page 247 on kingdom, church and cosmos is an example. Further, it is perilously non-resistant to contemporary spiritualities which affirm body, life and eros in the divine but do so in glad freedom from the burden of the concept of sin. Was Augustine, against whom Moltmann contends, so totally depraved and blinded by 'sin'? And does the Spirit, for whom Moltmann pleads, so affirm life that one forgets just how much the heart deceives? Perhaps it is the logic of the decision to write of the Spirit of 'life' rather than the Spirit of 'holiness' that is worth probing here.

Bibliography of works by Moltmann

(These works are cited in chronological order. Works later than 1987 are not included.)

Theology of Hope: On the Ground and Implications of a Christian Eschatology (London: SCM, 1967).

Two Studies in the Theology of Bonhoeffer (New York: Scribner, 1967).

Religion, Revolution and the Future (New York: Charles Scribner's, 1969).

The Future of Hope: Theology as Eschatology, F. Herzog (ed.) (New York: Herder and Herder, 1970).

Hope and Planning (London: SCM, 1971).

The Gospel of Liberation (Waco, TX: Word, 1973).

Theology and Joy (London: SCM, 1973).

'The Cross and Civil Religion' in J. Moltmann, H. W. Richardson, J. B. Metz, W. Oelmüller and M. D. Bryant (eds.), *Religion and Political Society* (New York: Harper and Row, 1974).

The Crucified God: The Cross as the Foundation and Criticism of Christian Theology (London: SCM, 1974).

Man: Christian Anthropology in the Conflicts of the Present (London: SPCK, 1974).

The Experiment Hope (London: SCM, 1975).

The Church in the Power of the Spirit: A Contribution to Messianic Ecclesiology (London: SCM, 1977).

The Open Church: Invitation to a Messianic Lifestyle (London: SCM, 1978).

Why Did God Make Me?, H. Kung and J. Moltmann (eds.) (New York: Concilium, 1978).

An Ecumenical Confession of Faith?, H. Kung and J. Moltmann (eds.) (New York: Concilium, 1979).

The Future of Creation (London: SCM, 1979).

Hope for the Church: Moltmann in Dialogue with Practical Theology, T. Runyon (ed.) (Nashville: Abingdon, 1979).

Experiences of God (London: SCM, 1980).

Jewish Monotheism and Christian Trinitarian Theology (Philadelphia: Fortress, 1981).

The Trinity and the Kingdom of God: The doctrine of God (London: SCM, 1981).

Humanity in God (London: SCM, 1983).

The Power of the Powerless (London: SCM, 1983).

Following Jesus Christ in the World Today (Occasional Papers No. 8; Institute of Mennonite Studies, October 1983).

On Human Dignity: Political Theology and Ethics (London: SCM, 1984).

Notes

[1] J. Moltmann, *The Coming of God: Christian Eschatology* (London: SCM, 1996).

[2] Richard Bauckham, *God Will Be All In All: The Eschatology of Jürgen Moltmann* (Edinburgh: T. & T. Clark, 1999).

[3] My review of Bauckham's work, above, appeared in *International Journal of Systematic Theology* (2.3), 2000. See also Stephen N. Williams, 'The Problem with Moltmann', in *European Journal of Theology* (5.2), 1996.

[4] A bibliographical article pertaining to the period covered by my account was published in *The Modern Churchman* (28.2), 1986; *Moltmann: Messianic Theology in the Making* (Basingstoke: Marshall Pickering, 1987) looked at Moltmann from 1960 – 1979, and *The Theology of Jürgen Moltmann* (Edinburgh: T. & T. Clark, 1995), dealt with the work up until then.

[5] See especially pp. 6–17.

[6] See pp. 21–36.

[7] See, for example, *The Power of the Powerless*, ch. 17.

8   For example, *The Open Church*, p. 30; *The Power of the Powerless*, p. 100.

9   Preface to *The Gospel of Liberation*.

10 M. D. Meeks, *Origins of the Theology of Hope* (Philadelphia: Fortress, 1974),
    pp. x–xi. As Moltmann uses 'man' in the older generic sense, I often
    follow his usage in expounding his thought.

11 See ibid., passim.

12 M. R. Tripole, 'A Church for the Poor and the World at Issue with
    Moltmann's Ecclesiology', in *Theological Studies*, 42 (1981), pp. 645–659.

13 *On Human Dignity*, p. 100.

14 T. Runyon, in *Hope for the Church*, p. 10.

15 *The Gospel of Liberation*, p. 30.

16 *The Future of Creation*, ch. 2. See also the helpful survey by S. Travis,
    Christian Hope and the Future of Man (Leicester: IVP, 1980), esp. ch. 1.

17 *Theology of Hope*, pp. 16, 30.

18 W. H. Capps, *Time Invades the Cathedral: Tensions in the School of Hope*
    (Philadelphia: Fortress, 1972), p. 49.

19 RSV, NEB, NIV margin.

20 'Spes Quaerens Intellectum', *Interpretation* 22 (1968), p. 40, n. 37.

21 *Theology of Hope*, p. 114.

22 *Man*, p. 17.

23 J. Barr, *Old and New in Interpretation* (London: SCM, 1926), ch. 2, 'The
    Semantics of Bible Language'.

24 Meeks, *Origins of the Theology of Hope*, passim.

25 See *Experiences of God*, p. 29.

26 Travis, *Christian Hope and the Future of Man*, chs. 2–4.

27 *Theology of Hope*, p. 329.

28 *Religion, Revolution and the Future*, p. 138.

29 *The Future of Hope*, p. 38; but note the relation of ethics to aesthetics,
    Theology and Joy, preface and p. 62.

30 See Meeks, *Origins of the Theology of Hope*, especially pp. 47ff. and 129.

31 See Bauckham, 'Moltmann's Eschatology of the Cross', *Scottish Journal of
    Theology*, 30 (1977), pp. 301–311.

32 'The Cross and Civil Religion', in *Religion and Political Society*, p. 41.

33 In E. H. Cousins (ed.), *Hope and the Future of Man* (London: Teilhard
    Centre for the Future of Man, 1973), p. 51.

34 See, for example, *Hope and Planning*, p. 41.

35 For a concise statement of Moltmann's convictions here see 'The "Crucified
    God": God and the Trinity Today', *Concilium* 8.6 (1972), pp. 26–37.

[36] See J. Pelikan, *The emergence of the Catholic Tradition* (Chicago: University of
      Chicago Press, 1971), pp. 229ff.; but also, briefly, C. B. Kaiser, *The Doctrine
      of God* (London: Marshall, Morgan & Scott, 1982), pp. 52f.

[37] For other succinct statements of lines of argument in *The Crucified God* and
      The Trinity and the Kingdom of God, see also G. Hunsinger, 'The Crucified
      God and the Political Theology of Violence', *Heythrop Journal*, 14 (1973),
      pp. 266–279.

[38] *Experiences of God*, p. 14.

[39] Especially ch. 6.

[40] Ch. 8.

[41] 'The Cross and Civil Religion', in *Religion and Political Society*, p. 19.

[42] *Concilium* 8.6 (1972), p. 30.

[43] *The Crucified God*, p. 313.

[44] See R. Bauckham, 'Jürgen Moltmann', in P. Toon and J. Spiceland (eds.),
      One God In a Trinity (Leicester: IVP, 1980).

[45] Tripole, 'A Church for the Poor and the World: at Issue with Moltmann's
      Ecclesiology', p. 659. Tripole's essay, in general, offers a well-judged
      criticism of Moltmann's ecclesiology, in my view.

[46] Romans 9 – 11. For the connection between justification and eschatology,
      see *The Future of Creation*, ch. 10.

[47] J. J. O'Donnell's exposition of Moltmann's trinitarian thought is actually
      entitled *Trinity and Temporality* (Oxford: Oxford University Press, 1983).

[48] Moltmann, *An Ecumenical Confession of Faith*, p. 18.

[49] See, too, *The Open Church*, pp. 125ff. *The Open Church* is a good general
      introduction to the themes of *The Church in the Power of the Spirit* and
      Tripole, 'A Church for the Poor and the World: at Issue with Moltmann's
      Ecclesiology', who offers an alternative exegesis.

[50] See *Hope for the Church*, p. 25.

[52] See Moltmann's *Two Studies In the Theology of Bonhoeffer*, where his sympathy
      is often indirectly shown, and G. C. Chapman, 'Hope and the ethics of
      formation: Moltmann as an interpreter of Bonhoeffer', *Studies in Religion* 12
      (1983), pp. 449–460.

[52] *The Church in the Power of the Spirit*, p. 132.

[53] Ibid., p. 134.

[54] *The Gospel of Liberation*, p. 31.

[55] *The Church in the Power of the Spirit*, p. 138.

[56] *Jewish Monotheism and Christian Trinitarian Theology*; *On Human Dignity*,
      ch. 12.

57 *The Gospel of Liberation*, p. 32.

58 *The Church in the Power of the Spirit*, p. 152.

59 George A. Lindbeck, *The Nature of Doctrine* (Philadelphia: Westminster, 1984), p. 54, though note a qualifying clause.

60 George A. Lindbeck, *The Future of Roman Catholic Theology* (Philadelphia: Fortress, 1970), p. 37.

61 *The Church in the Power of the Spirit*, p. 196.

62 *The Trinity and the Kingdom of God*, passim: *The Open Church*, ch. 4; in the context of sexism, *Humanity in God*, p. 121.

63 *The Church in the Power of the Spirit*, p. 336.

64 See *The Open Church*, chs. 4, 8; *Theology and Joy*, p. 85.

65 *The Church in the Power of the Spirit*, p. 360.

66 O'Donnell, *Trinity and Temporality*, p. 108.

67 Ibid., p. 112.

68 *The Trinity and the Kingdom of God*, p. xii.

69 In relation to Barth, this is illuminatingly laid out in David Ford's work, *Barth and God's Story* (Frankfurt: Peter Lang, 1985), and there is useful reference to Moltmann in the context of another helpful discussion of Barth in David Kelsey, *The Uses of Scripture in Recent Theology* (Philadelphia: Fortress, 1975), pp. 54ff.

70 *The Trinity and the Kingdom of God*, p. 64; see *The Future of Creation*, p. 74.

71 See J. Mackey, *The Christian Experience of God as Trinity* (London: SCM, 1983), pp. 202–209; D. Brown, *The Divine Trinity* (London: Duckworth, 1985), pp. 307f.; and R. Olson, 'Trinity and Eschatology', *Scottish Journal of Theology* 36 (1983), pp. 213–227.

72 See, too, *Hope and Planning*, pp. 117–118.

73 *Christian Hope and the Future of Man*, ch. 7. See also the response to S. Travis by Brian Hebblethwaite, *The Christian Hope* (Basingstoke: Marshall, Morgan & Scott, 1984), pp. 217f.

74 E.g. *The Gospel of Liberation*, p. 31; *Experiences of God*, p. 79.

75 *Man*, p. 20.

76 See, for example, *Experiences of God*, where the remarks of p. 36 lead on from the 'universalist' statements of p. 35.

77 E.g. *Religion, Revolution and the Future*, p. 61; *On Human Dignity*, p. 103; *The Experiment Hope*, p. 27.

78 We saw this in the autobiographical fragment in the preface, but see too, for example, *The Experiment Hope*, p. 36; *The Future of Creation*, p. 42.

79 E.g. a generally perceptive criticism of Moltmann is found in S. Sykes, 'Life

After Death', in R. McKinney (ed.), *Creation, Christ and Culture* (Edinburgh: T. & T. Clark, 1976).

[80] E.g. *The Experiment Hope*, pp. 36–39; *Religion, Revolution and the Future*, chs. 3, 8; *Man*, pp. 47–59.

[81] *Hope for the Church*, p. 30; Kung/Moltmann, *Why Did God Make Me?*, pp. 101f.; see too *Theology and Joy*, pp. 55, 62, and *Religion, Revolution and the Future*, pp. 58, 169f.

[82] 'Theology after Hiroshima', *Scottish Journal of Theology* 38 (1985), pp. 583–601.

[83] E.g. *Following Jesus Christ in the World Today*, p. 61.

[84] See G. C. Chapman, 'Hope and the ethics of formation', p. 452, who notes the significance of Moltmann's preoccupation with apathy and despair as the significant forms of sin. See too an author who preceded Moltmann and whose work presents us with one of the most interesting foils to Moltmann's position in our century, Reinhold Niebuhr, e.g. in *Faith and History* (London: Nisbet, 1949), pp. 174ff.

[85] For a brief introductory account, see Alan Richardson, *Creeds in the Making* (London: SCM, 1935; XPress Reprints, 1994).

[86] *Theology of Hope*, p. 200.

[87] *The Christian Knowledge of God*, pp. 249–252; *Christian Theism*, pp. 108f.

[88] G. Hunsinger, 'The Crucified God and the Political Theology of Violence', p. 278.

[89] Readers can be urged here to read the various writings of John Stott, e.g. *Christian Mission in the Modern World* (London: Church Pastoral Aid Society, 1977), ch. 1; *Issues facing Christians Today* (Basingstoke: Marshall, Morgan & Scott, 1984), part 1; and to note the article by R. W. McKim, 'Reformed Perspective on the Mission of the Church in Society', in *Reformed World* 38.8 (1985). It is an area where more work is needed, but these writings will provide helpful pointers.

[90] *Jewish Monotheism and Christian Trinitarian Theology*, p. 47.

[91] See S. Lukes, *Individualism* (Oxford: Blackwell, 1973).

[92] This brief review was originally published in *Modern Churchman*, 33.3 (1991), and is reprinted here by kind permission.

[93] This brief review was originally published in *Modern Believing* (1.1) (1994), and is reprinted here by kind permission.

3. THE TRINITARIAN THEOLOGY OF WOLFHART PANNENBERG: THE DIVINE FUTURE PERFECT

Timothy Bradshaw

Tim Bradshaw is Senior Tutor of Regent Park College, and member of the Faculty of Theology in the University of Oxford. He was formerly a lecturer in doctrine at Trinity College, Bristol. He is the author of The Olive Branch *(Carlisle: Paternoster, 1990),* Praying as Believing *(Macon, GA: Smyth and Helwys, 1998) and* Trinity and Ontology *(Lewiston: Edwin Mellen, 1988).*

Introduction

Born in 1928, Wolfhart Pannenberg, a Lutheran theologian, has now retired from his chair in Munich, but continues to write and lecture. He remains active also in world ecumenical affairs, and especially in colloquia focused on the interface between science and Christianity. His definitive theological statement is his three-volume *Systematic Theology* published in the original German from 1988 to 1993. This has been justly hailed as a classic, a major twentieth-century theological synthesis, to join those of Barth, Tillich and Rahner. Pannenberg's *Systematic Theology* effectively sums up and clarifies his previous theological monographs and essays, remaining very consistent in his interpretation throughout his career.

This means that much earlier work, such as his *Revelation as History, Jesus, God and Man* and *Basic Questions in Theology,* still express his theology and indeed he often refers back to such works in his *Systematic Theology.* His *Theology and the Philosophy of Science* in particular remains a vital work in explaining his integrative approach to faith and reason by way of hermeneutics. His *Anthropology in Theological Perspective* and the smaller early work, *What is Man?*, likewise remain clear expositions of his understanding of the human condition. As will become apparent, Pannenberg conceptualizes his theology by way of the category of history, and the history of thought always features heavily in any of his works. This means that the reader gains an education in the history of theology and other disciplines, as well as Pannenberg's own views. He is one of those polymaths whose range of learning is extraordinary, and who seeks to unite theology with the concerns of the 'secular' world – by showing that it is not in fact a 'God-free zone' at all.

One of the most important works not translated is the set of essays, *Grundfragen systematischer Theologie band 2*, containing essays which clearly paved the way for his final *Systematic Theology*. In particular these essays emphasized the fact that Pannenberg was unquestionably a trinitarian theologian, that the doctrine of the Trinity was at the heart of his understanding of the Christian faith. *Systematic Theology* is insistently, even radically, trinitarian.[1]

The intriguing nature of Pannenberg's theological project lies in this combination of open rationality and trinitarianism, including a thoroughgoing defence of the objective resurrection of Jesus whose identity thereby is declared to be divine. Pannenberg commits himself to arguing for this position on grounds acceptable to the secular thinker. His theology therefore coincides with apologetics, it asks questions of the secularist, while 'raising the question of God' as the most probable hypothesis to account for our experience of the world. At the same time he insists that the world has much to offer the church in terms of intellectual insight and new horizons.

In terms of the theological debates within Christianity, Pannenberg's approach rejects both liberal and conservative positions. The former fails to speak of God, and particularly the trinitarian God of Jesus Christ, amounting to a form of deism. The latter fails properly to relate God to the flow of human history. Both positions fall into forms of dualism, doing justice neither to God nor to human history and reason. Philosophically the liberal school remains in the grip of Kantian agnosticism, conservative orthodoxy being unduly Platonistic. Pannenberg claims to get beyond the impasse of the liberal and conservative dualisms by way of his new synthesis.

Since he appeals to reason, while believing that reason points to faith in the God who maintains all reality and truth, Pannenberg must be classified as a theologian and philosopher who does not embrace 'postmodernism' in the sense of relativism or irrationalism. He does believe in a meta-narrative, in ultimate universal meaning, and is prepared to argue for it. But this narrative is historical and so sensitive to cultural shifts and new insights arising as time goes on. Therefore he can claim the benefits which postmodernism attributes to its own critical rejection both of the Englightenment and of traditional theology.

In short, for such reasons and others which will emerge during the exposition of his thought, Pannenberg is an important dialogue partner for all serious students of theology, as well as a rich resource as a critical expositor of the history of theology in relation to secular thought, and indeed an acute cultural critic.

Revelation and reasonable theology

A new theological agenda

Pannenberg broke onto the theological scene as part of a working group, the Pannenberg Circle, which published a symposium edited by Pannenberg, in 1961, and published in English in 1969.[2] He contributed to the collection, including the introductory essay. This set out a major criticism of the ruling German theology and made a broad proposal for revision. The shift he sought to make concerned the *kerygmatic* theological stance of Bultmann and also Barth, at that time very influential in German Protestant theology. Pannenberg rejected the dualism between faith and reason he found in these theologians, and sought to reconnect the two ways of knowing through the category of history.

The doctrine of revelation developed in these different versions of theology stressed divine self-disclosure. In Bultmann's case this occurs in the moment of faith connecting with the word of the cross, in Barth's case in the person and work of Jesus Christ.

Protestant theology, in German *academe*, was in full flight from understanding Scripture as 'propositional revelation', or revealed truths from God, accommodated to our human understanding, as Calvin, for example, had classically taught. 'Revelation', says Pannenberg, 'is not God's making known a certain set of arcane truths, but – as Karl Barth puts it – the self-disclosure of God ... The new stress is the exclusive use of the concept "revelation" to mean the self-disclosure of God, without any imparting of supernatural truths.'[3]

The concept of revelation has been filled with an immediate, direct divine content, more akin to that of irresistible grace than the older, more detached understanding of inspired information telling us about God. Pannenberg speaks of 'the collapse of the older Protestant scripture principle as formulated in the doctrine of inspiration'. But he continues, 'Note that this collapse did not make untenable the basing of Christian theology on scripture as the norm of its *content*.'[4] This question of content, knowable by the mind, will prove increasingly important in Pannenberg's attempt to construct his doctrine of revelation. He accepts from Barth that revelation must mean divine self-disclosure, flowing from the divine initiative to us. 'The knowledge of God that is made possible by God, and therefore by revelation, is one of the basic conditions of the concept of theology as such. Otherwise', he goes on, 'the possibility of the knowledge of God is logically inconceivable; it would contradict the very idea of God.'[5] By God alone, can God be known, is a dictum approved by Barth and also Pannenberg, but developed rather differently.[6] Pannenberg also approves of Barth's emphasis on the unity of divine revelation, if it is truly to reveal its revealer; it must be unique rather than multiple in character: 'A multiplicity of revelation implies a discrediting of any particular revelation.'[7] In other words, when taken in this strong sense of divine full self-disclosure there can be but one revelation, not several.

The biblical narrative, however, speaks of many acts of God and words about God, given in many and various ways. The history of Israel mediates revelation about God, but there is a distinction between the mediating events themselves and God. Bultmann's theology of revelation collapses this range of historical

meaning into the experience of faith here and now. Barth unites
the medium and the message in the incarnation: God reveals
himself fully in the person of Jesus Christ, God and man,
accessible only to obedient faith. Pannenberg wishes to re-
appropriate the whole sweep of history as his focus, which he
argues is more biblical and more reasonable.

These considerations led Pannenberg to the understanding
of 'indirect self revelation' as the most accurate definition of
revelation. By this he means that the content of divine revelation
is given in the totality of history, and so finally known at its end
point, just as the plot of a novel is finally fully disclosed in its last
paragraph. But along the way we encounter a multitude of truths
that go to make up the whole. The indirectness of revelation
comes from the fact that we need to reflect on the meaning of
events in order to understand them, just as we need to reflect on
the meaning of a book or play. The content is the key element: our
understanding is required to unlock its meaning, and so there is an
indirect path to the truth, through our interpretation, rather than
instant direct personal union. History is rather like a play through
which we advance, seeking to understand the situation as we go
along, trusting that the final end will bring full disclosure of the
playwright.[8]

Pannenberg makes the powerful point that this view of
relevation chimes in with that of the biblical apocalyptic message,
that the end of history will bring the vindication of God's ways,
and the vindication of the faithful. He points out that biblical
'revelation' is an apocalyptic term, and that it focuses on the end
time: it is a thoroughly eschatological concept. The end-time event
will disclose the final truth of God and his ways, and will put into
place the puzzles and painful problems of history. That point will
be the self-disclosure of God, the revelation of the divine being in
the strong sense. Hence the title of Pannenberg's book, *Revelation
as History*; the totality of history will bring fullness of divine self-
revelation.

Pannenberg argues that history does have a meaning, as does a
play, and the fact that we are not yet at its end does not affect that.
Interpretation will therefore be tested according to its power to
explain events convincingly. One might, for example, ask whether

Shakespeare's *MacBeth* is most convincingly interpreted according
to the thesis that the drunken porter at the gate is the key figure;
the content of the play almost certainly ruling that interpretation
as an unlikely hypothesis! Pannenberg works with an objective
view of interpretation. He also rejects a special 'faith' mode of
knowledge as part of his rejection of dualism. If faith is in touch
with the truth, then it must be true on the universal field of
knowledge; there can be no 'retreat into commitment' as a lazy
substitute for the hard work of demonstrating the strength of the
Christian claim. Pannenberg regards such a move as quasi-gnostic,
appealing to an authoritarian special form of knowledge divorced
from normal links with the world and history.

Likewise history is one field of reality and truth. We cannot
assume a special form of it before examining and interpreting it.
The meaning of history will disclose itself to proper hermeneutical
consideration. Christianity must not be tempted to wall itself off in
a ghetto, but must rather be confident that its truth claims will
vindicate themselves in the world of open debate and investigation. Pannenberg believes that this honours God, the God of all
reality, more than the dualisms of either the classical Platonic kind,
or of the Kantian kind, which split critical reason from faith, and
split the noumenal realm of value from the phenomenal realm of
the observed world around us. In *Revelation as History*, therefore,
Pannenberg announced himself as a synthesizer, a theologian
seeking to knit together what so much theology since Kant put
asunder.

The keystone to his new synthesis was the resurrection of Jesus,
taken as an historical question, and interpreted against the background of its contemporary apocalyptic thought. As such,
Pannenberg suggested, this event was the end time come in
advance, and so the clue to the meaning of the totality of history,
and divine self-revelation. His second essay in the early program-
matic symposium detailed seven theses in which he crystallized his
view of revelation as history, anticipated in the resurrection of
Jesus, and open to understanding by good historical and hermeneutical reasoning. This last point has been nuanced somewhat in
the more recent *Systematic Theology*, but broadly speaking *Revelation
as History* still states Pannenberg's theological synthesis in a

nutshell. He rejects fideist epistemologies as authoritarian and irrational, and he rejects traditional natural theology. He seeks instead an historicist mode of interpretative reasoning which will reflect the truth of things coming to us in the flow of events. And he finds biblical warrant for this view in the prophetic and apocalyptic traditions. Philosophically he makes no bones about a shift from Kant to Hegel as supplying better resources for theology, keying in with a biblical way of understanding truth and reality.

Hermeneutical history

Pannenberg's doctrine of revelation is in effect a view of history pregnant with meaning, a move away from a Cartesian or Kantian kind of subjectivist base, towards a more objective historicist position. An event may be interpreted differently by different people, but Pannenberg holds that a single, objectively true interpretation can be reached in the light of the facts taken in context. It is crucial to his case that all events have their inherent meanings, disclosed by correct hermeneutical investigation. Pannenberg's stance on this has met with criticism, notably from an historian, Burhenn, who deems it wrong to maintain one true interpretation for all events (historians often remain agnostic about the historicity and significance of events), and argues that this option is a perfectly valid one.[9] Pannenberg, on the contrary, thinks that it is necessary to come to a decision about events under consideration, in particular when considering the resurrection of Jesus. The doctrine that history bears an inherent meaning in itself is vital to Pannenberg's whole programme of historical objectivity. Revelation does not depend upon the subjective creativity of the interpreter but is mediated through human cognition, and so indirectly, hence the content of revelation is objectively given. For Pannenberg, events evoke their proper interpretation: the stimulus to the rational reflection 'derives from the event itself'.[10]

History is therefore a hermeneutical process and the human interpretation of its events conceptualizes its current significance by means of rational reflection on the data. This is central to Pannenberg's attempted synthesis of a high view of revelation with freely operating rationality: the matrix of the synthesis is the stream of history, bearing revelatory meaning within its events. Freely ranging enquiring reason and objective revelation are united in the nexus of history in such a way that Pannenberg can argue his case that 'Christian speech about God can be verified only in such a way that it is the revelation of God itself which discloses that about man and his world in relation to which its truth is proved'.[11] The point is that Pannenberg shifts the centre away from man's arbitrary constructs to what history teaches: the flow of history is revelatory and it includes human thought formulating the intrinsic significance of events as they arise. As time goes on, events will be seen in a different light and gain fresh meaning, and their interpretation develops accordingly. In this way Pannenberg builds provisionality into his doctrine of indirect self-revelation as history. Again this emphasizes the determinative importance he accords to the flow of history, incorporating the history of thought to 'thematize' or formulate the developing meaning of the whole process. Revelation as history is objectively given but, since it is as yet incomplete, our insights remain provisional and subject to amendment from the open future. Particular clusters of events and their meanings before the eschaton are always provisional and will be taken forward into ever-new syntheses of meaning as future discoveries in the flow of human thought cast fresh light on the past, as the old is incorporated and changed into new configurations. We are all involved in a rolling process of 'history as hermeneutic'. The whole process of history read from its point of consummation, from God's point of view, constitutes revelational meaning and essence.

It is startling to ears dulled by the dogma of secular materialism, the empiricist metaphysic, to hear Pannenberg claim that an anticipation, or 'prolepsis', of the end-time event is necessary for us to understand the universe. Without some clue to the overall process of history, we are in Hegel's 'night in which all cows are black'. Revelation is, then, not just a 'faith' idea but is rationally necessary for thought in general. Here we see how radical Pannenberg is in his efforts to achieve a new synthesis. He has set himself the target of upholding both the freedom of critical reason and the normative majesty of divine revelation, which alone can provide the yardstick of verification for speech about God.

Revelation and history are two sides of the one coin: revelation is going to be recognized in the final future as the whole plan of historical meaning; the eschaton will declare the final significance of the web of history as having been God's essential revelation all along. In the meantime, the overall meaning to be given by this event has been anticipated in the life and fate of Jesus, and therefore Pannenberg does make his claim upon the intellectual decision of the historian and of the philosopher as well as the theologian. We are not operating in two realms, one of secular history and one of revealing grace: we are in a single frame of reference and knowledge, and the claim on the mind must therefore be pressed. Pannenberg thinks that people have a responsibility to make up their mind about the resurrection of Jesus one way or the other. Faith is no blind leap but is the most sensible conclusion and response in the light of reasonable reflection.

At the same time, Pannenberg contends, these conclusions are to be held, logically, as provisional in the light of the possibility of fresh counter-evidence. His insistence that all truth claims must be subject to reasonable evidence, is no doubt the cause of the criticism made by some that Pannenberg practises a form of 'rationalism'.[12] Pannenberg has indeed sought to reclaim the secular realm of reason for the theological realm of faith and insists on a reasoned approach to all matters of interpretation. For Pannenberg this demonstrates not only intellectual integrity but also a determination to speak to 'the cultured despisers of religion', as Schleiermacher called them in his day. In the foreword to *Systematic Theology* II, Pannenberg states:

> Christian theology has developed in the service of this truth claim, seeking to clarify it, to strengthen it by a systematic presentation of Christian teaching, but also again and again to test how far it may be made. Theologians can do justice to this task only if they examine the Christian truth claim as impartially as possible. They cannot begin, then, with a firm presupposition of the truth of Christian revelation. If they did, they would make this truth a matter of mere subjective conviction, which would be little more than an objective untruth, and perhaps even in many ways an attractive fable.[13]

Pannenberg basically believes that truth is truth, and will be able to sustain itself in the face of any proper test.

He argues that the historical and hermeneutical probability is that the Christian claim is true, and, therefore, that psychologically the Christian has certainty in his faith, while logically admitting that new counter-evidence may arise to undermine that claim. Christianity is treated on the same basis as all other such hypotheses. The key to Pannenberg's doctrine is that human cognitive and intuitive processes are woven into this whole process. History has its ongoing rationality in the stream of human consciousness, history synthesizes the real and the rational, fact and theory.

To use Toulmin's phrase, history is 'a field encompassing field' for Pannenberg; indeed the only such field. Nothing escapes the web of universal history: truth, reason, faith, morality – all are functions of the historical-temporal whole, which is still in process. This total fabric is a 'semantic network'[14] of reality and truth on its way to fullness of meaning. Human interpretation is that element of this whole which consciously reflects on its significance by taking up insights from the past into the future in the hermeneutical tradition of the history of thought. Reasoning capacities do not therefore stand over against history so much as reflect its truth on the way to the final revelation of its overall meaning. Reason springs from history and subserves its unfolding significance. Pannenberg says that events themselves contain the stimulus to reflective reasoned interpretation within themselves: we are not at the mercy of subjective fancy in the hermeneutical enterprise; sound contextual interpretation will prove itself by the test of time.

Pannenberg is only rationalistic, therefore, in a quite unusual sense, unusual to the Anglo-Saxon empiricist tradition, at any rate, because his rationalism, if it be such and it is a contested point,[15] comes in objectivist form.

> As I understand it, this would describe reason, not as *a priori*
> capacity, but in its historical structure of sketching and reflecting,
> but thus also in its essential (not however always factual) openness
> to a truth always presupposed but never grasped in the act of
> thinking out the sketch.[16]

Rationality is woven into the fabric of the universe, and we participate in this process. For Pannenberg, as for H. R. Niebuhr, 'time is in reason and reason is in time'; reason is not an absolute raised above temporal history and independent of it. Because this is so, reason shares the structures of historical experience. All our understanding, he says, requires that we project provisional overall pictures or worldviews, within which reason operates: we sketch out, albeit often unconsciously, a plan of the shape of how things are as a prerequisite for any analysis or interpretation. Moreover, the stimulus for this comes from the new events and advances in thought which the future brings. Hence the projecting is also reflecting the intrinsic dynamic at the heart of events. History is hermeneutical, and our consciousness participates in this process of the development of meaning. Faith has the same kind of structure in that it trusts the God of the unpredictable future: hope is its overarching presupposition or worldview, within which it grapples with the difficulties thrown up by events.

Jesus is the great example of a faith in the God of the apocalyptic tradition to vindicate his trust. Pannenberg also thinks that science depends on just such a structure of understanding, sketching out horizons within which theories can be tested, and indeed which will need revising as fresh evidence brings down the current theory, or projection, of how things are. This structure of reason, or of human experience, in the flow of time generally, is, for Pannenberg, thoroughly biblical, especially in the apocalyptic tradition, which looked to the ultimate future for its hope to make sense of the state of the world. The eschaton will gather up all the foreshadowings of the end and will show how all the preceding events mesh together. Indeed the preceding events of significance point ahead and derive from that future to which they point: the apocalyptic tradition, according to Pannenberg, engaged in just this 'sketching and reflecting' hermeneutic with its hallmark of trustful humility towards the future in all its inscrutability. In addition, emphasizing the totality of history constituting divine revelation, Pannenberg originally holds to the future orientation and determination of all things. Truth is in process and is proleptically structured: it lives from its future to the future. Human interpretation, an integral element in the rolling forwards of all truth, is controlled likewise by

this future-orientated historicist system. The present must bury
itself in the future humbly, and be ready to revise currently held
opinions. This is what Jesus did and what he lived out:

> The understanding of reason and knowledge here indicated means
> that both live in anticipation in regard to their relationship to truth.
> This proleptic structure, which determines the form of all acts of
> knowledge, is proper to the knowledge of the Christ-event also
> precisely in view of its content. All knowledge of this event, the
> more precisely it is aware of the nature of the event, will appreciate
> so much more its own provisional character and will press forward
> so much the more insistently beyond itself towards faith as the
> relevant attitude of man to God's revelation in the Christ event . . .
> Aware, however, of the proleptic quality of the revelatory event
> which is its basis, faith will take seriously the provisional character
> of the knowledge on which it rests.[17]

Pannenberg offers a very objectivist, systematic, historicist
worldview, an interpretation of the shape of reality which is
holistic, unifying and intent on softening, or removing, absolute
barriers of fact and thought. He continually resists dualism and
delights in synthesizing what some philosophies and theologies
have made into apparent opposites.

The Christ-event is the revelation of God in advance and at the
same time it is the philosophical clue to the universe. The
proleptic structure of the resurrection closes the structure of all
thought and reality. The very epistemological or hermeneutical
process involved in reaching this conclusion about Jesus (that is
historical-critical exploration, gaining meaning from an event
against its current thought-context, then projecting an overarching
horizon of universal interpretation) holds good throughout
Pannenberg's work. Bearing in mind that this hermeneutical
enterprise is not only the construction of man but is stimulated
by the meaning inherent in the clusters of events, we can see how
revelation as history is the same as the hermeneutical process of
history. Our provisional, human sketch-plans of the whole shape
of things are also God-sent, inspired intimations of the beyond.
They are fully human, fully divine.

The reality of God is always present only in subjective anticipations of the totality of reality, in models of the totality of meaning presupposed in all particular experience. These models, however, are historic, which means that they are subject to confirmation or refutation by subsequent experience.[18]

As one of Pannenberg's commentators, David McKenzie, correctly says: 'I submit that Pannenberg wants to link natural knowledge and revelation.'[19] This is exactly the case: indirect self-revelation is the same phenomenon as the 'secular' hermeneutical course of history finding true formulation through good, reasonable interpretative exploration of the facts in context.

Because of this, I suggest, it is not really helpful to see Pannenberg as ever having operated a theological method 'from below' in the normal sense. Rather he has used an integrating method: reason and faith share the same structure and fasten onto the same content. Faith could not begin without hermeneutical reason, the indirect filtering element in Pannenberg's doctrine of revelation as history. Revelation is, for Pannenberg, as history: 'above' is not distinct from 'below'; the sacred and secular, the 'eternal' and the temporal, cohere in Pannenberg's system. 'Below' is not isolated from the divine Spirit. Human projections and divine mediation of fresh insight are correlated through the flow of time. 'In that man's existence is animated by the question about his destination and fulfilment, he is already borne by the reality at which such inquiry is directed';[20] human projected answers to the question of reality are not only subjective creations, but are also evoked by the power of the future, the beyond. Nature and grace very much interpenetrate in the single continuum of history.

Pannenberg's very systematic epistemology rests upon his holistic, anti-dualist, ontology; his view of faith, reason and revelation depends on the shape of the universe and its origin in the free and faithful God of the open future. Knowing reflects being: the Enlightenment heresy, that our knowing somehow fashions the world, is attacked and turned round. Our derivation of meaning from events is not simply an anthropocentric enterprise rooted in arbitrary subjectivity, but it is rather evoked by, and confirmed by, history in the fullest sense of this word.

Pannenberg teaches, in effect, that historical *meaning* determines *being*, and that it does so from the future, giving rise to freedom and unpredictability in our universe. History determines being, but this is no merely fatalist worldview, because this history comes to us from the open future, not as a result of an iron law unfolding out of the past. Pannenberg's insistence that all truth and interpretation is provisional, in the light of the new insights yet to come from the future, is based on this ontology of the future constantly revising the past and taking it forward into fresh configurations. Just as this applies in the case of the evidence for the historicity of Jesus' resurrection, so too the principle applies hermeneutically, in terms of its interpretation: the meaning of God's self-revelation in Jesus is also subject to future develop-ment, indeed its meaning will fill out as time goes on. At the final eschaton we will see how the Christ-event always presented in microcosm the pattern and meaning of everything, the truly universal plan of reality.

According to Pannenberg's dynamically interrelating view of the universe, all things gain their being from outside themselves; all truth and reality is open to its neighbouring counterpart and to its opposite. In this sense, the universe is 'exo-centric' or 'ec-centric', not full of isolated atomic entities, but inter-penetrating and mutually dependent beings, perhaps what the Cappadocian Fathers might term 'perichoretic', using their trinitarian language. Whereas, says Pannenberg, modern man regards the essence of things to be in himself, the biblical tradition affirms the source of all life to be objectively outside ourselves. At the very end of time we shall see the whole revelation of God as history; we shall see that it was all along a meaning inseparably informed by the life, death and resurrection of Jesus. We shall see that all history gains its unity from the God of the open future, always beyond and free, yet always the indwelling source of historical vitality and significance.

The whole and the future are the overarching concepts in Pannenberg's historicism. The whole will be seen to embody the fullness of divine self-disclosure. The future is the source of all things, informs everything with freedom, and is the goal towards which all things tend. Within this overarching framework a tension, or dialectic, is constantly at work: the past and present are the thesis to which the future forms the antithesis, thus making a fresh synthesis, which then in turn constitutes the new present. This dialectical dynamic of history is at the core of Pannenberg's system and forms the basis of his interpretation of apocalyptic theology:

> In the development from the Jahwistic tradition to the apocalyptic literature it is not just the extent of events proving the deity of God that is increasing, but also the content of revelation that is revising itself. What had previously been the final vindication of God is now seen as only one step in the ever increasing context of revelation.[21]

A remarkably parallel picture of the progress of understanding through history was given by the secularist philosopher of history, E. H. Carr in his classic text, *What is History?* He writes:

> The absolute in history is not something in the past from which we start; it is not something in the present, since all present thinking is necessarily relative. It is something still incomplete and in the process of becoming – something in the future towards which we move, which begins to take shape as we move towards it, and in the light of which, as we gradually move forward, we gradually shape our interpretation of the past.

He concludes in striking similarity to Pannenberg, 'This is the secular truth behind the religious myth that the meaning of history will be revealed in the Day of Judgement.'[22] Pannenberg's theology of revelation as history is indeed the very same notion as his hermeneutical understanding of history.[23]

It might be said that Pannenberg seems after all to be using theological ideas as dress for a philosophy of history, which can be commended to secular interpreters. But this would be unfair to Pannenberg the theologian who regularly put the challenging question to his secular dialogue partners about the future and the fact that it 'raises the question of God'. Secularism, he suggested, can provide no solutions to account for the phenomenon of the new and unpredictable in history, nor indeed for the

phenomenon of human freedom. These factors in particular point
us to the hypothesis of the God of the open future.

Concepts of God, religion and revelation

In presenting his definitive theological synthesis, his *Systematic
Theology*, Pannenberg places his interpretation of revelation after
initial chapters dealing with the question of God in terms of
philosophy and religion. This reminds us sharply of Hegel's
approach to religion and its treatment first of the concept of
religion then the concrete religions themselves.[24] Pannenberg, in
fact, acknowledges his admiration of Hegel in this project, and
defends him from the charge of holding a purely intellectualistic
and abstract concept of religion: 'Awareness of God', for Hegel,
'the concept of deity, is indeed the basis, but the concept of
religion reaches its culmination in the cultus.' Cultus, for Hegel,
means all forms of bridging the gulf between humanity and
God.[25] The final form of religion will be that which God brings
about, in convergence with the human attempt to reach after the
divine. The path from concept to concrete reality could be said to
characterize Pannenberg's theological technique: a concept develops and refines itself, then is put to the test of concrete history.

. Revelation is going to manifest itself finally in all the debates
and controversies of life. 'The manifestation of divine reality even
within the unresolved conflicts of religious and ideological truth
claims is called revelation.'[26] This restates the thesis of revelation
as history, linked to all the phenomena of the historical flow,
isolated from no part of it. Christian theology must exist in this
continual struggle to uphold its truth claims against all manner of
criticisms and rivals, and divine self-disclosure comes in and
through this complex and contested context. *Systematic Theology*
insists that Christian theology cannot simply base itself on
assertions which are not subject to critical questioning by unfet-
tered reason. But 'the knowledge of God that is made possible by
God, and therefore by revelation, is one of the basic conditions of
the concept of theology as such,' says Pannenberg; 'Otherwise the
possibility of the knowledge of God is logically inconceivable; it
would contradict the very idea of God.'[27] This logical deduction,
that God, if he is God, must disclose himself rather than be an

object of human discovery akin to some sort of supra-object, does not close the question of how this revelation is made and how human kind apprehends it. Pannenberg rejects the distinction between natural theology and revealed theology, as if the former were the product of some 'God-free zone' of human enterprise. Revelation comes in and through the processes of history, subjective and objective. He affirms this as a matter of epistemology, rejecting a fideist starting point. Yet as a matter of logic, at the start of *Systematic Theology* I, he is able to say that 'recourse to the incarnation is indispensable,' explaining that 'Only from the standpoint of God's saving action that seeks to bring creatures into fellowship with himself can we maintain their participation in the deity of God (without prejudicing their distinctiveness), and therefore in theology as the science of God.'[28] Theology can only speak of God if we can know of God in the world's reality, and therefore incarnation seems indispensable to this enterprise. But, has it happened, and can we uncover it in the vast flow of history? This procedure seems to be how Pannenberg sets up his theological treatise, and how it unfolds methodologically.

We move from chapter 1, entitled 'The truth of Christian doctrine as the theme of systematic theology', to chapter 2, 'The concept of God and the question of its truth.' Chapter 3 takes us to 'The reality of God and the Gods in the experience of the religions', prior to chapter 4, 'The revelation of God,' and chapter 5, 'The Trinitarian God.' The pattern is clear. We move from the insistence that Christian doctrine prove itself, rather as a maths teacher might ask a child to demonstrate why the answer given is true. Doctrine cannot simply be asserted by authoritative *diktat*, not that of the Emperor,[29] nor that of the consensus of the church, nor the idea of a Koranically kind of inspired Scripture. But Pannenberg does regard the content of Scripture as basic, and all creeds, 'confessions and dogmas are in fact summaries of the central themes of scripture'.[30] The subject-matter of Scripture, through all the processes of interpretation, is what produces church consensus, according to Pannenberg, and his view that theology must continually renew itself in the light of the developing exposition of Scripture, and so regard itself as provisional, similarly echoes an evangelical note, *semper reformanda*. In other words, his *Systematic Theology* is a Christian theology, positing the doctrine of Christ and finding in Scripture its fundamental content: but these doctrinal claims must always be tested, must prove themselves as true in the process of human experience and history, in the light of the whole realm of human intellectual enterprise.

The shape of Pannenberg's thought emerges again as positing a question or idea, and confirming it, a kind of dipolar elliptical process that does not end until God confirms finally the truth of Christian doctrine at the eschaton. In this way, Christian truth-claims are ultimately provisional until 'that day'.[31] Theology articulates the Christian understanding, but also tests its truth and confirms it, rather than presupposing this truth as given beforehand. A kind of bracketing of initial certainty is entailed in terms of the objective intellectual quest, and this will ultimately confirm personal subjective faith.[32] Here we recognize that Pannenberg does not flow with the stream of fragmented 'postmodern' notions of truth which reject any 'metanarrative' in favour of individualist claims without criteria for evaluation. But the eschaton will be the ultimate determinant of that universal truth and meaning.

Pannenberg is keen to argue that truth cannot depend upon any individual act of faith, rather truth is connected to the concept of God, as he commends Augustine for teaching. This, in fact, is another way of putting his contention about revelation as history: divine being cannot be separated from divine self-disclosure in historical event and interpretation. He develops this point by suggesting that the concept of truth entails the criterion of truth: 'can that be a criterion of truth which is not part of the concept?' he asks,[33] and thinks that the concept itself becomes ontological. Truth relates to being, and to God: 'God alone can be the ontological locus of the unity of truth in the sense of coherence as the unity of all that is true.'[34]

But again, this truth will be confirmed definitively only at the eschaton, and the biblical understanding of truth 'does not seek to grasp it as that which is present behind the flux of time. It seeks to grasp it as that which shows and confirms itself to be lasting as time progresses'.[35] Christian dogmatics then takes the form of postulated hypothesis making sense of reality and conceptuality.

Dogmatic statements are assertions, but modestly made. They are propositions laying claim to the truth of what they assert, but are open to question by other disciplines and dialogue partners. Mindless acceptance honours these propositions less than their invitation to testing and confirmation. Dogmatics is really a systematic doctrine of God, and since the world exists, it also concerns the connection of God with this world, including the debatability of God in the light of human experience.

Pannenberg's system does not permit the idea that faith builds onto reason as if the two were initially separate and needed to be reintroduced. The two are intrinsically related. For Pannenberg, reason has the same hypothetical structure as faith,[36] and faith is suffused with reason: again, two sides of the same coin. Christian faith understands life in the world on the basis of the self-revelation of God in the resurrection event of Christ, and believers move forward through life believing this to be true and trusting in the revealed God of Jesus, the God of the open future. *Psychologically* believers are sure, but *logically* they are open to new evidence – which might contradict their working hypothesis and bring it down.

Philosophically, the historic 'proofs' of the existence of God no longer work as logically compelling arguments. They can be treated as merely projections of human longing for a primal reality sustaining all things, along with the atheistic criticism developed by Feuerbach. But Pannenberg understands the function of the proofs as pointing to the concept of God as essential to a proper human self-understanding. This can be in relation to human reason, or other human faculties, such as our moral sense, for example. Pannenberg cites Hans Küng's theory that all humans presuppose a deep trust that things hold together and are sustained, that the same conditions will continue hour by hour, making life possible. This deep trust in the coherence of things, alongside Pannenberg's own stress on the accompanying newness of events in history, is an anthropological axiom of humanity. It is constitutive of the human condition. The believer refers to this deep basis of things as God. Pannenberg also argues that human freedom is a phenomenon deeply problematic for the atheist to account for, and that it points to an origin in God.

This is not a claim to proof in any strict sense, but rather 'what is maintained is that we are referred to an unfathomable reality that transcends us and the world, so that the God of religious tradition is given a secure place in the reality of human experience'.[37] As interpreted anthropologically by Kant and Hegel, says Pannenberg, the proofs of God usefully bear witness to the need of humanity and human reason to rise above the mundane finitude of human existence to the thought of the infinite. The cosmological arguments are important because they refer all reality to the one origin. Pannenberg views the arguments as helping to clarify the concept of God in relation to the world, and so helping to develop a critical, purifying function for theology. The divine is constantly at work in all manner of ways, mediating itself in and through such conceptual philosophical theology, refining the concept of God – which will of course be decisively confirmed and verified at the eschaton.

God and religions

Not only Christianity, but religions in general must, likewise, be relevant to our theological considerations, and here Pannenberg takes an unusual course in his *Systematic Theology* by devoting an early methodological chapter to 'the reality of God and the Gods in the experience of the religions'. This chapter follows on from his treatment of natural theology. Such a radical move ought not really to have surprised us, since the religions are part of human history just as much as philosophies, and of course they make claims about the divine to be tested and evaluated as hypotheses without fear or favour.

Pannenberg, after all, has consistently taught that human existence, at its deepest level of being, is *Weltoffenheit*, that is, open to the world and what sustains it. This, in turn, points to an inherently religious openness to the future, the future anticipating the final promised end, summing up the totality of meaning.[38] He has consistently argued that God is indirectly 'co-given' in world history, not directly given or accessible, not, as Heidegger would have put it, 'at hand', like a commodity in the supermarket of the universe.[39] In ordinary experience of meaning, he teaches, the totality of meaning is only *implicitly* anticipated, that is to say as the implied grand context for any particular meanings, whereas in religious experience there is already present 'a form of explicit awareness of the total meaning of reality, even though it is only an indirect assumption within the awareness of the divine basis of all reality'.[40] Logical implication coincides here with religious sense in his understanding of a less than fully worked out *content* of religion. The combining of the logical unfolding of concepts with historical development may be an important clue to interpreting Pannenberg's thought. Again this is a clear link to Hegel's style of thinking, both logical and encyclopaedic, in its attempt to grasp the grand unfolding meaning of the universe.[41]

Pannenberg is very alert to the issue of the plurality of religions in the world, and the problem that this poses for Christianity. Contradictory truth claims compete with one another, and Christianity cannot escape being classified as one of them. Pannenberg insists on being honest about the clash of religious assertions, and he believes that glossing over this plain fact increases public secular scepticism about religion in the West.

> Only a so-called theology of religions in the industrial societies of the West closes its eyes to this truth, depicting the many religions as in principle unconflicting ways to the same God. In the event, this type of theology plays into the hands of the prejudice that the advanced secularism of the modern public has against all religious truth claims, treating the differences in religious confession merely as private matters of no public interest.[42]

Christianity must cling to the truth it perceives as coming from the revelation of God given by the resurrection of Jesus, but must constantly take responsibility for defending this truth in the light of the many challenges of other disciplines and criticisms.

Pannenberg has an unusual interpretation of the rise of the secular mindset in the West. He does not attribute this to the rise of science or to intellectual criticisms; rather, the savage European wars of religion, especially the Thirty Years War, set back the cause of religion as a public good as societies turned to secular structures to avoid religious feuding. Religion became a matter of private devotion, not a resource for public values and policy

making. In the era following 11 September 2001, the extremist
Islamic terror attack on the USA, this point has become of great
interest and importance as the political aspect of one branch of a
world religion was made painfully clear to Western secularists and
indeed Christians. It is less and less obvious now that all religions
do actually make the same truth claims about God. Likewise, the
assumption that religion is a private matter, detached from wider
public relevance and criticism, becomes decreasingly plausible.
The moral imperative to respect people of different faiths, and
none, can less easily blur into a homogenization of the truth
claims of these faiths, *as if* they were the same – albeit without
realizing it! Pannenberg, in other words, wants to distinguish
tolerant politeness from the question of truth as debated between
the positive religions.

He regards a religious dimension as being constitutive for being
human, not consciously known or conceptualized until the stage
of positive religion – when the concrete religious systems must of
course compete, as just indicated, to show which best makes sense
of human experience in the world. Human development of
cognition, of awareness of objects other than ourselves, presupposes a religious dimension, he argues: 'that which can become
the explicit object of religious consciousness is implicitly present
in every turning to a particular object of our experience'.[43]
Development of human experience of life entails rising levels of
consciousness of other things and of the self as a being in
relationships, and of being finite or bounded. Pannenberg draws
on a doctrine of the *imago Dei* originating in the work of Herder,
who interpreted this divinely given image not as an original state
of perfection but rather as a destiny given to us and fulfilled by
divine agency. From our earliest days, 'we are set before a
transcendent mystery in the sense that the silent infinity of reality
that is beyond our control constantly presents itself to us as
a mystery'.[44] Later in life this is recognized as having been
'nonthematic' knowledge of God, which is not, however, real
knowledge of God.

Like Schleiermacher, Pannenberg seems to be teaching that we
all have a 'sense and taste for the infinite', or a 'dissatisfaction with
the finite', but that this can be connected to the definite question

of God which will be gained from an actual religion. Pannenberg cites Paul's teaching in the book of Romans to back up this thesis that in the history of humanity there has always been some form of explicit awareness of God which is linked to experience of the works of creation, and hence our creaturely perception of creation. Pannenberg, again perhaps like Schleiermacher and his audience of 'cultured despisers of religion', is keenly aware of the need to take seriously the challenges and concerns of contemporary society. This is a generation, in the West at least, in which all talk about God is reduced to subjectivity. Accordingly Pannenberg wants to attend to the fashionable vogue for religions and the anthropological elements of truth that he might be able to take from this approach, so as to take them up into a theology focusing on the primacy of God and divine revelation. The history of religions and the conceptual development of monotheism, connected to the understanding of the unity of the human race, are significant in Pannenberg's analysis of religion. God is 'the all determining reality'.[45] As ever, he applies his principle of the need for truth claims to be tested and confirmed in human historical experience.[46] This includes conceptual testing, a point that can be forgotten in Pannenberg's analysis, and the concept of revelation as divine self-mediation has become decisive in the history of religious self-testing. God reveals himself in the world, human effort does not reach deity by unaided effort. This notion, he claims, has attracted such widespread agreement as to become a definitive concept.[47]

Placing revelation after a treatment of religion in his definitive *Systematic Theology* clarifies Pannenberg's approach, making him quite unusual among Christian theologians. However, it also places him within that tradition of theology so keen to make links with contemporary culture and to begin with the questions it is asking – that of other religions being one of growing importance. Pannenberg is acutely aware of the pluralist approach to religions now prevalent in the West, and the effect of this to relativize all religious claims into the realm of private taste. It is therefore vital in doing Christian theology to take up this issue with all seriousness. Pannenberg accepts that religions can pervert and mythicize the relationship of God to the world, as Barth stressed.

But he thinks that the revelation of God transcends the dangers of
human construction of idolatrous religion, and that in the course
of the history of religion, the God of Israel emerges as the God of
the universe. The claim of Christianity, one of the religious
claimants, is that it will prove itself as true. This is better put that
the God of the Bible will prove himself to be the one God of all
people, the one God disclosed in Jesus Christ. Historical revelation confirms the concept of the one God, the all-determining
reality. Christian theology takes the form of explicating and
confirming the truth claim about this God, starting with the
historical revelation. Theology is at the same time a theory or
hypothesis of the meaning of history, rooted in the person of
Jesus and the God he trusted.

The thesis of 'revelation as history' is reaffirmed in *Systematic
Theology*, with some attention to his critics' concern about the
displacement of the 'word of God' model of revelation. Pannenberg maintains that the final truth, now lying hidden in historical
events, will appear at the eschaton, together with the idea of
provisionality before that day. He emphasizes the varied nature of
the experiences of Israel in relation to God, and claims that his
view of 'indirect self-revelation' has the 'systematic function of
integrating the various experiences of revelation to which the
biblical writings bear witness'.[48] Again Pannenberg stresses that
the *decisive concept of revelation* is crucial, the self-revelation of the
very being of God. This truth becomes clear in retrospect as
the processes of interpretation engage with the historical events
set in context.

We are placed in a sort of historical dialectic: on the one hand,
the future will manifest the truth of God, 'on the other hand, there
are preliminary revelations of this final event that is still hidden in
the future',[49] in prophetic and apocalyptic insights. Jesus' proclamation of the kingdom of God is similar to these preliminary
disclosures of end-time events, but the coming of God's kingdom
actually occurs here, the power that shapes the future.

> The future of God is not merely disclosed in advance with the
> coming of Jesus; it is already an event, although without ceasing to
> be future ... In this special sense we can speak of an anticipatory

revelation, in Christ's person and work, of the deity of God that in the future of his kingdom will be manifest to every eye.[50]

Pannenberg also retains his original view that it is not necessary to have special, subjective, 'supplemental' inspiration to understand revelation: the content of that revelation is sufficiently convincing and self-interpreting; the apostolic message is Spirit-filled by virtue of its content, and so can impart the Spirit. The most proper understanding of the 'Word of God' is Jesus Christ, the quintessence of the divine plan for creation and history, and their final destiny, yet proleptically present. The Christian revelation and its intellectual outworking will constitute itself the consummate religion, of all religions.[51]

The trinitarian 'future perfect' of God

The structure of Pannenberg's theologizing reflects the contents of the theological truth he uncovers, an anticipation of final truth, provisionally held and yet certainly rooted in God. As we move forward, so our understanding develops and takes up insights we already have, refining them in the new light of fresh experience and insight. The final insight to which we move will prove definitive for all experience, will make clear all meaning and disclose all truth, making sense of the partial and fragmentary knowledge we gained on the way. For this reason his theology can hardly be dubbed 'foundationalist', as if working on a fixed and static base. It is more historicist and provisional, hence the term 'postfoundational' coined by F. LeRon Shults, not unhelpfully.[52] Pannenberg does presume a grand plan of history and truth, but disclaims access to it directly, suggesting instead that we are finding our way forwards in time gradually, and that we need to attend to the full range of human experience and expertise in the process. In this he is not 'postmodern', but seems to have a defence against the charges levelled by postmodernists against modernism. This is because, he says, we need revelation and yet do not have it 'at hand', we feel after it and need to revise our opinions regularly in the light of each new event and discovery.

New questions may not be avoided, indeed they are welcome as potential stimuli of new light. But God has a plan for history, and we know this in and through the life and fate of Jesus. There is a Logos, but this does not amount to some oppressive rational schema, or iron template, placed on history – rather a personal and tentative feeling after truth, indeed a humble self-deference at the heart of things.

Pannenberg's understanding of reality and thought can be described usefully as that of the *future perfect*: in other words, history always will have been what it turns out to be in the end. From the end point, looking back, it was always going to be the case, and a certain momentum was always at work to that end and from that end. In some ways this is confirmatory of what was always already going to be so. In another way, until that final or perfect moment, things could have been different, logically speaking, and the end was not wholly predictable. Hence we have an elliptically shaped structure, moving forwards to the end, then back again in confirmatory movement. In addition to this, we might add that the structure can also be seen as a *concept* being put forward and then confirmed by the course of *events*: Pannenberg's concept of revelation is posited and vindicates itself, but again that concept emerges from the course of history: the to-and-fro movement at work again, this time with the added level of thought and reality, the rational and the real in creative interplay, meaning enriching itself in the process. Pannenberg's difficult and controversial notion of retroactivity, of the definition of being coming from the future and being finalized at the end, amounts to an *ontology of the future perfect tense*, an ontology of ultimate meaning deciding being.

The unity of Jesus with his Father
Theology is itself about this process of self-explication of the divine meaning, and this shapes itself as the unfolding of the doctrine of the Trinity, implicit in the self-revelation of God in Christ, whose meaning is disclosed by way of human historical and hermeneutical analysis. Pannenberg considers the doctrine of the Trinity as arising from the interpretation of the ministry and history of the historical man Jesus. He certainly was in a deep

THE TRINITARIAN THEOLOGY OF W. PANNENBERG   151

relation to the God he called his 'Father'. Because of the 'revelational unity of essence' with God, it is no longer possible after Easter for those who accept the Easter message to think of God the Father without Jesus. But since God is eternal, his relatedness to Jesus as 'Son' must be eternal too: again we note this ontology, and epistemology, of the future perfect tense, ranging forwards to the perfected end, then backwards through the prior process with the perfected truth of the end. Therefore, two different aspects in the historical reality of Jesus come to be distinguished: the human aspect that took its beginning in time and the divine aspect (his sonship) that belongs to perfected eternity.

This is not only a question of cognition, but also of reality, a reality, however, that is claimed on the basis of the historical Jesus and is not independent of that particular history. Therefore Pannenberg speaks of a retroactive importance of the history of Jesus, especially of his resurrection, concerning the question of his identity as Son of God. If Jesus had not been raised, he argues, he would not be the Son of God, nor would we know of any Son of God. This is not only the question of knowing, or simply retrospection, since if such knowledge occurs, it also involves being; being is not independent of time. This even applies to the very being of the God whose kingdom Jesus proclaimed to be coming: if the kingdom were not to come about, then this God whom Jesus announced would not be real. But it has, so he is – and there is no real question about this real state of affairs: the future has been perfected, proleptically. Again, therefore, knowing and being are argued to be inseparable, interwoven in the question of the actual course of history. After the kingdom *will have come*, future having been perfected, we shall know that Jesus' God existed from eternity. But yet that eternal existence depends on the future of the kingdom. Had no world come into being, God conceivably could have enjoyed his existence without a world. But since there is a world, the existence of God cannot be affirmed without his kingdom, or sovereign divine rule, being established in this world; God being by definition the all-determining reality. This is the reason why the very existence of God will continue to be debated until the end, when his kingdom will have been decisively established.

Pannenberg's bold argument from the historicity of the resurrection, we recall, was that this event constituted Jesus as the Son, one in being with God, his Father, since this event is the end-time revelation of the totality of all meaning, a revelation identical to that of the being of God. The concept 'revelation' bears an enormous load in Pannenberg's proposal, being the bond between the final *apocalypsis* (unveiling) of the end-time point of perspective on all historical meaning, and the very being of God. Pannenberg adheres rigidly to the uniqueness of divine revelation as God's self-disclosure. Following the thought of Hegel, he argues that

> ... it is no longer permissible to think of a medium of revelation
> that is distinct from God himself. Or rather: the creaturely medium
> of revelation, the man Jesus Christ, is caught up to God in his
> distinctiveness and received into unity with God himself.[53]

The medium and the message bond together, and the resurrection of Jesus, adjudged probably to have occurred, constitutes Jesus at one with divine being.

While space prevents developing the idea, it might be that this difficult suggestion could be made less problematic by pointing out that divine knowing of all meaning is a holy knowing and indeed a judging, that it therefore presumes divine being, character and quality to make this act of discrimination and to reach the true meaning of the totality of things, the essence of life in effect. Also Pannenberg might here strengthen his hand by integrating the theological insight that to 'know' truly involves participation, involvement, sacrifice: those aspects of deity associated with theologies of 'the creative suffering of God'?[54] With these two seed-thoughts in mind, we might help ourselves to appreciate Pannenberg's move from the eschatological summation of the meaning of all things, to the very being of God – and the integration of Jesus into the divine being through the resurrection crisis, come in advance.

What is revealed is that God is the God of Jesus Christ who is the Son; and also that the structure of all reality is itself proleptic, at the heart of all being and knowing. The identity of Jesus is disclosed as that of the Son, because his unity with the Father is revealed as being 'taken up'[55] into the divine being. Pannenberg points to Jesus' 'filial dependence' on God as his Father, his extraordinary sense of oneness. In the light of the resurrection, this has special significance and confirms the identity of Jesus as the divine Son, again the future perfect shape of being and knowing interweaving. The human Jesus is constituted divine by the cosmic act of the resurrection, and this reads backwards ontologically because the meaning of who he is ultimately constitutes his identity. This identity 'must have been so' all along. The life and ministry of Jesus belongs to the being of God the Father.

Pannenberg originally postulated his Christology as an alternative to the classical Logos approach, which taught that the pre-existent Logos entered history from outside and assumed manhood, in a person called Jesus. This failed, he argued, to take seriously the humanity of Jesus, and failed to do justice to the God of the open future of history. Pannenberg instead focused on the resurrection as constitutive. He stressed that the Christological matrix is the Father-Jesus relation, not the Word-Jesus relation, although the latter may be a valid way of expressing what is true on other grounds. The historical relationship of the man Jesus and his God, the God of the open future, whose coming kingdom Jesus proclaimed, is the central relationship for trinitarian doctrine, which is of the essence of Pannenberg's whole ontology. He sought to reground the Trinity in eschatology, to reintegrate it into organic connection with finite reality. Thus the revelation of God in the event of Jesus means that 'the relationship of Jesus' openness to God is included in the essence of God'.[56] In the fate of Jesus, the God of Israel is revealed as the triune God. The event of revelation should not be separated from the being of God himself. The being of God does not belong just to the Father, but also to the Son. The Holy Spirit also shares in the being of God by virtue of his participation in the glory of God that comes to life in the eschatological congregation. Hegel and Barth are correct in the principle of grounding the doctrine of the Trinity in revelation and the doctrine of the Trinity formulates the concept of God as a historically experienced revelation. Moreover, Pannenberg argues that 'If God has revealed himself in Jesus, then Jesus' community with God, his Sonship, belongs to eternity.'[57] Pannenberg has retrieved the Logos theology in his later theology, since it is a way of expressing the place of the Son in relation to the Father, but still his stress is on the relation of the Son to the Father and that relationship lived out in history. There is a distinct softening of his radical emphasis on the futurity of God in his later work, as the implications of the future perfect structure, the final definition playing backwards to origins, gain strength.

So far we have seen how Pannenberg argues for the divine identity of Jesus as the Son in revelational unity of being with the Father. God is the Father of this Son and not otherwise. Here we have a doctrine of the Trinity which seems to connect the life of human history with the very being of God. The economic Trinity, the work of the triune God outside of himself, is inseparable from the immanent Trinity, God in himself. There has to be a distinction between immanent Trinity and economic Trinity, according to Pannenberg, because if God's revelation in Jesus Christ involves the trinitarian structure, then there must be a trinitarian structure in the eternal reality of God himself – prior to the existence of creation. On the other hand, the economic Trinity is not merely an image (in the Platonic sense) of the eternal trinitarian structure in the being of God. The immanent Trinity is dependent on the process of history, hence on the economic Trinity. This is so not only for our knowing, but also for God's very being as soon as he creates the world. Pannenberg considers the eternal reality of God itself to be dependent on the outcome of history – although such dependence occurs only on the condition that there is a world. It is possible and even necessary to think that God could very well do without a world. But that is mere speculation, since there is a world. Therefore, if God exists, he must show himself to be master of that world, since at present this is not beyond dispute; the truth of the proposition concerning the existence of God depends on the eschatological future of his kingdom or rule. Once again the future perfect tense, made into actual history and meaning, provides a key to trying to understand Pannenberg's assertion of a free God, whose being and lordship are dependent of the outcome of history. This makes it quite clear that any reappropriation of the Logos doctrine is very different from that deriving from the neo-platonic patristic era: Pannenberg is committed to divine relations of a real kind with the world. God is open to world history and its final destiny, and has bound his being to this destiny, while freely shaping it.

The reciprocal self-differentiation of Father, Son and Spirit[58]

Pannenberg has been consistent in taking, retroactively, the life and ministry of Jesus prior to the resurrection into his divinely revealed and constituted identity as the Son. He works this out in terms of the Sonship of Jesus and the Father-Son relation established by the resurrection. This relation contains a distinction rooting back to Jesus' historical life and ministry, his attitude of humble refusal to claim equality with God, or as Pannenberg puts it, his self-differentiation, or self-distinction, from God.

> If Jesus' history and his person now belong to the essence, to the divinity of God, then the distinction that Jesus maintained between himself and the Father also belongs to the divinity of God. The relation of Jesus as Son to the Father may be summarized with primitive Christianity as 'obedience'. It is therefore a relation proper to the essence of God himself ... Thereby the expressions 'Father' and 'Son' are to be strictly applied to the relation to God of the historical man Jesus of Nazareth ... God's essence as it is revealed in the Christ event thus contains within itself the twofoldness, the tension, and the relation of Father and Son, and the role of the Spirit gains increasing stress in the resurrection. The deity of Jesus Christ cannot, therefore, have the sense of undifferentiated identity with the divine nature, as if in Jesus, God the Father himself had appeared in human form and had suffered on the cross.[59]

This trinitarian insight is developed increasingly by Pannenberg. The self-distinction of Jesus from the Father is part of his union with the divine being. God is revealed as being the Father of the Son, with this particular relationship. Jesus trusted his Father, for example, as he sought to fulfil his vocation and went towards unjust death. He trusted the God of the open future, and by his resurrection he was vindicated against the unjust judgment of the world. This openness to God as Father, in all humbleness and obedient love, is key to Pannenberg's view of the Trinity.

The essence of God has the dialectic of the freedom of the God of the open future, the Father, and the Son, the man Jesus. God's revelational activity, his self-disclosure, embodies the temporal appearance as essence of the Father-Son relation, which is divine. 'God himself has come out of his otherness into our world, into human form, and in such a way that the Father-Son relation that – as we know in retrospect – always belonged to God's essence now acquired corporeal form.'[60] God is the God who releases from himself finitude into temporality, and yet is always distinguishing himself from these events in his freedom and ungraspability. Jesus, in the structure of his life, was wholly open to the future and was thus in harmony with it. Jesus' life, therefore, shows the proleptic structure, and this is of the essence of deity. Indeed, Christianity is the crown of all the religions because Jesus was the epitome of openness, which reveals God as the ever-new and free God of the future: the God who can be trusted even beyond death, the God who decides the truth of all being eschatologically. The history played out between Jesus and his Father, in the Spirit, therefore becomes the trinitarian history, and by the principle of the future perfect, always was going to be so, and so eternally always was so.

Pannenberg's trinitarian doctrine, it is again worth noting, is in fact a claim or suggestion, made to the secular as well as to the faithful, about reality. God really is this relational being, bringing all things into existence, and the clue to this lies in the resurrection of the man Jesus and his identity revealed as ultimate and divine. The pattern of humble self-distinction on the part of Jesus takes us to the heart of reality, to the very being of God. Pannenberg means the actual concrete history of Jesus, and his temporally lived life of prayer and witness, and ultimately death, when he speaks of this self-distinction. This is no platonic image reflected in history; the actual historical revelation is what is meant as being true for God, affecting God, and coming from God. The Logos is this structure of relationship.

Pannenberg puts much weight on the lordship of the Father, and of Jesus' pointing to that and laying down his life for it. Jesus refuses divine lordship in all humility; his lordship is to proclaim the rule and kingdom of the Father. The Father, however, hands over lordship to the Son, to receive it back: the Father therefore makes his lordship dependent on the Son's glorification of the Father. There is a reciprocal self-distinction at work here on the part of the Father: he not only 'begets' the Son eternally, but hands over all things to him, 'so that his kingdom and his own deity are dependent upon the Son'.[61] We recall that Pannenberg teaches that if a world does exist, then God must be its sovereign to meet the conditions of deity. This lordship, it is revealed, is Christlike and not mere worldly power-play.

Pannenberg, in his early theology, defined the Spirit as the aspect of God which knits together past and future and takes events beyond themselves into new experiences. In *Systematic Theology* the Spirit gains a central place by way of the Trinity. It may be said that primarily the Spirit figures as the one who raises up Jesus from the dead, through the act of the Father; all three persons are at work in the eschatological event of the resurrection. Pannenberg was well known for his widening of the understanding of the role of the Spirit, from a narrow role in enlightening the minds of believers into that of cosmic creator. In *Systematic Theology* the Spirit is central, relating differently to Father and Son – as perhaps the synthesizing agency relates differently to the past and to the future. Self-distinction does not mean exactly the same for each of the three persons.[62]

It is plain that we are dealing with a very trinitarian and relational theology and ontology, being led to God the Father who is not this God without the Son and Spirit. Mutual self-distinction defines this trinitarian deity, and Pannenberg opts for the Eastern rejection of three modes of one divine subject

> but as living realizations of separate centres of action. Whether we must also view these centres of action as centres of consciousness depends on whether and in what sense we can apply the idea of consciousness, which derives from human experience, to the divine life.[63]

Pannenberg does not wish to abolish the monarchy of the Father in a trinitarianism that abandons the distinctiveness of the persons. The monarchy of the Father is served by the Son and

Spirit, yet the former is not what it is without the latter. This is true for the economic life of God and for his inner essential being. The mutual self-distinction explains this for Pannenberg:

> The Son is not subordinate to the Father in the sense of ontological inferiority, but he subjects himself to the Father. In this regard he is himself in eternity the locus of the monarchy of the Father ... The monarchy of the Father is not the presupposition but the result of the common operation of the three persons. It is thus the seal of their unity.[64]

Here we have an important unfolding of Pannenberg's logic, in that his focus moves from the originative past of the Father as the begetter of the Son and Spirit, towards the *result* of their common life and operation; the final outcome becomes decisive. Given that God is not the victim of the temporal flow, unless perhaps some Process thinkers opt for that, it is surely a fresh idea to ponder the Trinity with this future orientation, instead of the 'past' having the controlling emphasis. Pannenberg, of course, is connecting this trinitarian self-definition of God to the actual end of history: the economic Trinity shapes the very being of the essential, or immanent, Trinity. The final end will be decisive, and in fact this end is already disclosed – the raising of Jesus, who abandoned himself utterly to the lordship of God in loving trust, was accomplished by the Spirit at the behest of the Father. This is the true power at the heart of the universe, a power that will break injustice and sin and will vindicate righteous trust and restore the suffering. Pannenberg boldly proposes that the monarchy of the Father is established through the mediation of the Son and the Spirit, and that the Father's identity is finally established in relation to them, and never in isolation: monarchy is not a monad!

It is worth noting here that Pannenberg does not accept the feminist criticism of the language of the Fatherhood of God.[65] Starting as he does from the Jesus of history, his life and work, he stresses the fact of Jesus' prayer to God as Father being a Jewish tradition. It is therefore related to the patriarchal constitution of the Israelite family, with the father as the head of the clan and responsible for their care.

The aspect of fatherly care in particular is taken over in what the OT has to say about God's fatherly concern for Israel. The sexual definition of the father's role plays no part. A mark of Israel's faith from the very outset is that the God who elected the patriarchs ... has no female partner. To bring sexual differentiation into the understanding of God would mean polytheism: it was thus ruled out for the God of Israel.[66]

Pannenberg argues that because God's fatherly care can be expressed in motherly terms, it 'shows clearly enough how little there is any sense of sexual distinction in the understanding of God as Father'.[67] He does not agree that because Israelite culture was time-bound and patriarchal, that the term Father is also relativized: such a demand would be valid only if our language for God were a mere human projection, reflecting prevailing social mores. He argues that the Hebrew understanding of God was prior to and a presupposition for their singling out of terms from their culture as appropriate, and not just a product of that culture. Hence the term 'Father' is still valid today, despite the breakdown of forms of family and society and much disreputable human fatherhood. Jesus' use of the term is decisive, and indeed 'this self-distinction from God finds its clearest expression in the prayer of Jesus to the Father'. The whole life of Jesus, the way he fulfilled his vocation in loving obedience, cohered with his teaching and praying, and it was suffused with the presence of the Spirit. The full humanity of Jesus is always stressed by Pannenberg: Jesus is not a pre-existent heavenly being who assumed a different and alien creaturehood. Jesus' deity arises precisely because of his human historical and eschatological meaning. This is carried back into divine eternity, but without turning the human Jesus into something else. But unless human creaturehood is to be deemed eternally in relation to God, another distinction has to be made, according to Pannenberg, this time between Jesus' relationship to God's eternal deity as the correlate of the Father, and his human creaturely reality. This is the root of what Christian theology means by the two natures, divine and human. Again we note the analytical technique and theme, running through Pannenberg's theology, of *union and distinction*: this time the figure of Jesus, constituted divine by the resurrection, needs to be distinguished into two natures – the divine aspect having been abstracted, taken up into the eternal. But likewise the conceptual and the historical are united, yet distinct, as are the Father and the Son, and those with the Spirit. The divine history is also revelation as history, the economic Trinity – united to the immanent Trinity, yet distinct and self-differentiating into history. The future gains perfection, and then is disclosed as having been immanent in the past, all along. Once we have grasped this subtle dialectical conceptuality, Pannenberg's theology opens up more easily.

The trinitarian God of history

Pannenberg teaches that the real life of God is in play in the history of Jesus, since that actually is the decisive, unique revelation of the divine trinitarian relationship of Son to Father in the Spirit. We are taken into the very being of God through the economy of the trinitarian God. With Barth and Rahner, Pannenberg goes with the theological logic that the economic Trinity cannot be split from the essential Trinity, and that the history of Jesus with the Father does not merely reflect a higher divine life, but is that divine life of union and humble self-differentiation.

However, he logically widens and deepens this theology, since the whole of history is under the lordship of God and its total meaning is determinative for the being of God – while God freely brings this history into being from the future, another instance at the deepest level of the pattern of the future perfect. He says,

> the linking of the immanent Trinity to the economic Trinity cannot be restricted to the history of Jesus up to his resurrection from the dead. The executing of the world dominion of God by the exalted Lord and his end-time handing back of the kingdom to the Father are now to be seen from the standpoint of the historical controversy concerning the deity of God, of the heavenly Father whom Jesus proclaimed.[68]

He applauds the work of Moltmann here, who showed that the Spirit's role of glorifying the Son and the Father in history is also real within the very trinitarian life of God, and argued that the consummation of salvation history integrates into the consummation of the trinitarian life of God in itself. When all things are in God and God is all in all, then the economic Trinity is subsumed in the immanent Trinity. Jenson is cited as agreeing that the immanent Trinity is the eschatologically definitive form of the economic Trinity.

Here we are clearly in danger of dissolving the divine trinitarian life into the totality of history, of absorbing the immanent Trinity into the economic Trinity. Pannenberg insists that the two are distinct, but yet the same. The immanent Trinity, he asserts, is to be found in the Trinity of salvation history: 'God is the same in his eternal essence as he reveals himself to be historically.'[69] History is real and decisive for God, and the end-time will both reveal and accomplish this self-definition, the economic trinitarian life. But yet this life is always going to be what it is already, perfected and yet to come into perfection. The order of knowing and the order of being are juxtaposed to enable Pannenberg to have his economic trinitarian cake, and to eat it essentially! Union and distinction, knowing and being, are two of the dialectical movements to watch as Pannenberg seeks to elaborate his historicist interpretation of the trinitarian life of God. Pannenberg denies that he is rendering the Trinity into a product of history. 'Refuted herewith is the idea of a divine becoming in history, as though the trinitarian God were the result of history and achieved reality only with the eschatological consummation.'[70] Quite so, that does seem a possible interpretation of his metaphysics. But he continues by way of rebuttal and defence of God as not being the product of the process,

> In our historical experience it might seem as if the deity of God whom Jesus proclaimed is definitively demonstrated only with the eschatological consummation. It might also seem as if materially the deity of God is inconceivable without the consummation of his kingdom, and that it is thus dependent upon the eschatological coming of the kingdom.

That possibility is not the case, however, the reason being: 'But the eschatological consummation is only the locus of the decision that the trinitarian God is always the true God from eternity to eternity.' This seems to confirm the usefulness of our interpretative tool of the future perfect: the perfection of God is not really at stake, salvation history was always going to confirm the identity of God as this trinitarian, holy God; and yet on the way forwards, from the past into the future, this was provisional – but only provisionally provisional, until the final confirmation is given, the decision located at the end. The eschatological consummation gives the confirmatory decision, the constitutive decision, the ontological decision, that the trinitarian God is – and so always must have been – the Lord of all reality.

Once more we wrestle with Pannenberg's combination of history and logic, with time and eternity, with knowing and being. 'The world as the history of God', is his phrase, confirming the earlier 'revelation as history'. In his mature theology Pannenberg has undoubtedly moved to re-emphasize the eternity of God, the 'perfect' end of the future perfect, to protect himself from the charge of dissolving the divine life into the world-process. We can perhaps say that God is genuinely in this process, while not its victim, and while transcending it: just as a person is necessarily a body, and would not be human without this body, and yet transcends the body and is not reducible to it. The body is necessary, but not sufficient, to the person. In the case of Pannenberg's God, the world came into being by his free choice, but once it exists, then God's very nature demands that it be subject to divine lordship. Its eschaton will reveal that this was true all along, and that God was always God, despite the contested nature of this fact in all the ambiguities resulting from the freedom of historical creatures. This kind of model may help clarify how Pannenberg can both reject the idea of divine becoming in history, while insisting that 'today we see that differentiating the eternal Trinity from all temporal change makes trinitarian theology one-sided and detaches it from its biblical basis'.[71] His theology seeks to hold the transcendence of the divine being together with his immanence in the world, but also the eternal self-identity of God together with the debatability of his truth in the process of history. He seeks to achieve this through a radically trinitarian theology, which will at the same time be an ontological structure which runs through all reality as the best possible interpretation of how things really are.

Relational self-mediation of the divine persons

Self-mediation

The Sonship of Jesus was revealed and established by Jesus' resurrection and union of being with the Father, and within that by his self-distinction from the Father, in the Spirit. This trinitarian relation in distinction is the very being of God, a relational being.[72] God revealed himself as the Father, never without the Son or the Spirit.[73] There is no deeper understanding of the deity than this climactic self-definition of God.

For Pannenberg the reality of the Trinity, of the one God, is constituted by the threefold dynamic movement of moments in God. He rejects a prior *una substantia* which is shared by three entities, albeit 'modes', 'persons', or 'relations'. Nor does he sympathize with more modern interpretations which presuppose the Trinity as a self-unfolding of a divine subject. Instead, the self-differentiation of God is constitutive for the trinitarian persons and for their own divinity. This fact, he teaches, 'which is to be taken from their historical revelation must also determine the portrayal of the inner-trinitarian connections'.[74] The 'external' revelation of God will reflect his inner being; indeed Pannenberg advocates, technically speaking, a widening of the doctrine of attribution. In its classic form this theory was concerned with the activity of the trinitarian God externally, but the fact that 'in revelatory occurrence for each of the persons their own divinity is conveyed through the other persons means that we have to talk of an inner-trinitarian attribution as well, an attribution of the one deity to one or several of the persons through the respective third person ...'[75] It is noteworthy here that this procedure of 'attribution' or 'appropriation' is not, as in the classical methodology which Pannenberg rejects, a matter of abstraction from historical revelation, by the human mind.[76] Rather, it is the inner meaning of the revelational events, with their significance having been realized by reasonable interpretation. The event of this historical revelation has this meaning.

The unity of God is, then, one of self-mediation, not a matter of a prior essence, which is shared 'subsequently' in terms of logic. Revelation is, we recall, indirect self-revelation, whereby the indirectness comes not because of the medium, but because of an indirectness in content, which after consideration yields its inherent meaning, as the 'stimulus to the reflection derives from the event itself'.[77] The mediation of divine essence *ad extra*, or into the created order, would seem to be congruent with the dynamic of God's eternal being – which is affected by history. In the person of the Son,

> the one God comes forth from his Godhead. He stands over against the Godhead in the form of the Father. He does not, of course, lose his relation to the Father in the unity of the divine essence, for in coming forth he is obedient to his sending by the Father and remains united with him precisely by his self-distinction from him. In the Son, therefore, the inner dynamic of the divine life finds expression in its concreteness as Spirit and love.[78]

The economic trinitarian action really is the essence of God, outwardly.

God's being is a living dynamic, in which the persons do not exist for themselves but in ec-static relation to the over-arching field of deity. Their relationship to the divine essence that overarches each is mediated by the relations to the other two persons. This self-mediated deity, as has been pointed out, means that

> as the Father, with respect to Jesus, is the one God present to him through his Spirit; so for the Spirit the one God is revealed in the community of the Father and the Son; and so for the Father the reality of his own Godhead, that is the reality of kingdom, depends on the operation of the Son and the Spirit.[79]

This self-mediation, in terms of the 'persons' of the Trinity, has been interpreted most helpfully by Hegel, according to

Pannenberg. 'Hegel was the first to so elaborate the concept of "person" in such a way that God's unity becomes understandable precisely from the reciprocity of the divine Persons.'[80] The essence of the person is 'to relinquish its isolation',[81] cites Pannenberg in agreement, and continues the quotation: 'Morality, love, is just this: to relinquish its particularity, its particular personality, to extend it to universality – friendship is the same ... the truth of personality is just this: to win it through immersion, through being immersed in the other.'[82] This Hegelian doctrine is reflected in Pannenberg's teaching of the 'dialectical Sonship' of Jesus, whose particularity and deity were found to be coordinating aspects. The particular man Jesus has the universal significance of deity, and his characteristic was utter self-abnegation, the losing of himself in the Father: thus he is Son. In the losing of himself, the Son finds himself as the Son of the Father, the utterly free God. The resurrection would be the temporal thematization, also according to Pannenberg the retro-active ontological establishment, of this dedicated second person as raised to consciousness of God as Father, in the dynamic of God's being. This Son, being aware of his Father, is therefore, hence, indirectly or mediately, aware that this state of affairs is God's work, hence is aware of the Spirit. The very fact that the Son worships and serves the Father in the Spirit indicates the self-distinction of the Spirit from Father and Son. This is the character of Pannenberg's mutually self-giving unity of God. This 'process of self-dedication' gives us the insight as to the real, living, intense unity of deity. It may seem paradoxical, but self-differentiation constitutes the divine unity.

Personal integration in God

Pannenberg has been glad to rehabilitate Hegel's triune self-differentiating, self-integrating deity. But he criticizes Hegel for failing, as he sees it, to overcome the subjectivism of the modern idea of 'person'. This criticism of Hegel, following Pannenberg's adoption of his relational idea, is significant in that it drives Pannenberg's criticism of the Kantian heritage to its farthest point. Pannenberg's momentum towards the 'post-Kantian synthesis' reaches its climax, arguably, with his doctrine of the

personal character of God, and thence, derivatively, with his
doctrine of man.

Pannenberg discusses in several places the philosophical and
theological debate between Fichte and Hegel over the nature of
God as 'Person'.[83] The issue between Fichte and Hegel was
whether the infinite God could be a Person.

> In the dispute over atheism of 1798 Johann Gottlieb Fichte
> maintained that God cannot be thought of as a person without
> contradiction, because the idea of person includes the notion of the
> finite. As 'person', a being is always thought of in comparison with
> something else – a world of objects or persons. The idea of the 'I'
> essentially and inalienably includes a 'Thou' and an 'It'.
> Consequently no 'I' seems capable of being everything; it always is,
> as person, limited by other things, and hence finite.[84]

We have seen that Hegel's view of the person sought to overcome
this difficulty.

> According to Hegel, the person does not in every respect have its
> counterpart outside itself, as limitation of its own being; it is rather
> the nature of the person to be related to its counterpart even to
> give itself up to that counterpart and thus to find itself in the other.
> Moreover, a person finds himself again in the other in the degree to
> which he has surrendered and given himself up to that other. Thus
> in the personal life the contrast to the other, the limitation, is
> abolished or overcome.[85]

Indeed, for Hegel, the truly personal would be infinite: finite
personhood is partial, since we only partially overcome the
contrast to the other. Pannenberg seems to accept this counter-
argument of Hegel in some passages, thus:

> Hegel overcame Fichte's argument through a deeper understanding
> of person ... and ... the decisive step is already taken in the
> *Phenomenology*, the step which overcomes the criticism of Fichte on
> the personality of God understanding the subject as not limited by
> the other ...[86]

Pannenberg, however, argues in his article 'Person und Subjekt', that Fichte's criticism of the notion of God as personal is only apparently overcome by Hegel's reconception of the notion of subject.[87] Fichte himself retracted from his early position of asserting a self-positing ego, and Hegel's concept of the self-positing subject, which is with itself in its 'other', fails finally to escape Fichte's later critique, according to Pannenberg. Either 'the other' is not clearly distinct from the self-positing subject, or else there is genuine, original distinction, which vitiates the true identity, and the subject then is no longer absolute. If the subject, by finding itself in its 'other', becomes through this 'other' an other, then the subject is no longer for Pannenberg the all-embracing absolute, but rather 'the process of the history of its change, through which his self is granted to him'.

Pannenberg dislikes Hegel's identity of subject as self-insulated and absolute. He wishes, as it were, to open up Hegel, to out-Hegel Hegel, in a sense, to increase the emphasis on openness and relationality by moving away from the central insulated subject as self-positing. Pannenberg's amendment of Hegel runs along the line of history, the process which comes from the future. The becoming of the subject, the 'history transcending its subjectivity' points us in the right direction to the true heritage of Hegel.

He sets out his key triadic understanding of the ego, the self and the person as follows:

> Instead of being a postulation of the ego, the self represents itself in a process of change in a story or history, in the course of which it is not clear what the self will become. But the ego, far from bringing forth the self, for its part needs the self to gain stability and continuity. For this it needs a manifestation, present to the ego of its not yet completed self, and that, as we shall see, is the person. Thus we reach a thought of the person which is different to that of the subject and as shall be seen allows a better solution to the problems of Trinity and Christology which are connected with the concept of person.[88]

Such a move will overcome the contemporary absolutizing of subjectivity, that Kantianism against which Pannenberg's whole agenda operates. Pannenberg wishes to elucidate a doctrine of person which retains the modern experience of creative subject-ivity, includes it, but does not absolutize it. Pannenberg desires to do away with the notion of the core ego as the ultimate substratum of reality.

> It is tempting to regard the inner world of the consciousness as the true 'I', in distinction from the body, but this is unduly restrictive: from the angle of the listener, the physical aspect is always included. The post Kantian emphasis on subjective perception makes the experiencing ego, or I, absolute, but this detaches it from its social and historical context: the ego is developed in the process of objective experience ... in individual experience the social nexus precedes the use of the term 'I'.[89]

Pannenberg is defining 'person' as an anticipatory reality, an overarching category, the *locus* of which is the end of one's life, whence our definition: who we are as who we will be.

This overarching category, a descriptive, phenomenological one, embraces the 'I', the experiential ego, and the 'self'. Pannen-berg rejects the 'ego' as the integrative factor: it is the 'self' which, as the stable pre-figuration of the overall 'person', integrates our ego experiences. As we proceed in the protean experiences of life, 'in our self-consciousness we identify ourselves with our self, which gathers together the totality of our self-experience and which is therefore constant, this self, and through this in each moment we let our ego be integrated through our self'.[90] Pannen-berg radically destroys Kantian subjective idealism. 'It is not the "I" which postulates itself ... but the self integrates the "I", and only through this gives it identity.'[91] This means that Pannenberg is advocating a triadic definition of person. The 'I' or 'ego' is the subjectivity which experiences the protean events of life. The 'self' is an objective reality which integrates these experiences of the 'ego' and which is the proleptic being of the 'person', and his identity given to the 'ego'. The 'person' is the overarching reality, which subsumes the 'ego' and 'self' in their dialectical relation through the temporal process. The 'person' really exists at the end of a life, because, as is the case for all Pannenberg's ontology, the end is determinative, retroactively, for what went before. The 'self' is the 'person' proleptically prior to the finally decisive end-point of the fulfilled 'person'. Pannenberg intends to break clear of the definition of person as the conscious centre, the core ego, which he sees as dominating philosophy and theology since the Enlightenment, and which represents the hidden anthropocentric metaphysic of modern thought. It seems hard to over-emphasize the 'Copernican revolution' he attempts here.

He is with Hegel in seeking to leap over human subjectivity, and his thought is far more Hegelian than Kantian in cast. But he sees himself as revising Hegel in opening up the central category of subject or concept of Hegel, by the use of the anticipatory category derived from apocalyptic thought and from its empirical fit with the realities of history. The 'person' includes the 'ego' and 'self' and is ultimately constituted by their temporal course as a whole.

> The person can neither be identical with the I in its difference to self nor even with the self in distinction to the I. The person cannot be identical with the mere fact of the I consciousness; in the word person we mean more than the punctiliarly appearing I. The word person is related to the whole life of an individual. We are already an I. We still become a person although we are already one. Person refers to the mystery which goes beyond the presence of the I, the mystery of the as yet incomplete totality of his unique life history, the totality on the way to its particular definition. Person, then, is neither the I nor the self each taken for itself. A person is the presence of the self in the moment of the I, in the claim of the I through our true self and in our proleptic consciousness of our identity. Person is the I as 'countenance' through which the mystery of the as yet unfinished history of an individual is on the way to his destiny.[92]

A person is therefore a primarily future entity existing proleptically as the objective 'self' which provides the identity for the subjective 'ego' or 'I'.

Here it might be suggested that Pannenberg's idea of personhood might be paralleled, paradoxically perhaps, with a black feminist writer, bell hooks (sic).[93] She develops a theory of writing in order best to portray personhood by way of bringing together narrative in the first person, then revisiting the same events but in third-person narrative. The meaning of her life gains richness, her self-understanding is more than merely the immediate experience of the present moment: she writes both forwards, then backwards in reflection, reading back a richer, fuller being into who she already was, and is becoming.[94] The irony in this parallel is of course that Pannenberg attracts criticism from the 'post-modern' school as being an Enlightenment thinker, rationalistic and lacking in the sensitivities to the human condition, now being disclosed by feminist authors!

Pannenberg's triadic view of 'person' is applied to his doctrine of man, to his Christology and to his trinitarian doctrine. In regard to the Trinity, Pannenberg sees the Son as having his deity in relationship with the Father, the God of the open future. Father and Son are not each divine in themselves, 'but only through the community of the Spirit which unites them. The unity of the divine being is not absorbed in personal relationships but is mediated for each of the persons through their relations to the other persons.'[95] The Son is the proleptic objectivity of the Father oriented towards the Father whom he experiences in the Spirit. For the Father, the Son is the realization of his divinity. Pannenberg disclaims any attempt to distinguish in God the ego and the self-being because such distinctions belong to finitude. Nevertheless, the triadic model of person remains meaningful in understanding the Trinity.

To sum up, Pannenberg seeks to avoid the Scylla of substance and the Charybdis of subjectivity, and aims instead to define divine being as his history of dialectical threefoldness. 'The persons' of the Trinity, 'are referred to the other persons. They achieve their selfhood ec-statically outside themselves. Only thus to they exist as personal selves.'[96] Interestingly and consistently, Pannenberg asserts that the Christian doctrine of the Trinity was a breakthrough not only for the history of theology but for the whole human understanding of personhood: that it is constituted in relation to other persons, that each 'I' lives by its relation to the 'Thou' in social context.

He stresses that the trinitarian life is more personally relational

than the human, which is not so exclusively constituted by the
relation to one or two other persons as it is in the trinitarian life of
God. The mutual relations of the trinitarian persons are such that
the existence as persons is wholly for and from the others. The
identity of the Son is wholly given in relation to the Father, and
vice versa. This is divine love and divine dynamic being. It is actual
love, not an abstract idea of love. Divine love constitutes the
concrete unity of the divine life in the distinction of its personal
manifestations and relations:

> we may know them only in the historical revelation of God in Jesus
> Christ. But on this basis they and their unity in the divine essence
> make sense as the concrete reality of divine love which pulses
> through all things and which consummates the monarchy of the
> Father through the Son in the Holy Spirit.[97]

The centre of reality, the all-determining reality, for Pannenberg, is
no cosmic mind but rather the life of divine self-giving and
responsive love.

It is scarcely an exaggeration to say that all the rest of
Pannenberg's doctrine flows from the Trinity. This gives us the
unity of God, which is not to be presupposed as a prior reality or
idea so much as concretely constituted in and through this life-act
of self-mediation and identity-in-the-other. This is the essence and
existence of God. The biblical view of the unity of God focuses
on the divine self-identity, 'I will be who I will be', as he translates
God's words to Moses (Exodus 3:14). This is not a timeless
concept, but the faithful God whose actions and purposes express
his character of holiness, wisdom and patience. Divine unity finds
its deepest identity in divine love, the unity of the true infinite,
which transcends that which stands over against it in love.

Here is the key to eternity and time, since they coincide at the
eschatological consummation of history, the point at which 'there
is room for becoming in God himself, namely, in the relation of
the immanent and the economic Trinity, and in this frame it is
possible to say of God that he himself became something that he
previously was not when he became man in his Son'.[98] Here is the
most profound suggestion in Pannenberg's theology, that God

becomes, and yet that in this process he becomes himself, more deeply what he always was, and was always going to be, in the divine, future perfect.

Here we see the creative love of God in all its faithfulness (a term preferred to 'immutability', which is too static to do justice to the movements of divine life and richness). If God wills the independence of his created order, the success of his creative love depends on the faithfulness of his creative love, on the outpouring of his eternity in time. God's creative love 'makes space' for his creatures, and his patience waits for their response, in which their destiny and so their true being is fulfilled, and given.

The issue of divine transcendence and immanence likewise finds its most hopeful resolution in the trinitarian way of love, uniting God's transcendence as Father and his immanence in and with his creatures through the Son and Spirit. This upholds the permanent distinction between the divine and the creaturely. The omnipotence or power of God likewise is no oppressive force, but works most deeply through the Son and Spirit, with creation free to be itself to fulfil its destiny. The 'all-determining reality', Pannenberg's description of God, actually has the connotation of the all-shaping or orientating reality, giving the world its destiny and seeking to bring that to fulfilment.

Creation's fulfilment is understood incarnationally, that is to say both freely attained and divinely shaped. The incarnation of the Son, read back from the resurrection of Jesus, overcomes the dualism between eternity and time, as the divine presence of the Father's kingdom is present to creation through the Son:

> The present not only contains all the past within it, as the idea of Christ's descent into Hades shows, but it also invades our present in such a way that this becomes the past and needs to be made present and glorified by the work of the Spirit.[99]

The pattern of the resurrection of Jesus, confirming the past and made present by the Spirit, a pattern we have characterized as that of the future perfect, explains the divine relation to created time. Pannenberg believes that this overcoming of dualities, such as time and eternity, finite and infinite, results from the love of God.

This trinitarian love embraces the tension of the infinite and finite without setting aside their distinction. This is not a matter of synthesizing opposites through the logic of an idea or concept, as with Hegel. The dynamic of love alone can leap over the frontiers of logic: the Holy Spirit of the divine Trinity is not Hegel's Absolute Spirit, or *Geist*, pure mind or thought. Pannenberg here makes a determined effort to demarcate his theological system from that of Hegel, quite rightly pointing out that the Trinity of love is superior to that of thought, and is at the heart of being and knowing. The Trinity is a concrete, rather than ideal, life and action. The common life of love of God constitutes itself by way of self-distinction, of mutual acknowledgment and indwelling. The self-differentiation among the persons is not a centripetal flight, but a harmony of union in distinction. Hegel's concept of the ultimate union of opposites is taken up, not into thought but into love and mutuality, the real takes in the rational, but that ultimate reality is love.

Here is the heart of Pannenberg's theology. All other doctrines flow from this and are explained by the Trinity, since that is the source and destiny of all truth and being. He says at the end of the first volume of his *Systematic Theology* that his explication of the doctrines of creation and eschatology must be by way of the trinitarian persons, who will in turn be lit up by their connection to the world and history. Theology as a whole may be expected to offer us an understanding of what it means that God is love. This great emphasis now dominates his thought rather differently from his earlier writings, in which divine *freedom* took centre stage as the dominating divine characteristic. From this understanding of the Trinity, Pannenberg's doctrines of creation unfold.

Human becomings

Pannenberg's interpretation of Jesus, his meaning and identity, results in the conclusion that his particular identity was that of the divine. But we are all human becomings, according to Pannenberg, in a sense moving forward to the defining moment that will establish who we really are and what our lives actually mean. That can be established only at the end, from the future, and by God. This is our life from God's point of view.

Our identity lies, therefore, not only within us in the present moment, but ahead of ourselves and in God. In this Pannenberg deliberately rejects the Marxist and pure materialist view of humanity, according to which all is determined by iron laws dictated by the past. Pannenberg believes that the future is open, that we need not feel imprisoned by the constraints of the past. It is important here to stress that Pannenberg believes this is a powerful argument for the existence of God, and trust in God; in practice he thinks that Christians should be far more intellectual in speaking about their faith than they are. The God-hypothesis is the best available to make sense of things.

Pannenberg teaches that the truest identity of the Christian disciple is a baptismal identity,[100] an identity founded outside oneself and in the God of Jesus, who himself trusted in God the Father for everything. This combines a freedom with a bonding to God, who leads us forward in life towards our destiny, towards the fullness of our being. We are human becomings, we are to become what we are, and ultimately this will be disclosed by God at our death and resurrection. The baptismal identity means that our destiny is bound up with that of Jesus, crucified and risen as the very Son of God the Father. We therefore share in this 'orientation' (*Bestimmung*) towards God, for ever.

Again the black feminist writings of bell hooks cited above may help us to get our imaginations inside what Pannenberg is formulating with his future orientation, and his casting backwards from the future perfect in order to explore personal identity and meaning, even being. She used writing in order to heal her wounded self and gain a space to be her self, to find that self.

> A distinction must be made between that writing which enables us to hold on to life even as we are clinging to old hurts and wounds, and that writing which offers to us a space where we are able to confront reality in such a way that we live more fully.[101]

Such writing is not an anchor or escape, but it truly rescues and enables recovery, she says.

I needed to confront that shadow-self, to learn ways to accept and care for that aspect of me as part of a process of healing and recovery. I longed to create a groundwork of being that could affirm my struggle to be a whole self and my effort to write … I spent more than ten years writing journals, unearthing and restoring memories of that shadow-self, connecting the past with present being. This writing enabled me to look myself over in a new way, without the shame I had experienced earlier … Resurrecting the shadow self, I could finally embrace it, and in so doing come back to myself.[102]

The focus here is on a healing process, and this may in fact be one which Pannenberg might usefully take up in his eschatological view of human becoming, given our common human brokenness. The pattern of writing being described is one which assumes a union and distinction of the ego and the self: the writer is seeking to bring them into harmony, to overcome pain and deep hurt, as she revisits the past and reunites that with the present, in order to face her future as a more integrated person. We might 'stretch' this human and humane description so as to gain an idea of the divine healing and remaking of our persons, from the future back through our past, to give us our true and redeemed identity.

This complex area of human existence, the fact of being already and not yet, is an area not only for further theological exploration, but also shows the pastoral and ecclesiological significance of much of Pannenberg's enterprise. He takes us into the thought of such complex metaphysicians as Hegel and Heidegger; but he explores honestly the scope of human experience of being in the world and especially as we walk forward in time, ultimately to meet with God, the God from whom all reality comes.

Heidegger's influence on Pannenberg may not have been appreciated fully. The understanding of human beings facing up to the ultimate future, facing death as their final completedness, and living in the light of that, is partly reflected in Pannenberg's view of us moving into the future with total trust. But Pannenberg is more rational than Heidegger, in that for him, if evidence arises to counter the hypothesis of the Christian hope, he would have to adjust his position. For Heidegger, human life (*Dasein*) gains its meaning in the light of the completion of death. Pannenberg as a Christian regards death as not the final end. Death itself cannot give us our ultimate meaning and being, but God can.[103]

Our true self is what it is now only provisionally; anticipating the fullness of who we will be, to be revealed at the end of our life-journey. Our consciousness, which bridges time, does not disintegrate because of its anticipation of the future. The moment-ary experiences of the ego are held together in the anticipatory whole, the self, as we journey into the future and to the summative completeness of our life.

Pannenberg's doctrine of retroaction is decisive here. If the end is the whole, events in the past cannot be regarded as frozen and static; they are open in meaning to a continually expanding horizon of interpretation as history proceeds. In contrast to a positivistic view of history, trying to investigate the bare event, Pannenberg asserts that event and meaning are inseparable, so that events can never be completed until meaning reaches its fullness at the final completion of things. The real and the rational cohere organically and separate only for the purposes of analysis. Jesus and the resurrection is the great example of this confirmation or retroaction. What was revealed of Jesus at the resurrection must also be true 'backwards' of Jesus in his life and ministry, particularly of his filial dependence on God as his Father. This is the future perfect tense applying to Christology: the risen Jesus is the crucified Jesus, so the one who is revealed as the Son of God in his resurrection from death must always have been the true Son of God, ontologically.

This reveals the being of God. In rising from death Jesus reveals God's purposes fully, revealing and forging the destiny of all his brothers and sisters to be in fellowship with God – so he must always have been one in being with God. The resurrection of Jesus anticipates the end of all things, and so the nature of the whole of history: that means fellowship in and with God, which transcends the present and makes its incompleteness clear. The resurrection also discloses the very shape of prolepsis, the anticipatory nature of our being in history, of our faith in the God who comes from the future to vindicate that trust. We are open-textured, open to

the world, open to God in the world and from the future
wholeness, which the world is becoming.

Moltmann, with his logic of promise, and Pannenberg, with
that of anticipation, can be said to complement each other at this
point. Moltmann regards the category of anticipation as inadequate on its own, arguing that anticipation forecloses genuine
openness for the future, and the ongoing future of Jesus Christ.[104]
Paul Fiddes points out that for Moltmann the resurrection creates
anticipation of the kingdom.[105] Moltmann needs the context of
promise along with the anticipatory concept, and he prefers to
speak of the resurrection as a promise event, revealing the coming
God and opening up a path to fulfilment which Jesus is treading
towards his parousia. But the two can combine by way of linking
what Fiddes terms the 'overplus' of promise beyond the present,
and the anticipation of a future wholeness. Both can act as a
challenge to ideologies which try to impose a total scheme on
events for the sake of human power-games. The eschatology of
meaning gives at least partial validity to the postmodern project
of questioning all settled interpretations of history.

By insisting on the category of retroaction rather than retrospection, Pannenberg goes beyond saying that we know after the
event. He claims that the totality disclosed and brought about by
the final event is the reality which all along was what was to be the
case, and that from this completed whole, as well as towards it, we
have our true being. *Dasein*, in Heideggerian terms, is not only the
guardian of being but has its being from *Sein* ('being') itself. The
fieldforce of future possibilities embodied in the Spirit of God can
actually overcome the momentum of increasing entropy and open
up new structures of life.[106]

But Pannenberg works out this understanding together with an
apparently static view of eternal life. For when he comes to
consider what it means for a person to participate in God's
wholeness, he understands it as the re-experiencing of one's past
life from God's point of view. What was once experienced in the
successiveness of time is now viewed from a new perspective, set
in the context of the whole of history and comprehended in the
eternal present of God in which there is no distinction between
past, present and future. In an early work Pannenberg asserts

that in this sense 'eternity is the truth of time, which remains hidden in the flux of time'.[107] In his most recent work Pannenberg maintains this doctrine, speaking of the unifying of all individual moments of our life's history into the simultaneity of 'God's eternal present, to be seen from the standpoint of the divine ordaining'.[108]

John Hick dubs this view one of recapitulation; but this may be unfair, since reviewing one's life from God's perspective would open up possibilities and depths of experience that had been unknown before. It would not be a mere repetitive circularity. So Pannenberg writes of 'an element of compensation' within the transfiguration of life.[109] Pannenberg argues that Hick has misread him,[110] because the simultaneity is not just a matter of the divine memory, as in Tillich and Process thought, and that it can apply to all who lived according to the Jesus way. But Pannenberg does not answer the central point about the lack of any really new experience. This question relates to the issue of final meaning decisively constituting being; Hick and Fiddes here ask whether it is doctrinally satisfactory that the end of time closes this wholeness into its final form, thus foreclosing on new experiences in the life of God after death. Meaning has reached 'closure', to use the postmodern concept, rather than opening up new possibilities for the redeemed human being in God. The future is not future any more to us, once we have arrived at our future perfect end. The self has found its fulfilment in personhood finally. Identity is reached. But why should this be frozen, rather than expanded, deepened, actualized in the Sonship of God?

Pannenberg can certainly point to his constantly emphasized concept of the meaning of a person gaining in depth after individual death: the resurrection of Jesus shows that the meaning of the man Jesus did not close at his execution, rather its potential remained open to divine vindication. His understanding of the ego, the self and the person as a dynamic becoming into and from the future of God, *could* be developed after death because God's being does not freeze in a stasis, and therefore our life meaning is related to the relational life of the Trinity of love. Pannenberg has options open to develop, ironically some possibly along the lines of the healing process for the individual that are found in the redemptive act of writing, as portrayed in bell hooks' discovery of first-person and third-person remaking of personal identity, from future to past and back.

Pannenberg with Jüngel,[111] as Fiddes points out, have been brought to a vision of eternal destiny which fails to balance 'closure' with 'openness' because he conceives the whole as a simultaneity of time in which there can be no real development, adventure or progress. He also assumes that the whole as possessed and known by God is a sort of fixed maximum. God has perfect freedom in having no future outside himself, and no future that is different from his present. But, with Fiddes, we can understand the wholeness of time as a healing in which there is not a total loss of successiveness, and the wholeness of life as a perfection which is ever expanding. Such a wholeness can still be the source of successive time as we know it in history; it can still transcend it and be 'retroactive' upon it.

Then we can envisage the Holy Spirit as not only holding created beings open to the future, but having the same role to play within the divine perichoresis. This movement of love distinguishes itself from the Father and the Son through always opening up the Father-Son relationship in new ways to new depths and to a new future. God, we might say, continually becomes what he is. Part of this future will be the inclusion of created beings within the divine life. The Spirit holds God open for a future which will be retroactive in God's self, making God what God already is.

Fiddes reminds us that Barth used the term 'the healing of time';[112] he has used the language of simultaneity while insisting that this is not a total absence of time. Pannenberg uses ideas of simultaneity in Augustine and Boethius: Augustine's eternal present assumes the Platonic tradition of opposing time to eternity, thus only hinting at simultaneity; Boethius follows Plotinus in conceiving eternity as the simultaneous presence of the *totality* of time.[113] Boethian simultaneity is not strictly time-lessness but the embrace or concurring of the whole past, present and future in an undivided present. It is this totality of time in eternity that is the ontological basis for the separation out of the tenses of time in the course of history.

Barth criticizes attempts to develop a notion of eternity in opposition to time, since this is lost time and so problematic; the timelessness of classical metaphysics is a kind of idolatry, a mere projection of human fallibility, where we should be attending to what we can learn from the 'time of revelation', given by God.

We can agree that eternity is the wholeness of time in the sense of overcoming the division and separation between past, present and future; the metaphor of healing of time retains the *distinction* between time's phases in a way that simultaneity cannot. We might think of God's eternity as a relation to time in which there is indeed succession, a before and after, but in which God's being is not fragmented by time's passing as ours is; instead God would always be integrating past, present and future within perfect love. Love is important in considering time.

Timeless moments, 'epiphanies of eternity', Fiddes suggests, heal rather than dissolve time: reading a poem or listening to music can be done as if time had slipped by or away. But we need successiveness in listening to musical phrases and combinations, to rhythm and repetition and rhyme, for the experience to occur at all. We have not escaped from time but experienced a new relation to it.

Relativity theory tells us that time is characterized by its relations – to space, to velocity, to the observer – rather than being something absolute. Our hope of sharing God's eternity would then be the hope of participating to some extent in God's own unbroken relation to the multiple time-paths of creation. Barth's idea of 'pure duration' seeks to express the affirmation that the kind of distinctions we know between past, present and future are overcome in eternity.

The special theory of relativity makes clear that as far as participants in time are concerned, there can be no common 'now' between two time-frames. A person cannot witness the 'nows' of someone else in another time-scale, since instant communication is not possible: the theory assumes that no material object can exceed the speed of light, so simultaneity itself must be relative to the observer. This leads Pannenberg to propose that unlike finite beings, God is the supreme observer who 'does not need light to know things', so that God's eternity is 'simultaneous with all events in the strict sense'.[114] All events – past, present or future, of whatever time-frame – are present to God, and embraced in a divine eternal present. But Fiddes argues that relativity theory need not be pressed to support a simultaneous eternity. Instead, the relation of God to multiple time-systems may be envisaged as an unsurpassable participation, taking the journey of time seriously in each as God indwells each. God may relate to all time-scales, participating in them concurrently, moving at the same moment along their individual time-paths, where we are limited to our own. Barth says that God can enter time on the ground of being already a triune 'event' which makes for our history, within the divine communion of life. So God makes room for all histories in the universe, or universes. God can intermesh with them all because God has an eminent temporality. Eternity is then about the integration of time through participation, rather than either simultaneity or extension of time.

Pannenberg stresses retroaction not just retrospection because the parts are made by the whole, and anticipation is an ontological category. Things do not simply increase in meaning as history moves onwards, but they are what they are out of the wholeness of the future. There is a qualitative richness to the meaning of life as it runs to its end, and receives itself from that end – and so from the lord of the ultimate destiny of all things.

Pannenberg certainly can point to his constantly emphasized concept of the meaning of a person gaining in depth after individual death: the resurrection of Jesus shows that the meaning of the man Jesus did not close at his execution, rather its potential remained open to divine vindication. Pannenberg's understanding of the ego, the self and the person as a dynamic becoming into and from the future of God, *could* be developed after death, because God's being does not freeze in a stasis, and our life's meaning is related to the relational life of the Trinity of love who in history embraced our humanity in his Son. Ultimately we face not the end, but the Father, as we share sonship with Jesus.

Ultimately, therefore, we participate in a life, not a closure of being. We share in the sonship of Jesus, and so we share in the worship of the Father in the Spirit, a doxological destiny of praise. Pannenberg in fact concludes his *Systematics* on this very note, speaking of earthly praise of God by his creatures as anticipating 'the praise of the heavenly community of the perfected'.[115] Pannenberg's consistent view of religious language has been that it is primarily doxological, glorifying God.[116] Pannenberg can surely argue that this heavenly praise does not indicate a fore-closure of experience, and in this way he might seek to turn the blade of Fiddes' criticism. Pannenberg looks forward to 'the revelation of his love in the consummating of creation for participation in God's own eternal life'.[117]

Pannenberg's long emphasized structure of history as finding its meaning in the future, given by God at the eschaton, required a genuine and full end, and even raised the logical question as to what might be after this end.[118] Fiddes is surely correct in his reflection that Pannenberg makes much of simultaneity as the eternal mode of relating to time,[119] and that the final end of history seems to give little scope for creaturely experience to be taken forward. 'Openness', a key feature of historical being, does seem to be closed. But the eschaton for individuals does not only mean completion of identity and personhood, given by God. It is also a transformative and purgative passage into a new mode of being, when sin falls away and joy in worship becomes all in all. The shared sonship means facing the Father in wonder, love and praise – implying clearly some sort of duration included in the life of the eternal God.

Time and eternity figure constantly in Pannenberg's theological discussions, and while he reckons with the problems of simul-taneity,[120] he believes that this phenomenon, so close to the idea of the eternal in his view, can embrace duration, and does not lead to a 'freezing of the frame'. He has used Augustine's famous treatment of hearing a melody to illustrate the wholeness and completeness of reality shaping and defining the course of history.[121] Duration is real but is also bridged; diversity is held together by unity, the unity of the future wholeness which we anticipate. As we hear the melody, we are in the midst of its flow, and yet the overall shape of it gives it a structure and wholeness, and yet that will in fact be given to us at the end: the future whole suffuses the present and past.

Our fragmented lives, our sense of dislocation, result from our sin, the desire to make 'me, now' the centre of things, rather than deferring gladly to the God of the open future as the focus of all things. Creaturely life depends on variety, on multiplicity, yet held in unity rather than chaos.

Pannenberg understands that this unity of temporal duration in fact arises because of the eternal participating in the flow of the multiplicity of time. Here he draws on the thought of Plotinus. He believes 'that the flow of temporal moments cannot be conceived at all without presupposing, with Plotinus, the eternal simultaneity of all that is separated within time'.[122] Divine eternity participates in time, while creating time: the sonship of God faces the Fatherhood of the free God of the future, with the Spirit bringing forward events into their self-transcendence and movement towards their promised destinies. Pannenberg stresses the immanence of the eternal in the flow of time: surely this participation can work the other way, and the temporal creature will find participation in the life of the eternal? God makes space for his creatures in the fulfilment of their destiny, a destiny gained by the Son. Christians, Pannenberg says, 'expect a future in which all their temporal life will be permeated by praise of God and will be glorified as incorruptible fellowship with this eternal God'.[123] Implied in this destiny of worship is an opening up of richness and wonder beyond what the totality of our lives has known. Here we see in a glass darkly. Pannenberg teaches that death for us is death, not the escape of a soul which survives, in neo-platonic fashion.[124] When we die, we entrust our selves, our persons, our very existence to God. We lay ourselves down in death with Jesus, in baptismal pattern. We are held by God in death: 'Herein the identity of creatures needs no continuity of their being on the time line, but is ensured by the fact that their existence is not lost in God's eternal present.'[125]

Therefore Pannenberg may need to consider developing a theology of the new way of being in and with God, or of being rather less agnostic about this. He says that the life of the future world is not the resumption and endless prolongation of this life, along the same temporal time-line; it will unfold its dynamic through growth in the vertical dimension of our present life.[126] Yet, as Fiddes argues, some form of duration and experience seems

necessary in the new life within the eternity of God.[127] Pannenberg
has not yet explained a way to integrate, or 'take up', ongoing
openness into his eschatology, but he does suggest an openness
which is enriched after the whole of earthly life gains its 'final'
meaning, so that the sons and daughters of God can indeed be lost
in wonder, love and praise, as he expects. He certainly intends no
static idea of the afterlife,[128] and stresses the common resurrection
of the dead rather than simply that of individuals – for the divine
intention is the kingdom of God over all humanity. Our ultimate
identity, constituted by the meaning of our lives, is given by the
God of the future, and in context of our relationships with others.

Jesus' divine identity

Our humanity is most truly revealed in the life and fate of Jesus,
where we see the future-facing obedience and openness to God
the Father disclosed and vindicated by the event of the resurrection. We have just seen how the destiny of humanity is with the
Son, in glorifying and worshipping the Father. The path Jesus trod
in his life, particularly his 'filial dependence' and humble self-
abnegation before his Father, both open the way to, and establish
the nature of, true humanity. And humanity, as we have seen
above, includes an implicit religious dimension. The trinitarian
destiny of Jesus as the Son includes his disciples; he is the
eschatological second Adam. The structure of his humanity is
transparent and true for us.

As to the birth of Jesus, no-one has full personal identity from
the moment of birth, says Pannenberg. Who we are or were is
seen and decided only in the course of life and in view of its end.
In the case of Jesus, the Easter event gave his particular identity,
that of the divine Son. Therefore, only in the light of this outcome
may we say, then, that the child Jesus who was born of Mary was
the Messiah and the son of God. The history of his earthly work
and life 'is not something accidental in relation to the identity of
his person'.[129] The human historical flesh-and-blood life of Jesus
is part and parcel of his identity as the divine Son, and of his
revelation of humanity. For Pannenberg, the doctrine of the virgin

birth of Jesus by Mary is a piece of legendary narrative, it is not philosophically impossible, but merely unnecessary and improbable. The sinless life of Jesus is vindicated by the Father at his resurrection and so is read back through all his life, and we can take the doctrine of the virgin birth as a symbol of this fact.

The new eschatological Adam is 'the definitive form of humanity', says Pannenberg, seeking to echo the Apostle Paul, who thereby 'has given expression to the universal significance of the person and history of Jesus in the light of the Easter event'.[130] The new Adam relates to all humankind, emerging from the particularity of the Jewish history and context. Jesus' expositions of the Torah broke open the truth expressed in Israel's witness of the link between fellowship with God and human fellowship. Our participation with Jesus is through baptism and faith.

The eschatological identity of Jesus maps the man Jesus into the divine Son, in relationship to the Father. The resurrection, as has been unavoidably stressed, given its prominent emphasis throughout his work, constitutes and confirms this mapping of the human into the divine: this is who God the Son is – defined in relation to the Father and shared with the human race in utter reality. Jesus in his experience of life focused on the Father, in union with him and yet in self-abnegating distinction from him. This was in fact the identity of Jesus, although he could not have been consciously aware of the fact early in life. 'The history of Jesus led him deeper and deeper into this identity of his person as the Son of the Father.'[131] The identity of this man was that of the divine Son, and this became clearer and clearer to Jesus as he went on, trusting his life totally into the hands of his Father.

Pannenberg's historical and hermeneutical argument justifying the claim that the identity of Jesus is that of the Son of the Father rests on his appraisal of the evidence for the resurrection. Historically he uses the tools and methods of critical scholarship on the texts, and reaches a conservative conclusion. He points to contradictions in the New Testament texts about the resurrection as evidence that the material has not been manipulated and ironed out by its writers. He does not regard the empty-tomb tradition as primary nor alone convincing, although he is more dismissive in his earlier *Jesus – God and Man* than in his definitive *Systematic Theology*.

In this latter work he points to difficulties for critics, including the debates found in the New Testament between Christians and their opponents, regarding what happened to the body. His opinion is that we must assume that the tomb was empty, until critics provide further counter-evidence.[132] His main plank of argument is the appearance traditions, which, he maintains, are not explicable in terms of psychological hallucination. Whereas the appearance tradition is primary, and the tomb tradition more ambiguous, the two interweave both for historical argument and theological interpretation.

> Though primitive Christian conviction as to the resurrection of Jesus rests not on the finding of his empty tomb but on the appearances, the tomb tradition is significant for the total witness to the Easter event. It creates difficulty for the theory that the appearances of the risen Lord might have been mere hallucinations. It also resists any superficial spiritualising of the Easter message, though leaving room for the thought of a changing of the earthly corporeality of Jesus into the eschatological reality of a new life. We thus cannot explain the finding of the empty tomb as a product of the Easter faith and must recognise that it happened independently of the appearances. Accordingly, even if this tradition developed in the light of Easter faith, we must still assign to the report the function of confirming the identity of the reality of Jesus encountered in the appearances with his resurrection from the dead.[133]

The Christian doctrine of the resurrection of Jesus entails the continuous narrative of Jesus through crucifixion, burial and being raised by his Father and the Spirit. The tomb tradition plays an important part theologically in this thesis. Pannenberg firmly rules out the risen Christ's existence as simply a resuscitation and extension of earthly life. The Christian claim is of a new mode of existence for the continuing identity of Jesus – now taken into divine being.

> The Easter message certainly states that the resurrection of Jesus was an event of transition from this earthly world to a new and

imperishable life with God, yet the event took place in this world, namely, in the tomb of Jesus in Jerusalem before the visit of the women on the Sunday morning after his death.[134]

This very biblical suggestion that the identity of the crucified Jesus endures, while being radically transfigured into a way of being capable of relating to human disciples, explains very clearly why Pannenberg calls the resurrection 'a metaphor',[135] in both his early and definitive works. The resurrection is a new and unheard of event, one which our concepts and categories can only reach after, stretching human language to its limits. Yet in spite of the metaphoric language, a real event was in view.

Philosophically he defends the possibility of the unique event not predicted beforehand nor experienced subsequently.[136] He rejects that historicism, which imposes a grid of causality on all events, ruling out something totally new. The future is open and unpredictable, with a constancy and yet the capacity for the novel. His conclusion is that the resurrection of Jesus did occur in all probability – that always being a necessary caveat for any historical judgment.

The meaning of this probable event, as has been sketched out earlier, is shaped very strongly by the contemporary Jewish apocalyptic expectation. In his *Systematic Theology*, however, Pannenberg is rather more subtle in treating this shaping than in his earlier monograph, *Jesus – God and Man*. In his definitive work he nuances the several strands of Jewish apocalyptic and their interaction with that of the risen Jesus in the early church's appearance tradition. The Hebrew eschatology of resurrection hope encompassed several expectations, corporate and individual, a presupposition of judgment and the justification of the right-eous, and also the self-vindication of God in the face of apparently prospering evil in history. Jewish apocalyptic therefore gains a richer interpretation in *Systematic Theology*, and 'the relation to the Jewish idea of eschatological resurrection life, however, was profoundly altered by the linking of this idea to the reality of Jesus encountered in the Easter appearances'.[137] The crucible of this mutually defining reality of Jesus' resurrection in apocalyptic context brings together the individual and the corporate, the particular and the universal resurrection, beyond just the Jewish people, for judgment and future hope.

Divine reconciliation

The immense focus on the resurrection has led to some commentators asking whether the death of Jesus has sufficient theological importance in Pannenberg's theology.[138] There can be no doubt that the death of Jesus has a real effect on God. For Pannenberg, the history of the world and of Jesus is real for the trinitarian God. We recall that 'The Trinitarian idea of God is congruous with historical process ... The Trinitarian doctrine describes the coming God of love whose future has already arrived and who integrates the past and present world, accepting it to share in his own life forever ...'[139] So deeply shared is this generous love that God's being is affected by the incarnation, in what Pannenberg calls the self-actualization of the trinitarian God in the world. The death of Jesus the Son is best understood in Pannenberg's theology from the angle of the Trinity in terms of its deepest meaning; the self-actualization claim does not mean that the divine life is self-ish, very much the reverse – the trinitarian persons find themselves in relation to the other persons, looking outward for the other. Hence,

> the action of the trinitarian persons is not oriented directly to themselves but to the other persons. In the economy of salvation the same is true of the sending of the Son by the Father, of the Son's obedience to the Father, and of the glorifying of the Father and the Son by the Spirit. Hence the self-actualization of the one God is one of reciprocity in the relations of the persons and the result of their mutual self-giving love to one another.[140]

The self-giving of God's very being is enacted in time. His lordship is implemented in the world in this way. The death of the Son is God's way of actualizing his rule in the world without oppression and with respect for the independence of creatures, on the part of God.

The unjust execution of Jesus is not external to God's very being, but is the deepest act of the self-distinction of Jesus from God, an orientation of his life now consummated in this obedient acceptance of death – in total trust of the Father. At the cross, God's own history of self-mediation and self-definition is affected. Pannenberg can say:

> On the cross the Son of God certainly died and not just the humanity that he assumed. Nevertheless, the Son suffered death in his human reality and not in respect of his deity. In the death of Jesus the deity reached the extreme point of the self-distinction from the Father by which the Son is also related to the Father, so that even his humanity could not be held in death.[141]

The death of Jesus for Pannenberg unquestionably has the most profound impact on the divine life of self-distinction, and expresses this self-distinction. He speaks of the sufferings of human existence as a *natural result* of the self-distinction of the eternal Son from the Father as the one God, a movement that reached its deepest depths in the incarnation of the Son and the suffering obedience of Jesus. The divine life expresses itself in the history and fate of Jesus, reaching a point of utmost self-distinction – if not self-alienation – at the cross. At that point the divine bears the pain of the negative. The divine life of the Trinity comprises union and self-distinction and reveals infinity as such, an infinity inclusive of temporal history.

Here the hand of Hegelian metaphysics is quite evident, and Pannenberg has been very clear about his debt to Hegel. The question arising from this view of the cross as the self-actualization of God, taken together with the constant emphasis on the self-differentiation of the Son from the Father, is whether Pannenberg is simply rehearsing a version of Hegel's self-distinguishing Spirit or Geist, as it lives through finite history. God distinguishes himself from himself in the process of time, and so reveals himself to himself. But Pannenberg's trinitarianism, with its dynamic of the threefold personal self-definition as ultimate, and the Son's self-humbling, works against a final metaphysics predominating over the personal God of love. We might also argue that this self-humbling way of the Son, worked out in history, can be used against those who criticize Pannenberg for 'closure', when openness is needed for understanding divine life and creaturely life. This continual self-humbling, distinction in union, is not transcended or taken up into Absolute Spirit: God's trinitarian personhood is not therefore 'finalized' or totalized.[142]

Pannenberg's definition of the Son as the self-differentiating identity of God uses the vocabulary of Hegel, but he must argue that the content of, for example 'union-in-distinction' and of a finite particular identity being 'taken up' as infinite,[143] has been revised in a more Hebrew and Christian relational direction. This issue was brilliantly expressed by P. T. Forsyth in his theology of the eternal *kenōsis*, or self-emptying of God the Son, which is the divine great personal moral act, not a matter of a necessary metaphysical substance unfolding in order to reintegrate. This great moral act of sacrificial *kenōsis* is really divine greatness or increase (*plērōsis*), as Forsyth points out: 'It is only by such a moral *act*, and not in the course of some ideal *process* ... could he incarnate himself in human life.'[144] Critics who regard Pannenberg's doctrine of the death of Christ as thin in theological content seem to miss this vital point of its trinitarian significance.

Reconciliation by Jesus is a matter of his whole life, death and resurrection, for Pannenberg. The cross cannot be isolated from the whole pathway of redemption taken by Jesus and ultimately by God the Son. Reconciliation is achieved by the man Jesus in obedience to the Father, so through human historical agony and sweat, Jesus, the agent of the rule of God in human sin and misery, enacts the eschatological judgment of God on the living and the dead, as our representative. The resurrection means that God has vindicated Jesus in judgment, whereas the world condemned him.

Pannenberg is happy to speak of the death of Christ as expiatory of our sins. Whereas we might think that the awful sin of killing Jesus would only increase the divine displeasure, Pannenberg teaches that

> Expiation for the people of God in the death of Jesus means, then, that in spite of participation in the crucifixion and other sins, access

to eschatological salvation is still open on the condition of
acceptance of the eschatological message of Jesus and confession of
Jesus.[145]

Jesus has widened the scope of the purely Jewish hope of salvation
by God to all who accept Jesus. Jesus bore death as the consequence of our sin, 'thereby effecting representation in the
concrete form of a change of place between the innocent and
the guilty'.[146] Pannenberg does not flinch from affirming a kind of
substitutionary dynamic at work, and further vicarious penal
suffering: 'This vicarious penal suffering, which is rightly described
as the vicarious suffering of the wrath of God at sin, rests on
the fellowship that Jesus Christ accepted with all of us sinners and
with our fate as such.'[147] Pannenberg here correctly stresses the
representative character of Jesus' work, in Pauline fashion. The
link of common humanity before God the Father is utterly crucial
to any strong doctrine of vicarious atonement. The inclusive aspect
of Jesus' participation with humankind is given by the incarnation,
the exclusive aspect comes to expression in this expiatory death of
the innocent one for sinners, setting him apart as unique in his
saving work.

The past event becomes the present event now through
apostolic proclamation of this gospel, itself a level of the saving
reality of Jesus. This relates to the human historical level of the
work and fate of Jesus, and then to the same history as the medium
of the eternal Son of God, who is at work in it as he became man in
Jesus. The apostolic proclamation can also be understood as the
active presence of the exalted Lord, but based solidly on the
history of Jesus, also the divine Son.[148] By way of this threefold
view of levels of the one saving history, Pannenberg again nuances
his earlier emphases somewhat, since he had made much of the
present absence of Jesus pending the eschaton; the presence of
Jesus the Son by way of the apostolic, Spirit-filled proclamation
improves his theology of the process of reconciliation.

Again it may be asked, perhaps especially by the pastoral
theologian, whether Pannenberg may have more resources than
he deploys, especially in regard to human redemption and healing.
Jesus reconciles, but this also includes the binding up of the

wounded, the knitting together of the hurt mind, the restoring
of the betrayed and abused. Pannenberg focuses strongly on
the meaning of Jesus in the objective sense, his meaning for the
universal being of history and of God. But subjectively his
eschatology of reconciliation could include and make more of
the making whole of the battered and bereaved by the humble
caring Son, in relation to the sovereign Father whose divine
intention is to heal and recreate, in the sustaining presence of the
Spirit, whose very nature is to hold together. This kind of
development seems consistent with Pannenberg's theology, and
to flow from it. 'Come to me, all who are weary and burdened, and
I will give you rest', says Jesus in Matthew 11:28. These words
provide another window on the trinitarian love of God, inviting
his people to his Sabbath completion of creation.

Relational creation

Pannenberg's future oriented ontology intends to emphasize that
the novel event is possible, that the world is not simply the
implementation of some immutable law working itself out. Freedom is a vital principle undergirded by Pannenberg, as is
contingency (the unpredictable aspect of things), as well as the
ordered reliability of the world process. God is not working from
'the past' by a remote decree of predestination, nor 'from above'
as if by way of copying a divine template from eternity into time,
in neo-platonic fashion. That is the problem with the 'classical'
understanding of the Trinity over against the world. It is too
detached and unable to offer sufficient integration into the world,
hence the great problems over producing a doctrine of incarnation, in effect forcing two contradictory substances together.
Liberal theology is no better in Pannenberg's eyes, because it fails
to speak of God's reality in history and time. God is unknown
behind the Kantian screen hiding the inaccessible 'noumenal'
from the 'phenomenal'.

The spatio-temporal world is characterized by life and dynam-
ism, and Pannenberg claims that his future orientation of the
world, open to God and suffused by the sustaining divine life, is a

good hypothesis to describe this world's reality. The exocentric character of all reality has been noted in Pannenberg's theology; a pattern of uniting and differentiating, of self-transcendence towards a new synthesis. Such a pattern of life cannot be explained reductively, trying to explain the more advanced phenomena simply in terms of the more basic realities. This of course is the problem with atheistic evolutionism: the phenomenon of mind or beauty or goodness is impossible to explain just by reference to the flux of the atoms in the primal soup. Advances from the primitive past demand explanation of some kind from beyond that past, and this comes to us in the freedom or contingency of the future, ultimately the God of the open future. God is personal, argues Pannenberg, in that he is not manipulable but free, and this quality, known only to persons, comes from God.

In his early works Pannenberg sketched out a distinctive and fresh doctrine of the Spirit, relating the Spirit to creation.[149] He rejected the narrowing of the role of the Spirit to that of enlightening the minds of believers to the saving message of Christ, which he found prevalent in both church and theology. He recovered the biblical doctrine of the Spirit's role in sustaining the created order, in restraining chaos, in knitting up what was torn apart. The Spirit in particular is associated with the self-transcendence in the world; going beyond what is presently at hand towards that which beckons. He also associates the Spirit with worship and doxology, again in strong continuity with both biblical and patristic sources. The ultimate beckoning of the Spirit is towards the Father by way of wonder, love and praise. The Spirit is fundamentally the origin of all life, and the intellectualized focus given, in the West particularly, to the work of the Spirit had the effect of banishing the Spirit's relevance to the material order. This focus has long been an Eastern Orthodox complaint about Western theology, and indeed is seen as responsible for the development of a God-free, and so value-free, approach to technology and science.[150]

Scientific developments must, for Pannenberg, be taken seriously by theology. Indeed theology has a responsibility to respond to scientific, as well as philosophical, accounts of reality. Ultimate dualism is not an option, especially given the Christian claim that God is the God of all reality, not simply a small section. And we have seen already that Pannenberg cannot contemplate a dualism of knowing, in which the Spirit enables a segment of humanity to know in depth, while the others are not given this secret gnosis. He regards such an approach as 'authoritarian' and irrational, and not honouring to the God of creation.

Science suffers if theology pulls out of engagement with it, leaving it to go its own way free of insight and value, as if the material world were polystyrene to be cut into whatever shape took the fancy of human technologists. As someone who grew up in the time of the Third Reich, this fear no doubt plays a part in Pannenberg's mental furniture. Science and God belong together. Whereas modern theology has managed to overcome the shock of Darwinism and seeks to adapt to a new shape of reality, science also needs to take seriously the insights of theology and philosophy. Human intuition has an important part to play in our thinking, as well as mathematical constructs with their amazing precision but impersonal character. The depersonalized 'God' of Spinoza resulted from this kind of precise iron law being applied to events in the world, including interpersonal 'events'. But humanity knows that we are more than items related by 'laws' of nature.

Theology must point to God as the way of looking at reality in order to balance the mathematical dominion of our horizons. The idea of God is comprehensive in scope: God is by definition all-encompassing, involved with all that is. What is not divine is finite, and so we have a doctrine of creation to reflect on this relationship between the transcendent and the finite particular world. It is interesting to note that Hegel logically moved upwards from the finite particulars, to laws of nature, to minds, and then to absolute Mind or *Geist* as the ground for reasoning minds, which could deduce scientific laws.[151]

Pannenberg avoids the intellectualistic route quite deliberately, an important difference in method from Hegel. However, we note the shape of Pannenberg's subtle dialectic with finitude over against the transcendent which alone can make sense of the particulars of the world. Pannenberg similarly connects his doctrine of creation to theodicy: a doctrine of creation will help to corroborate the reasonableness of the belief in God. It will also help to sustain faith in the goodness of the world, against suspicion, cynicism and the belief that reality is meaningless. Similarly it will give credence to the claim that the universe has a goal and a final end, that it is worth 'supporting' and believing in. Pannenberg has a very important point to make to the Western world here, as it lurches into hedonistic anomie and faces the need to address the Islamic world with a theological voice rather than simply with technological superiority. The question of God is indeed now in the public political forum, and needs to be connected with the world's future destiny and current values.

The creative sonship of God

Christian theology, in its doctrine of creation, has come to lay massive emphasis on its beginning and origin, at the expense of the ongoing sustaining of the world, and indeed of its final cosmic destiny beyond the human. The Eastern Orthodox are less guilty of this imbalance than the Western traditions. Pannenberg is keen to reinstate the theology of the continual creative activity of God, and not treat the two views as antithetical alternative versions of the doctrine. The continuing preservation of the world by God is an essential part of Christian doctrine, without it a kind of deism would develop, removing God from the process of the world.[152] Creation does not exist of itself, and Pannenberg teaches that the conception of creation out of nothing applies to continuous creation as much as to the originative act of creation.

Indeed, there are real problems with the great stress on the idea of divine creation as the establishment of all reality as finished and finalized in form. The ancient view of divine preservation focused on the conservation of the originally given order of things. The species of plants and animals were assumed to have been fixed at the outset of creation. Here the 'mythical' form of explaining the world dominated, in that everything was thought to have been established at the same time and for ever, as if by the copying of a divine template. But here the modern theory of evolution is clearly very different indeed from the ancient view.

Pannenberg turns a necessity into a virtue by pointing out that continuous creative activity by God seems to be required, over against a fixed and finished model of creation. He argues, however, that this is a biblical way of looking at things. As well as the divine originative event, the Bible speaks of divine upholding and supervising of the world in the prophetic writings, the Wisdom literature, even on the lips of Jesus in the Gospels. In the Bible we get a picture of both a divine initiation and the history of divine activity: certainly not the idea of the divine watchmaker letting the creation simply tick over by itself. God is deeply involved in the world process. Pannenberg points to the scientific understanding of new forms of existence in nature, akin to a continuous creativity at work for the theological interpretation of reality, and indeed to the prophetic understanding of God bringing about the new and unexpected event.

This connects to the contingency and freedom of creation, an emphasis long held by Pannenberg. Contingency means that the process is open to new and enduring forms of life and patterns of events. And, of course, for the Christian, God alone explains the possibility of all this richness and potential of the universe, as it reaches forwards into what is new, while being sustained by the order of the structures and patterns of reality. Pannenberg sees creation by God as embracing at least these activities; of initiation by an eternal act, and sustaining and drawing forward to its destiny. The eternal act is of the eternal God. This act of the eternal God conveys freedom and contingency, not a fixed programme which is to unfold by a law of necessity inherent in the process. It must not, on the other hand, be seen as resulting from a whim on the part of God, a capricious act of freedom. What is needed is both the eternal and the free aspects of God, invested into the created order, so as to constitute a covenant partner of God, autonomous and free, while most truly so in the orientation to the divine destiny.

Pannenberg finds the best hypothesis to account for this synthesis of divine being and free act in his core doctrine, that of the Trinity, truly the centre around which all other doctrines revolve. Pannenberg rejects the model of God as a monad with a will which implements ideas in the divine mind to enact the created order. This is overly anthropomorphic and individualistic. With all Eastern Orthodoxy in heaven and on earth applauding,

Pannenberg says that the Trinity provides the best way into the doctrine of creation, a better model than that of the individual mind. The trinitarian approach offers a better way and is coherent with the biblical idea that the Son was constantly cooperating with the Father in creating the world. The theme of the divine self-differentiation of the Son from the Father becomes central again. This dynamic life of God is in fact also the *raison d'etre* of the creative act, uniting the act of God with the being of God, divine relativity reaching out in love to bring into being another.

This fresh emphasis in the doctrine of creation is made plain in core doctrinal statements prior to *Systematic Theology*:

> Through the self-differentiation of the Father from the Son and Spirit, without which the one God does not have his full reality, God as Father gives at the same time a particular existence to the creatures, an existence which has not lost from the very beginning any chance of autonomy through its dependence on a continuously working omnipotence of the Father God and creator; but rather with the designation to partnership with God receives a personal worth vis-a-vis God himself.[153]

The Son's humble, eternal self-differentiation from the Father is worked out in history as the self-subordination to the kingdom of God in the ministry of Jesus; and here we see the creative origin of all that is distinct from God, the reason that there can be something which is not divine. The eternal act of self-differentiation is the possibility in God for the existence of a creation not of the divine being.

This is a very stimulating notion addressing a real theological problem: what in God can make non-divine being possible, apart from the naked will of God? The answer is not a platonic form in the divine, reflected outwards, but a living relationality in God. This is the originative principle of creation's space and time. In the freedom of the divine love and self-differentiation we see the freedom of God enacting creation to convey and bestow contingency into the universe. The Son is the generative principle responsible for the otherness of the creation, the autonomy of created beings. In generating ever-new creatures, a network of relationships emerges in the world, with the creative dynamic formed to interweave, unite and differentiate.

This is why creation can issue from the hand of God, and yet be free and independent – but in dependence on God, as human implicit religious sense testifies. The resolution of unity and diversity stems from divine Wisdom, the Logos.

> If the Logos is the generative principle of all finite reality that involves the difference of one thing from another – a principle grounded in the self-distinction of the eternal Son from the Father – then with the advent of ever new forms differing from what has gone before there comes a system of relations between finite phenomena and also between these phenomena and their origin in the infinity of God.[154]

This Logos, or creative word, is not simply transcendent and external to the creaturely forms being brought into being, he is also at work in them as he 'constitutes for each its own specific existence in its own identity'.[155] The transcendent immanently shapes reality, for transcendence itself is also relational, mutually indwelling at the core of life. All reality is open textured and porous, relational, and this fact stems from the Trinity at the centre of the universe, whose creative act brings particulars into being with an order and a life, and a propensity to complexity and future orientation.

Relating this to the scientific project, Pannenberg believes that the uniformity of the forms of the world is a natural law governing phenomena, but that this is indifferent to individuals. The Logos is not the abstract order of the world but its concrete order bringing forth concrete particular creatures. The creative principle of the cosmic order is not then a timeless structure like natural law or a mathematical system. It is the principle of the concrete, of particulars. In fact the unity of the Logos with the one particular man Jesus happens because the man is universal in his meaning, coinciding with the Logos, while being actual and concrete. Pannenberg stresses this point of concrete historicity to obviate any hint of idealism in his reappropriated and refashioned Logos doctrine.

The last pages of the first edition of his *Jesus – God and Man* gave an initial version of this doctrine matured in his final work:

> At the same time, Jesus in his dedication to the Father and to his mission to humanity is also in some sense exemplary for the structure of every individual event. Everything is what it is only in transition to something other than itself; nothing exists for itself. Every particularity possesses its truth in its limit, through which it is not only independent but is also taken up into a greater whole.[156]

Pannenberg's view here is that every datum of reality and truth is inwardly related to all other such 'events' in the continuum of the whole of world history; the boundaries of being and thought are really porous. Moreover, the whole is not merely the sum of these individual parts but, on the model of something organic rather than mechanical, the whole breathes life and meaning into the individual particulars, as the life in the parts of the body.

The passage continues: 'Through giving up its particularity, everything is mediated with the whole, and transcending its finitude, with God who nevertheless wanted this particularity to exist within the whole of his creation.' The individual particulars of historical being and thought go beyond themselves to be taken into the source of life. 'That which lives must go outside of itself in order to maintain itself; it finds its existence outside itself,' continues Pannenberg in this elaboration of his dynamically unitive synthesis. All individuality is qualified very radically in favour of the whole and this total finite fabric cannot be assigned any final independence over against the absolute which draws all things into its essence. It has always been Pannenberg's contention that human thought is, likewise, essentially related to objective being. The real is rational, and humanity participates in the objective Logos of the universe rather than standing over against it. Developing his doctrine of the relativity of being by applying it consistently to knowing as well as to being, to epistemology as well as to ontology, he continues: 'At the highest level the same is true of human subjectivity, namely it must empty itself to the world and the "Thou" in order to win itself in the other. Jesus' saying about losing and finding life … has universal ontological significance.'[157] Pannenberg's definitive statement of this view is careful to avoid the Hegelian tones of the above.

The Logos principle, the self-differentiating movement of Son from Father, replaces unbending law with relationality and individuality, and replaces mental ideal with concretely real and potentially loving. The created order stems from the divine being and the overspill of generosity acted towards an other, at a different level but inwardly related. This is part of the gift of being a creature, that God has permitted it space to be itself and to create itself, while being sustained and called to its origin.

The spiritual field of relationality

The Spirit's role in originating and sustaining creation applies also to the initiation of the world and to its ongoing preservation. Pannenberg links the Spirit to life, rather than mind. He cites the Spirit as breath in Genesis: a dynamic force, a creative wind blowing through creation and giving it life. The animals and plants are sustained by this life, likewise humans, who are also souls or creatures; alive and yet consciously dependent on God's Spirit as the transcendent source of life. Pannenberg makes the interesting point that the old Stoic view of Spirit, with its material connotation, is closer to the biblical notion than the intellectualized view taken by some important theologians such as Origen. Their legacy was a detachment of Spirit from the non-mental order of being. To help overcome this narrow mentalistic emphasis, Pannenberg looks to a new and adventurous model, that of fields of force, taken from physics.

The biblical idea of Spirit is closer to this sort of view of a dynamic force, which shapes the realities within its field of influence.[158] This is like the Hegelian idea of the particulars of the physical body being in the life of that body, and vice-versa: the life suffusing the body and bestowing life on it in a mutual model of dependence but superiority. The difference again is that the force-field idea seems to want more sovereignty accorded to the field over the items in its influence, items needed if the field is to have force over any particular thing. Pannenberg intends his language of force-field to function in a way that is more than merely metaphorical, since the Spirit really is the life or dynamic coursing through the universe in patterns.

It must be pointed out that eminent scientists who are also Christian theologians disagree strongly with Pannenberg on his use of this scientific concept. John Polkinghorne, for example, says that the field theory used by Pannenberg, the theory in which particles were to be considered as 'singularities of the cosmic field', is now considered out of date by physicists. Polkinghorne tells us that fields are carriers of energy and momentum, 'and this is the basis of my criticism of regarding field theories as if they were immaterial or even, in some sense, "spiritual"'.[159] Polkinghorne rejects Pannenberg's defence that matter is not a strictly physical concept but a philosophical one, because 'all the physical entities of the universe are excitations in fields,' and fields must participate in the material.[160]

Pannenberg thinks that the independence of the field concept of force from the notion of body makes its theological application possible, allowing all actions of God in nature and history to be described as field effects. But this independence has been powerfully rebutted by Polkinghorne. Pannenberg's model of the force-field, it seems, will lead him back to something more like Hegel's integrated life and body logic.[161]

In any event, Pannenberg teaches that just as spiritual experience has an ecstatic element, reaching outside itself, so it is with all life in general. All things reach out for nourishment beyond themselves. The Reformation idea of faith is just the same: we have our salvation outside ourselves, in God. This might be a common rhythm of life in all cases. Moreover, the ecstatic, self-transcending movement of all organisms is not something inherent in that entity, but it arises in response to some other entity approaching it and inspiring it with new life. The Spirit gives this life, the Word gives particular form; the Spirit works in all creatures, prompting their self-transcendence and bridging them forwards towards new emerging potential not previously possible.

Pannenberg believes that theology must acknowledge that something new happens in every single event, if the concept of evolution is to be compatible with a biblical theology of God and nature. Newness occurs in the emergence of new forms of life in the evolutionary process. He is advocating emergent evolution, made possible by the Spirit at work in all things, especially in the creative role of bringing forth qualitatively higher forms of being from lower. Evolution by way of mechanistic process is not compatible with Christian theology. When geared to the future, however, to the free God who invests his being into the process to convey newness and freedom, then evolution is a very helpful understanding of how creation proceeds.[162] Organisms depend on their contexts for life, but they also develop the capacity of self-organization in the swarm of complexity.

Human beings developed likewise, not as a matter of chance, and they reached the highest stage of independence and self-organization. Humans gained the capacity to discern between objects and to discern the objects themselves as self-centred entities. In this way they learned to discern themselves in the swarming world of complexity all around. They came to understand that the world around, and they themselves, were limited, and therefore were inherently religious, since limit or finitude presupposes transcendence of that limit. This marks us out from animals.

The problem of evil, also exclusive to humanity, arises not primarily from our finitude but in revolt against the limit of finitude, the refusal to accept our boundaries, the desire to be as God. The source of evil and suffering, says Pannenberg, lies in the transition from God-given independence to self-independence.[163] Pannenberg links physical evil to entropy, the tendency of things to move to chaos without new energy. 'Those that cannot take on new energy and thus transcend themselves come under the neutralizing sway of entropy.'[164] Basically, we cut ourselves off from the Spirit by turning inwards, by ceasing to trust in the goodness of things, by shutting ourselves off from the divine life. Christ, the new man, reverses this with his filial union with his Father, and his humble self-differentiation from God. He fulfils creation, and at the same time discloses and establishes the identity of God.

Conclusion

Pannenberg's theology is a very rich mine of resources. To read his theology is in itself to gain a theological education, and to be led along chains of reasoning which are complex, but always interesting and seriously profound. His theology has developed only in terms of nuancing; there have been no radical changes of mind since his early works. He now sounds more orthodox, as the Trinity has taken such a prominent place – the doctrine of God which decides all other doctrines.

Pannenberg's future orientation of reality has been a stimulus of the strongest kind, shaking up conventional theology and offering interpretations of apocalyptic which are much needed. His constant way of thinking has been to assert a hypothesis and then formally allow the challenges of secular thought to have their say and to become dialogue partners. Theology is therefore provisional; new evidence may arise to bring down the theological house, and Pannenberg would have to evacuate. This is his great defence against those who accuse him of being an Enlightenment thinker: modern, but not postmodern, not sufficiently pluralistic, still under the illusion that the grand narrative is available. But Shults is correct to defend him as 'post foundational' rather than foundational:[165] God is the centre of his theology, the relational and ultimately mysterious God whose being is Father, Son and Spirit, in subsistent relationality. Being is relational, it is love and self giving. This is no rational foundation, but an invitation to participate in life and in love. Pannenberg's theology takes us ultimately to praise and worship: to be part of the divine relationality of mutual serving and self-humbling. Self-differentiation means that this is no oppressive grand narrative being imposed on the world, rather a humble act of divine generosity and sustaining. It may even be possible to take the postmodernist critics at their word and point to the divine life of differentiation as difference, continually pointing away from person to person, to the other, to the new. No, this is not a modern rationalist theologian, but a subtle relational sage focused on the Trinity, whose meditations enrich us. History and meaning are provisional, in his theology; indeed they are 'deferred' and so are in accordance with the strict criteriological canons of Derridean orthodoxy!

Pannenberg's thought has striking resonances with Pauline

theological emphases in many places, and these may be worth noting. Creation is awaiting its climax, almost pregnant with meaning, eager to give birth to its true self and to be what it is intended to be, in harmony with the Creator. This will be a liberation, and a fulfilment of adoption as sons, a participation with the life of the Son, who is Jesus. Paul entrusts all into the hands of the Father, from whom nothing can separate us in Christ. This is the destiny of the people of God. Furthermore, the great theme of the second Adam, the new humanity of Jesus, is precisely taken up by Pannenberg. Most notable is perhaps the place accorded to the resurrection of Jesus. According to Paul, the gospel concerns God's Son,

> who as to his human nature was a descendant of David, and who through the Spirit of holiness was declared with power to be the Son of God, by his resurrection from the dead: Jesus Christ our Lord. Through him and for his name's sake, we have received grace and apostleship to call people from among the Gentiles to the obedience that comes from faith (Romans 1:3–5).

That could be a summary of what Pannenberg is saying in his trinitarian theology.

God is the eternal Trinity, who has freely created the world and in so doing allowed that to affect his being and to draw perfected humanity into his own life of self-giving love. Jesus, and those sharing his life, a field known ultimately to God, are perfected in love as this destiny is fulfilled – a destiny originating in God and so never in doubt: the future was always going to be perfected, springing as it did from the love of the Father, Son and Spirit.[166]

Bibliography of Pannenberg's major works

What follows is not an exhaustive list of Pannenberg's publications but a note of his major works with pointers to those giving an introduction to his theology. (The works are cited in chronological order.)

Theology as History (New York: Harper & Row, 1967). Edited by J. M. Robinson and J. B. Cobb, these essays form a dialogue between Pannenberg and several American critics, with a very useful introductory appraisal from Robinson.

Jesus – God and Man (London: SCM, 1968). Pannenberg's classic Christology, heavyweight and very worthwhile.

Revelation as History (London and Sydney: Sheed and Ward, 1969). A symposium edited by Pannenberg with two seminal essays by him outlining his position on this topic. Trans. David Granskou and Edward Quinn.

Theology and the Kingdom of God (Philadelphia: Westminster Press, 1969). Four essays by Pannenberg. Chapter 1 is a fine overview of his system. Edited by Richard John Neuhaus who gives a good profile of Pannenberg by way of introduction.

Basic Questions in Theology, 3 vols. (London: SCM, 1970–1973). Heavy-weight essays mainly on methodology and the question of God.

Spirit, Faith and Church (Philadelphia: Westminster Press, 1970). Edited by Pannenberg, C. E. Braaten and A. Dulles, contains useful essay by Pannenberg on the Spirit.

What is Man? (Philadelphia: Fortress, 1970). Pannenberg's early treatment of the subject. Less demanding than his later *Anthropology in Theological Perspective*.

Apostles' Creed (London: SCM, 1972). A good introductory book.

Theology and the Philosophy of Science (London: Darton, Longman & Todd, 1976). Pannenberg's highly regarded work examining mutual scientific, hermeneutical and theological presuppositions and their interplay.

Faith and Reality (London/Philadelphia: Search Press, 1977). A collection of essays, notably one on the Spirit.

Grundfragen Systematischer Theologie, band 2 (Gottingen: Vandenhoeck & Ruprecht, 1980). A very important collection of essays, as yet not translated, emphasizing Pannenberg's trinitarianism, and in effect laying the pathway for his *Systematic Theology*.

Anthropology in Theological Perspective (Philadelphia/Edinburgh: T. & T. Clark, 1985). Pannenberg's *magnum opus* on man.

Systematic Theology, 3 vols. (Edinburgh: T. & T. Clark, 1991–98). Translated by G. W. Bromiley. Pannenberg's classic and crowning work, his final theological statement.

Beginning with the End: God, Science and Wolfhart Pannenberg (Chicago: Open Court Publishing Co., 1997). Edited by C. R. Albright and J. Haugen. A collection of essays by critics, with responses by Pannenberg, focused on his scientific and theological explorations.

Notes

[1] The previous edition of this monograph predicted this would be the case on the basis of his early works.

[2] *Revelation as History.*

[3] Ibid., p. 4.

[4] *Systematic Theology*, vol. 1, p. 46 (my emphasis).

[5] Ibid., p. 2.

[6] See *Revelation as History*, p. 5, where the doctrine is traced back to Hegel.

[7] Ibid., p. 6.

[8] Pannenberg accordingly describes reason 'in its historical structure of sketching and reflecting', 'in its essential openness to a truth always presupposed but never grasped in the act of thinking out the sketch' (ibid., p. 198).

[9] R. Burhenn, 'Pannenberg's Argument for the Historicity of the Resurrection', *Journal of the American Academy of Religion* (September, 1972), p. 372.

[10] *Revelation as History*, p. 15.

[11] *Basic Questions in Theology*, vol. 2, pp. 206–207.

[12] John Macquarrie, *Twentieth Century Religious Thought* (London: SCM, 1981), p. 393; and most recently Jacqui A. Stewart, *Reconstructing Science and Theology in Postmodernity: Pannenberg, ethics and the human sciences* (Aldershot: Ashgate Publishing, 2000).

[13] *Systematic Theology*, vol. 2, p. xiii.

[14] *Theology and the Philosophy of Science*, p. 223, e.g.

[15] See e.g. F. LeRon Shults, *The Postfoundationalist Task of Theology: Wolfhart Pannenberg and the New Theological Rationality* (Grand Rapids: Eerdmans, 1999).

[16] *Revelation as History*, p. 198.

[17] Ibid., p. 199.

[18] *Theology and the Philosophy of Science*, p. 310.

[19] D. McKenzie, *Wolfhart Pannenberg and Religious Philosophy* (Washington, DC: University Press of America, 1980), p. 14.

20 *Basic Questions in Theology*, vol. 2, p. 225.

21 *Revelation as History*, pp. 131–132.

22 E. H. Carr, *What is History?* (Harmondsworth: Penguin, 1961), p. 121.

23 Pannenberg formulates his teaching: 'the meaning that we ascribe to our own individual histories and to the events of social history depends on anticipation of the totality which is developing in history, i.e., on its future, and these anticipations constantly change with further experience because as we move ahead the horizon of experience broadens. Thus as time advances it brings to light what is constant and true in the world of our beginnings, and what is unreliable' (*Systematic Theology*, vol. 1, p. 55).

24 G. W. F. Hegel, *Lectures on the Philosophy of Religion*, ed. Peter C. Hodgson (Berkeley, Los Angeles, London: University of California Press, 1988).

25 *Systematic Theology*, vol. 1, p. 173.

26 Ibid., p. 171.

27 Ibid., p. 2.

28 Ibid., p. 6.

29 Pannenberg interestingly reminds us that the emperor Justinian and the church 'made a codification of dogmas legally binding, thus not merely presupposing their truth but establishing it ... In that year [541] Justinian declared that the dogmata of the first four councils carried an authority equal to that of the holy scriptures' (*Systematic Theology*, vol. 1, p. 10).

30 Ibid., p. 16.

31 Agreeing with Barth at this point, he says, 'God alone has the competence to speak the final word about God's work in history' (*Systematic Theology*, vol. 1, p. 16).

32 'As a rule faith precedes theological reflection. Nevertheless, theological ascertainment of the truth is not made superfluous by the certainty of faith ... Personal assurance of faith always needs confirmation by experience and reflection. By nature it is always thus open to confirmation in the sphere of argument relating to the universal validity of the truth which is believed. No truth can be purely subjective' (*Systematic Theology*, vol. 1, p. 50).

33 Ibid., p. 53.

34 Ibid.

35 Ibid., p. 54.

36 See e.g. 'Faith and Reason', in *Basic Questions in Theology*, vol. 2, pp. 46–64.

37 *Systematic Theology*, vol. 1, p. 93.

38 This thesis was set out as early as *What is Man?*

39 *Theology and the Philosophy of Science*, pp. 301 ff.

[40] Ibid., p. 333.

[41] Christian claims, for Pannenberg, 'are open to possible confirmation in the history of human experience and reflection, but also open to provisional confirmation in a logical account of their contents' (*Systematic Theology*, vol. 2, p. xiii).

[42] Ibid., p. xii.

[43] *Anthropology in Theological Perspective*, p. 72.

[44] *Systematic Theology*, vol. 1, p. 114.

[45] Ibid., p. 159.

[46] 'In other words, the gods of the religions must show in our experience of the world that they are the powers which they claim to be. They must confirm themselves by the implications of meaning in this experience so that its content can be understood as an expression of the power of God and not his weakness' (*Systematic Theology*, vol. 1, p. 167). This seems difficult for the 'theology of the cross', but Pannenberg takes this into account and applies a kind of 'test of time' criterion.

[47] 'In the course of religious history the concept of revelation has become a description of the result of the self-demonstration of God in the process of historical experience. The fact that history is the sphere of the self-demonstration of the deity of God was a discovery of Israel, into whose inheritance Christianity has stepped' (*Systematic Theology*, vol. 1, p. 171).

[48] Ibid., p. 243.

[49] Ibid., p. 247. Interestingly, he says 'As all things have their beginning in the word, and their consummation in sight, so, too, does the future world of God.'

[50] Ibid., p. 247.

[51] As Pannenberg says, 'just as the thought of revelation becomes a comprehensive one for God's action and thus takes the place that myth has in other religions' (ibid., p. 257).

[52] Ibid.

[53] *Revelation as History*, p. 5.

[54] For a fine treatise on these see P. S. Fiddes, *The Creative Suffering of God* (Oxford: Oxford University Press, 1988).

[55] The Hegelian notion of *Aufhebung*.

[56] *Revelation as History*, p. 143.

[57] *Jesus – God and Man*, p. 154.

[58] Self-differentiation and self-distinction are used interchangeably below. Both are translations of *Selbstunterscheidung*, having the meaning of putting

oneself humbly from God in status, or 'not [considering] equality with
God something to be grasped' (Philippians 2:6).

59 *Jesus – God and Man*, pp. 159–160.

60 Ibid., p. 156.

61 *Systematic Theology*, vol. 1, p. 313.

62 Ibid., p. 321.

63 Ibid., p. 319.

64 Ibid., p. 325.

65 Edith Humphrey makes the point similarly in her fine essay, 'Called to be
One: Worshipping the Triune God Together', in Timothy Bradshaw (ed.),
Grace and Truth in the Secular Age (Grand Rapids/Cambridge: Eerdmans,
1998), pp. 219–234.

66 *Systematic Theology*, vol. 1, p. 261.

67 Ibid.

68 Ibid., p. 330.

69 Ibid., p. 331.

70 Ibid.

71 Ibid., p. 333.

72 This theology of God was explained clearly in some untranslated essays
entitled *Grundfragen Systematischer Theologie*, band 2, published prior to his
Systematic Theology.

73 Here the full import of Pannenberg's foundational work is seen: 'One can
think of revelation in the strict sense only if the special means by which
God becomes manifest, or the particular act by which he proves himself, is
not seen as distinct from his own essence' (*Revelation as History*, p. 7).

74 *Grundfragen Systematischer Theologie*, band 2, p. 124.

75 Ibid., pp. 124–125.

76 Ibid., p. 123.

77 *Revelation as History*, pp. 14–15.

78 *Systematic Theology*, vol. 1, p. 430.

79 *Grundfragen Systematischer Theologie*, band 2, p. 125.

80 *Jesus – God and Man*, p. 181.

81 Ibid., p. 182.

82 Ibid.

83 *Apostles' Creed*, pp. 27–28; 'Person', in Kurt Galling (ed.), *Religion in
Geschichte und Gegenwart* (Stuttgart: UTB, 1996), p. 232; 'Person und Subjekt'
and 'Die Subjektivität und die Trinitätslehre', in *Grundfragen Systematischer
Theologie*, band 2.

[84] *Apostles' Creed*, pp. 17–28.

[85] Ibid., p. 28.

[86] *Grundfragen Systematischer Theologie*, band 2, p. 109, n 33.

[87] Ibid., p. 86.

[88] Ibid., p. 88.

[89] *Systematic Theology*, vol. 2, p. 194.

[90] *Grundfragen Systematischer Theologie*, band 2, p. 91.

[91] Ibid., p. 91.

[92] Ibid., pp. 91–92.

[93] bell hooks spells her name in lower case very deliberately.

[94] bell hooks, *Wounds of Passion* (New York: Owl Books, 1997).

[95] *Grundfragen Systematischer Theologie*, band 2, pp. 92–95.

[96] *Systematic Theology*, vol. 2, p. 430.

[97] Ibid., vol. 1, p. 432.

[98] Ibid., p. 438.

[99] Ibid., p. 446.

[100] Ibid., vol. 3, p. 274.

[101] bell hooks, *Remembered Rapture: The Writer at Work* (New York: Henry Holt, 1999), p. 11.

[102] Ibid., p. 12.

[103] See, e.g., *Metaphysics and the Idea of God* (Edinburgh: T. & T. Clark, 1990), pp. 84ff.

[104] *Theology of Hope*, pp. 77–89, 171–177.

[105] Paul S. Fiddes, *The Promised End* (Oxford: Blackwell, 2000).

[106] *Metaphysics and the Idea of God*, p. 87.

[107] *What is Man?*, p. 74.

[108] *Systematic Theology*, vol. 3, p. 610.

[109] Ibid., p. 639.

[110] Ibid., pp. 638–639.

[111] E. Jüngel, *Death – the Riddle and the Mystery* (Edinburgh: St Andrew Press, 1974), pp. 121–122.

[112] Karl Barth, *Church Dogmatics* II/1 (Edinburgh: T. & T. Clark, 1957), pp. 617–618.

[113] *Systematic Theology*, vol. 1, pp. 402–404.

[114] Ibid., vol. 2, p. 91.

[115] Ibid., vol. 3, p. 646.

[116] E.g., *Basic Questions*, vol. 1, p. 237.

[117] *Systematic Theology*, vol. 3, p. 645.

1990), ch. 4; and *Systematic Theology*, vol. 2, p. 91.

[122] *Metaphysics and the Idea of God*, p. 90.

[123] *Systematic Theology*, vol. 3, p. 602.

[124] Notwithstanding, he says, that since 1513 the Roman Catholic Church has condemned the idea of the mortality of the soul as heretical: 'it is doubtful whether a man's personal identity, and his responsibility at the judgement seat of God after death, is dependent on the assumption – so hard to reconcile with our present human knowledge – of a soul independent of the body, and hence surviving even the body's death ... The identity of our present "body" with the future resurrection reality remains inconceivable as long as one only adheres to the linear sequence of time' (*Apostles' Creed*, p. 172).

[125] *Systematic Theology*, vol. 3, p. 606.

[126] *Apostles' Creed*, p. 175.

[127] It might even be suggested, perhaps provocatively, that 'closure' of life to new experience, as it reaches its future wholeness, equates more to Nietzsche's doctrine of the eternal recurrence, than to Christian worship!

[128] 'The transformation of our mortal life', he says in an early work, 'does not mean a frozen rigidity, as would be the case if eternity were to be viewed as timelessness' (*Apostles' Creed*, p. 175).

[129] *Systematic Theology*, vol. 2, p. 303.

[130] Ibid., p. 315.

[131] Ibid., p. 389.

[132] Ibid., p. 359.

[133] Ibid., p. 359.

[134] Ibid., p. 360.

[135] *Jesus – God and Man*, pp. 66–114; *Systematic Theology*, vol. 2, pp. 346ff.

[136] See David McKenzie, *Wolfhart Pannenberg and Religious Philosophy*
       (Washington, DC: University Press of America, 1980), ch. 4. This remains
       an excellent commentary on Pannenberg's argument in relation to
       philosophical and hermeneutical issues.

[137] *Systematic Theology*, vol. 2, p. 349.

[138] Stanley J. Grenz summarizes some of these critics, including Moltmann and
       Sobrino, in his *Reason for Hope: The Systematic Theology of Wolfhart Pannenberg*
       (New York/Oxford: Oxford University Press, 1990), pp. 146–148.

[139] 'Der Gott der Geschichte', in *Grundfragen Systematischer Theologie*, band 2,
       p. 122; or more recently: 'The reality that is achieved in the eternal
       fellowship of the Trinity and by the economy of its action in the world is
       one and the same' (*Systematic Theology*, vol. 2, p. 393).

[140] Ibid., p. 394.

[141] Ibid., pp. 388–389.

[142] The problem in this regard, as Fiddes has pointed out above, is *creaturely*
       openness, in eternity, within the dynamic life of God.

[143] Pannenberg at times gets very close to Hegel's position. For example: 'Only
       in the transition through the death of his individual existence as man is
       Jesus the Son.' But the next sentence redeems it: 'His human individuality
       has definitiveness, not as its particularity endures, but only as he offers it
       up for the sake of God and in the service of the coming kingdom'
       (*Systematic Theology*, vol. 2, p. 433); see p. 435 for his criticism of Hegel with
       regard to this doctrine, which he considers as deficient with regard to the
       particularity of Jesus' death and its liberating effect on individuals.

[144] E.g. P. T. Forsyth, *The Person and Place of Jesus Christ* (London: Independent
       Press, 1909, 1955), p. 318.

[145] *Systematic Theology*, vol. 2, p. 426.

[146] Ibid., p. 427.

[147] Ibid.

[148] Ibid., p. 441.

[149] See, e.g., his brilliant section in *Jesus – God and Man*, pp. 169–179.

[150] John Zizioulas, the distinguished Greek Orthodox theologian, has signalled
       his appreciation of Pannenberg's theology against the equation of Spirit
       and mind, in *Being as Communion* (New York: St Vladimir's Press, 1985),
       pp. 71, 78, 173, etc.

[151] For a brilliant cameo account of Hegel see Edward Caird, *Hegel*
       (Edinburgh and London: Blackwood, 1883. Reprinted: New York: AMS
       Press, 1972).

[152] We are reminded of Charles Kingsley's positive response to Darwin's work, on the ground that it brought God back into the processes of the world's development.

[153] 'Der Gott der Geschichte', in *Grundfragen Systematischer Theologie*, band 2, p. 126.

[154] *Systematic Theology*, vol. 2, p. 62.

[155] Ibid.

[156] *Jesus – God and Man*, pp. 395–396.

[157] Ibid.

[158] *Systematic Theology*, vol. 2, pp. 79ff.

[159] John Polkinghorne, 'Fields and Theology: a response to Wolfhart Pannenberg', in *Zygon*, vol. 36, no. 4 (December, 2001), p. 796.

[160] Ibid., pp. 795–797.

[161] Toulmin's notion, not born of natural science, of the 'field encompassing field', may serve Pannenberg rather better than the scientific category.

[162] *Systematic Theology*, vol. 2, pp. 115ff.

[163] Ibid., p. 172.

[164] Ibid.

[165] *The Postfoundationalist Task of Theology: Wolfhart Pannenberg and the New Theological Rationality* (Grand Rapids: Eerdmans, 1999), ch. 5.

[166] For a philosopher's objections to the category of 'the future' as real in any way beyond that of speaking, see David Mellor, *Real Time* (Cambridge: Cambridge University Press, 1981).

4. POSTMODERNISM AND THEOLOGY

Mark W. Elliott

Mark Elliott is *Lecturer in Christian Studies at Liverpool Hope University College. He was formerly Assistant Director of the Whitefield Institute, Oxford. He is the author of* The Song of Songs and Christology *(Tübingen: Mohr Siebeck, 2000), co-editor of* 'The Reader Must Understand' *(Leicester: Apollos, 1997) and contributing editor of* The Dynamics of Human Life *(Carlisle: Paternoster, 2002).*

Postmodernism and philosophy

In this short study[1] I do not intend to look at the phenomenon of postmodernism as a movement. I am no philosopher, literary critic, sociologist, psychologist, or architect, and there are plenty of studies which attempt to show postmodernism's effects, and so on. Across these various disciplines, the amount of books with postmodernism in the title means it is becoming increasingly difficult to represent all the corners where it can be found. Admittedly, not all books with the word 'postmodern' or its cognates in the title are necessarily all about postmodernism. Very often they are about something else, with the word 'postmodern' thrown in to catch the eye. This contribution is one such, in that my focus shall be on representing the work of theologians, by which I mean those whose primary interest is how one can or may discourse about God.

It will become clear at a very early stage, however, that one thing which postmodernism has done is to question the line of demarcation between theology and other disciplines, particularly philosophy. Of course, postmodernism by definition, or by lack of it, if you like, resists description. It has no wish to be dissected like a corpse, or even poked at while lying anaesthetized on a table. An anatomy of postmodernism would be a hard thing. Perhaps it is better to trace its effects across various disciplines. Starting with architecture, it has moved through literary studies, sociology and on into medicine and physics. Yet it is no respecter of these demarcations, or any nice parcelling-up of subjects, and for this reason appears to think of itself as bigger than any one subject. In truth this is not so much from a wish for holism as from a passion to differentiate and separate subjects into these component parts, to single out each little bit of knowledge as different from anything else. In that way any attempt to categorize is pre-empted.

In the first section I shall be concerned with the non-theological manifestations of the 'postmodern'. Here the territory is not uniform. For instance, in architecture 'postmodern' has become increasingly a pejorative term for (at worst) the nostalgic, the hesitant and conservative, or (at best) a style which is eclectic. Architecture can be labelled 'deconstructive', but that often simply means 'disorientating'. (For what 'deconstructive' means for the person who coined the term, Jacques Derrida, see below.) Some say that also, in philosophy, for example, it is rapidly becoming discredited on the grounds that it is too vulnerable to hard criticism and the logical rigour of tenacious argument, but, due to the mushrooming of and cross-fertilizing between disciplines, it is hard to see this trend applying to those parts of university and college curricula where 'theory' is discussed in relation to a practice: if anything, 'postmodernism' remains in the ascendant. As for sociological studies, it is not so much in sociology as a discipline but actually as a movement within society itself (which sociology reflects) that the objective presence of 'postmodernism' or 'postmodernities' in different parts and walks of life can be discerned: the flexible working practices, the dismantling of social hierarchies with an ordering being re-established in different ways often according to 'taste', mirrored in the growing erosion of the low-brow/high-brow boundaries.[2]

To return to philosophy; Hegel can perhaps be described as the great modernist, the one who thought that philosophy ended with his own theories as the completion of all philosophies, that a universal reality was true for everyone, and that philosophy reflected society; that what went on in history shaped and developed thought; and knowledge in turn (with knowledge of the conditioned-ness of all wisdom as the foundation of knowledge) allows for civilization and advance.[3] All who have reacted to him in terms of refusing to accept his continuation of the enlightenment project (as distinct from those who preferred some other strand of it – such as Kantianism, or empiricism), can be labelled 'postmodernist', although they probably would have disclaimed the term for themselves. Some enlightenment thinkers do fit into the fold of postmodernism, Spinoza, for example, but they are exceptional. For Gilles Deleuze, Spinoza is the philosopher, as one who worked his ontology – the way all things are – from *ethics*, a recurring postmodernist theme, to which we shall need to return. Postmodern philosophy is unashamedly open to contemporary outside influences, 'opening the shutters' to let in insights from experience as lived, not as observed in a 'controlled' way. Therefore from as many *human* sciences as possible; it despises 'pure' philosophers for trying to operate in a philosophical vacuum, for refusing to disclose their interests. It is not that personal experiences are so much valued as, rather, the mediations of experience and the re-creation of experience in the working of texts, of *discourse*. From ordinary conversations to writing and imaging creatively – a wide range of things can be grist to the postmodern mill. Thus David Clines in his commentary on Job argues in the preface for allowing popular hymns to be entered along with learned monographs on that most life-centred of biblical books.[4]

Of course, philosophy can often be evidently and to a large degree Christian. For instance, certain Neo-platonists' awareness of God's being profoundly interested in humanity in a purifying way may well owe something to Christianity, particularly in such a contemporary form as we find it in Gadamer. However, as Nancy Murphy has observed, theology often takes its weapons from the armoury of philosophy, and not just from weapon-makers who at first sight seem sympathetic to a theological agenda.[5] To switch metaphors, philosophy itself can be seen like a parfumerie of the abstracted essences of the various disciplines as they impinge on the big questions. Is theology just a way of communicating these ideas, or smuggling them in to church circles?

Admittedly, there has been a fair bit of worrying about what theology is there for. Theology has become preoccupied with self-examination particularly in Anglo-Saxon circles over the last two decades.[6] Its existence may be understood as due to a failure of nerve; a loss of engagement with the substance of doctrines due to a losing of moorings in any one confessional tradition; a weariness in combatting more and more penetrating questions from the secular camp; loss of contact with lay Christianity that wants to see answers, strategies and solutions.

Ideally, theology ought to be both a response to as well as a reflection of whatever passes for wisdom at any given time. It is my contention that theologians should seek to examine ideas on the grounds of origins, consequences and logical coherence, but also in their correspondence to a reality which is presented, albeit to some extent in outline form, by the Scriptures and the Christian creeds and tradition as commentary on these. To think of the early church notion of the Rule of Faith or the Pauline one of 'the Mind of Christ' does not mean that theology has to be hopelessly outdated about the kind of ideas which are to be affirmed.[7] So, although the term 'postmodernism' is often synonymous with all that is wrong in modern thinking, this essay, while largely devoted to offering information, will argue that it raises pertinent questions and at times reinforces easily forgotten points of Christian orthodoxy.

Postmodernism: a pseudo-philosophy?

According to Terry Eagleton, 'Postmodernity is a style of thought which is suspicious of classical notions of truth, reason, identity and objectivity, of the idea of universal progress or emancipation, of single frameworks, grand narratives or ultimate grounds of explanation.'[8] Or, with Lyotard:

> the term 'modern' to denigrate any science that legitimates itself
> with reference to a metadiscourse of this kind (i.e., 'a discourse of
> legitimation with respect to its own status, a discourse called

philosophy'), making an explicit appeal to some grand narrative,
such as the dialectics of the Spirit, the hermeneutics of meaning, the
emancipation of the rational or working subject, or the creation of
wealth.[9]

Yet are these metanarratives not necessary for human existence?
According to some, even postmodernism has its own meta-
narrative, namely that we are in transition. But Lyotard denies
this expressly. Postmodernism has little time for any *meaningful*
stories, and it therefore negates the possibility that whatever
postmodernism is, it is a metanarrative. Stories are, since Sartre,
only entertainments based on the imagined perception of events,
lacking connections. European cinema stands out from Holly-
wood not so much in its rejection of the 'Happy End' (a loan
word in German!) but in the rejection of endings.[10] Meaning-free
flux cannot provide a story without ourselves, like little demigods,
around to create it. Human existence does and can do without
over-arching themes into which our lives have to fit.[11] Instead, like
all we build and invent for convenience as we go along, so too
with our life-stories, when we get time to look back and make the
connections between our experiences. (Although perhaps our
built-in capacity to *see* order in the past suggests that we also to
some degree *act* meaningfully in the present.)

While the origins of this word are cloudy, 'postmodernism'
seems to have first become current in theories of architecture. It
came to mean a reaction against buildings which gloried in the
newest technology and materials at the expense of everything
else (modernism), and was more humanity-centred, appealing to
nostalgia and conveying a sense of all-knowingness by including
features from different periods of yesteryear. Its origins in what
might be called the aesthetic experience are significant. That is,
meaning is found in an experience of the sublime which is near to
the religious and the mystical.

Whereas a modernist is someone who thinks that that which
is irrational can be explained rationally, a postmodernist thinks
that that which is rational can be explained irrationally.[12]
This 'seeing as', as coined by Wittgenstein, means that our culture
and community provide categories through which to shape our

experience, and thus determine to a large extent just what reality is for us. The confidence of phenomenologists (Husserl) that we could see things as they are has been displaced since Wittgenstein and Merleau-Ponty by a realization that our categories do so much, and by the insistence of Gadamer on the priority of our interpretative 'baggage' (hermeneutic). However, postmodernists such as Baudrillard go a step further. Not only does the map precede the territory, it creates the territory!

Christopher Norris has argued that Anglo-Saxon critics of Derrida have often failed to do justice to the nuances of his arguments. My point would be that they have not read him closely, nor the other significant deconstructionists such as Deleuze, Baudrillard, Nancy. Postmodernism entered philosophy through a reaction of poststructuralists[13] to the attempts of structuralism to speak of human language as embedded, or given, in reality – especially as propagated by some linguists and French cultural anthropologists. The structuralist idea that reality, language included, is a subtle system of pairs of opposites ('black/white', 'strong/weak') was exposed as affirming an oppressive relationship where one half is always dominant. Structuralists thought that words are just arbitrarily chosen sounds and only exist as distinguished from other words' sounds (e.g. 'tree' as opposed to 'tee', 'try', 'spree', etc.). Poststructuralists then extend this to claim that the same goes for the concepts, the meanings which are 'signifed' by words. These have no meaning except for that given them in the course of a text and by the reader's interpretation.

The idea that there is more to a text than that which the author meant was first taken up by structuralists. Accordingly, the meaning was to be found in, not behind, the text (the author, his context) in question. The poststructuralists denied that any meaning or resolution could be found – that the tensions in a text are such that meaning is torn apart, de-constructed. One might want to call James Joyce's *Ulysses* a text which lends itself easily to structuralist criticism, and *Finnegans Wake*, or 'difficult' poetry to poststructuralist. By this I mean that while the word-play in the former offers a puzzle largely resolvable by close reading, in the latter the reader is encouraged or forced to fill the gaps of meaning herself. Valentine Cunningham has observed how *Finnegans Wake*

has obtained near-scriptural status among intelligentsia.[14] Such a
'mystical' text is revered partly because it is *anti*-revelatory. Joyce's
love of alluding to the profound in and through the profane is
carried on by Jacques Derrida.

The postmodernist believes that attempting to explain a text
convincingly in part or as a whole is always defeated by the
mystery of that which does not fit neatly into the explanation.
Meaning is always being deferred on to another meaning, since all
language is 'metaphorical' – that is, definitions of words use other
words which have a more obvious connection with what we can
see (thus 'involve' is defined as 'wrap, entangle') and thus never
get more precise than approximations.[15] In other words, language
is thought of in terms of a dictionary format. This means that
words are taken to be signs in themselves, rather than operating in
sentences or utterances. It gives priority to the sense that language
is about words as locked up in a storehouse over their actual use.
Saussure thought of the former (*la langue*) as the subject of
linguistics proper; a language is a 'given' and cannot vary that
much.[16] He attacked the idea that words point to some realities to
which they correspond; he proposed that they operated in a
sentence system to say something about a real thing, and to effect
something (warning, threat, command, promise). All this negativity about the possibility of finding the meaning results in the
positive principle: the encounter with the written text itself is
primary. Meaning gets created in each new interaction with a
reader.[17] In this vision, as Kevin Mills describes it: 'the mental
images evoked by language are, however, also signifiers: they
represent the world of objects. Language can never make contact
with the world: all that it can do is *represent a representation* of it'.[18]
However, when Derrida wrote: 'There is nothing outside the text'
(*Il n'y a pas dehors de texte*), he did not mean, literally, that there is
nothing real or meaningful beyond texts, but only that all
knowledge is mediated by our language and that all human
interaction is about codes and systems of signs which use us
more than we use them. Language is not about representing 'the
way things are', but is representing nothing because it is really
'something' in itself.

For postmodern philosophy, all human concepts are defined by the other: concepts have taken over from just being what helps us to describe or talk about reality to becoming part of reality itself. However, Derrida is unhappy with what he calls the 'white mythology' in which concepts become elevated into the heavens, and people (Platonists, Christians) think they have a hot-line to heaven when it is just intellectual excitement (Derridean mysticism would not get so carried away). Deleuze, therefore, insists that we remember that it is we who make concepts, and remake them as our tools.[19]

Nowhere is the contention that concepts just come as reactions to others, as pairs in binary opposition, of more political consequence than in the 'gender debate'. For example, there is the theory of Hélène Cixous that patriarchy establishes in the heavens 'male' and 'female' as opposites and that this had perpetuated inequality. Such feminist/postmodernist suspicion of essentialist thinking, coming to expression ever since phenomenology earlier this century, means that all classifications are to be avoided and only functional observations are allowed: for example, women bear children, men are called to recognize 'the other, the feminine' within.[20] Postmodernism has challenged any such differences as arbitrary: it is the very stuff of hierarchy that there are 'deeper meanings', and Derrida for one has been feted by feminists such as Julia Kristeva.[21]

The abandonment of division between high and low culture is another example. In architecture, postmodernism, as Charles Jencks noted in 1977, was a reaction versus the *technological*, not necessarily versus the *avant-garde*.[22] Daniel Bell has shown that this has led at times to a culture *versus* business and science antagonism. Habermas's attempt to mediate across this gulf by an aesthetic that could be commonly accepted once worked out was hailed with scepticism by Lyotard. As C. Strube has observed, postmodernism refuses all that looks totalizing and prefers Kant's view of aesthetic judgment, with a resistance against seeing a correspondence between this and how reality should be shaped.[23] The boundary between the image and the reality is threatened by what Jean Baudrillard has called *simulacra*. For example, 'Disneyland is there to conceal the fact that it is the "real" country, all of "real" America which is Disneyland … Disneyland is presented as

imaginary in order to make us believe that the rest is real.'[24]
Baudrillard also contends that sex and work are not opposites
since a link between desire and consumer demand is made (an area
explored already by Bataille and Marcuse); sex is now seen as
existing for its own sake as is work (post-Marx). Little by way of
positive remedy for society's ills is offered, since it is false to think
we can restore truth behind *simulacra*. In political life, the soft end
of postmodernism may be a communitarianism where 'the
common good' takes priority in a softening of individual drives
to domination, its harder edge a sort of Foucaultian libertarianism
in which the rights of minorities are paramount.[25]

Postmodernism has often seemed either too clever for its own
good, or wilfully self-contradictory. Following Nietzsche in *The
Will to Power*, all experience caused (pain, sweetness) precedes its
cause (a pin, a sugar lump); this destroys the assumption that the
cause is hierarchically superior to its effect. However, Jonathan
Culler notes that Nietzsche's point does not abandon the principle
of causation: 'The deconstruction appeals to no higher logical
principle or superior reason but uses the very principle it
deconstructs.'[26] In other words, postmodern thinking is parasitic
rather than creative; it is reactionary, fighting its battles point by
point rather than by working out a grand strategy.

It is here where the mordant critique of John Ellis bites.[27]
Taking Derrida as his protagonist, Ellis insists that it is pure
charlatanism to blame one's readers for misunderstanding less
than perspicuous passages. He adds that to argue that all points
are equally wrong results in a mysticism of a not very interesting
sort. Ellis also takes issue with the left-wing subversiveness and its
method of distrust 'which sometimes seems nothing more than
the standard advice to the researcher in any field'.[28] One thinks of
Karl Popper's principle of verification by falsification. But sometimes, and this is what is dangerous about deconstruction, it goes
further. 'Deconstruction' will not finally reject an idea shown to be
fallacious – the whole resulting complex (even *confusion*) is the
result to be held on to. Sentimentally, it wants to keep the door
open to the old theory, as if it may, although discredited, still have
something to say. The association with pluralism here is perhaps
why so many evangelicals have been against postmodernism. But

this is to confuse theology (talk about God and ultimate things –
where pluralist claims cannot stand) with philosophy or theories
of reality (penultimate things) in which postmodern insights are
sometimes acceptable and helpful. Think about the analogous case
of gender-specific language: while it is important that the world be
understood in its fully 'sexualized' way and the contribution of
women taken as seriously as that of men,[29] there is no need to call
God (who is beyond gender) 'she'; 'he' should be used for God on
the grounds that he must have some pronoun, and since when
God comes into language he does so in the form of Jesus.
Saussure, as Ellis reminds us, clarified how conventions of
language systems mean that we are fairly bound to a limited range
of meanings that a word can carry – the example he gives is that
the meaning of the German *heisses Wasser* to *warmes Wasser* is not as
in the English 'hot water' to 'warm water'. *Heiss* is a little *too* hot.
(Think of all the nuances anyone who works from dictionaries and
not from living with the foreign language can miss!) Saussure did
not go on to say that the relationship between the idea and the
thing spoken of (signifier and signified) was arbitrary, as some
postmodernists think. The point is that Derrida takes his leave
from Saussure in his view that meaning is always being extended.
Like Humpty Dumpty, like poets, we are always trying to map our
language to *our* new realities which confront *us*.[30]

The deconstructionists may have done us the service of
showing how important language is to our thinking and being:
but it is not everything. Derrida has also made it clear that the
common error of Rousseau and Levi-Strauss was to believe in an
aboriginal state of purity which was pre-writing. The fact that such
a state is illusory accords with the Christian conviction that the
present state of human beings is one of not having such innocence
as a memory: there is no continuous link back to such a state.
Surely, Ellis goes on, if we are going to prioritize speech and
writing, the speech comes first. However, as a matter of historical
inquiry, Derrida may have a point; that, even if there was a time
when there was no writing, we have no access to it, since oral
cultures leave no clear traces; we as humans are cut off from our
primordial culture and we have to start with writing, as given
systems of signs out of which language arose.[31]

George Steiner has also shown how deconstruction has imported those well-known principles of aesthetics – 'each to his/her own' meaning is merely that which we bring to reality ourselves, as if the very concept 'reality' were a delusion every bit as much as 'the existence of God'.[32] Nevertheless, to give it its due, 'deconstruction' does suggest that there are more things in heaven and earth than in our philosophy.[33] The limits of language are well known to those who have redress to physical expressions of love, or to those who live with violence and consumerism. There is something in the notion of infinite regress when it comes to arguing over the truth. For when we (the evangelists) try the old trick of telling the relativist that her view of truth as relative is on her terms just one poor little view, the law of infinite regress means someone can then tell us that our observation is no more true than false. Perhaps for that reason (following Wittgenstein)[34] a principle of 'by their *fruits* shall you know them' operates; ethics is the final or perhaps the only court. Deconstruction goes so far as to claim that, *inter alia*, the holocaust would have been avoided if people had not taken themselves so seriously and had internalized the ethical law rather than talked or preached about it. Along with the anthropology of *homo ludens* (playful man) is a wilful immaturity which perhaps unknowingly shares Hegel's optimism that out of the negative always comes something positive – that the deconstructive negative critique is relativizing, that the Shakespearian fool on the stage of the world drives the plot. Surely to feel content with such a state of affairs is to be desensitized. Most recent definitions of postmodernism emphasize the plurality of 'truth' and relativism, the 'nihilism with a grin',[35] the suspicion of institutions (especially of white patriarchy) and their metanarratives, indeterminacy in the universe, the treasuring of that which is sublime or inexplicable in words, the radical 'death of God and death of the author', the irrational and uncanny, reality as more about the symbolic freight things carry than the material things themselves, a sophisticated form of existentialism.[36] However, beyond these sound-bite assessments, is there anything of wisdom in postmodernism? My interim conclusion would be affirmative: postmodern writers do not do well when they suggest that how it is is also the way it should be;

but in relating how it is, they often provide a great service.[37] I think of Gillian Rose's challenging insights into the world of medicine as a closed culture where power is exercised over our bodies and where information is often reserved: hospitals operate in angelic hierarchies of death. The holistic medical movement with its platitudes and passivity does not fare much better under her scrutiny, as she attacks postmodernism as a whole for arrogantly thinking that philosophy or reasoning led to the holocaust, and so on. More likely, it was a refusal to reason, to see philosophy as engaged at the political level, in those kind of realities; reason as offering a way out of conflicting desires, a way forward. Yet Rose remains a *postmodern* writer, in that her concerns, her description is delivered in the terms of miscommunication, loss of meaning (with linguistic difficulties as a metaphor), of desire and identity through personal relationships *and* work, and so on.

Postmodernism and Christianity

The Judaeo-Christian tradition

Postmodern writers are often far less hostile to Judaism and the Jewish elements within Christianity than to Greek philosophy and the Western metaphysical tradition with its belief that texts can be reduced to 'one meaning'. Deleuze and Foucault give the impression that the West has Christianity to blame for exalting the One over the Many and the one voice over a plurality. Also, partly in reaction against the discredited Hegelian account of history, postmodern thought is notoriously ahistorical, regarding all metanarratives as fictional.[38] According to postmodernist Paul de Man in his introduction to Jauss's *Aesthetics of Reception*, texts are not able to leap across history and be applied to contemporary experience: not only are *we* shaped by what has happened since (Gadamer) but so is the text (Jauss) in the sense of its inner tensions having been shown up by the history of its exegesis.[39] It is therefore impossible to retrieve the 'original message of the Bible', not least because the biblical writers were too close up to have a view of the whole.[40]

What is preferred then is a Judaism without the history of salvation; a sort of exile-conscious, Talmudic Judaism which feels at three removes from the divine source. For Derrida there is a long silence between the Hebrew Bible and 'the place' to which it aspires; the law is shattered, prophets have disappeared and the poet has to make it up as she goes along, using her imagination. Nevertheless, it is fascinating to observe (with Derrida in particular) the continuing appreciation of the rabbinic tradition, and of the Christian mystical tradition with the implied premise that in order for God to be invisible, he must actually be there. Graham Ward has shown how Derrida mediates between the extremes of mysticism.[41] At one end, we can move from the world to God, delighting in Hebrew anthropomorphisms and in the idea that the upper and lower worlds mirror each other, as per Plato. Negative theology, which describes God in terms of what he is not, offers absolutely no understanding of God. In the middle stand Karl Barth and Derrida, who seem to agree that the Word or words are traces of a revelation that will come in the future. It is distinctively Jewish (and one might want to argue, authentically New Testament Christian) to do philosophy in the light of a catastrophe that relativizes the history of philosophy. Yet this is what the holocaust stands for.

Edith Wyschgorod criticizes Heidegger's dehumanizing vision which reduces all to individuals cut off from their world, as if we were all philosophers ready for death, integrating it into our life so that we act soberly, positively. The prisoners at Auschwitz never stood a chance of exercising their free-will or capacity for self-determination. Each one of us has to learn from the holocaust that the 'I' becomes social in the sense that we are tied to the whole human community.[42]

Judaism contributes to the postmodern delight in commentary's delight in re-presenting and the belief in the endlessness of that part of reality which is created by words. Even if we are biologically limited (although evolutionary theory may question this), with words we can deal in counterfactuals (what if?), fiction and uncover layer upon layer of associated meaning.[43] So works psychoanalysis with its need for arbitrary limits ('Your one hour is up!') and its endless possibilities prove its kinship with Jewish

Talmud and Midrash with their fascination with the Infinite. As distinct from the wish, represented by the mystical kabbalists to find the ultimate truth, the meaning of life (the Logos, we might add), it is ethically oriented – and this is perhaps the greatest impact which Judaism (or, controversially, the Old Testament spirit) has had on postmodernism. It becomes outward-looking to the point where it is at risk of veering into therapeutic pragmatism (whatever works is right).

The Bible

The Bible has been used to try out a whole range of new approaches, including poststructuralism. Stephen Moore has made interesting use of Lacan and Derrida in an approach to John 4. He demonstrates how Jesus' assertion of the superiority of spirit over flesh and an opposition between these two is contradicted and undermined by the fact that the text alludes to Jesus on the cross where that opposition is denied or overcome (John 19, 20). The spirit (God) has taken on flesh and achieved atonement; although previously immune to longing, in doing this God becomes subject to a desire for the Father in his abandonment. However, is this a contradiction, or could the difference between Jesus' talk and his action be explained as mutual qualification, dialectic or even paradox?[44] Part of the poststructuralist agenda is to resist the privileging of orality over literality. It asks: are Jesus' words in John 4 any more 'direct from God' because they are read in inverted commas? and replies: Surely not. Deconstruction describes reality as what is clearly given in history, however mysterious. 'In the beginning is the hermeneutic.'[45] One might argue that in John 4 (or indeed Genesis 1), textual metaphors just put off being able to say what is 'really meant' by deferring or passing along a chain of metaphors. In that sense, for Derrida, scriptural texts are often crooked and lead us into the desert of God's absence which is our freedom. Put simply, ultimate mean-ing is not accessible to beings in history because the Word is spoken in eternity. Words are traces only – the Torah is revealed in the sands of the desert – and their meanings are never fixed.[46] All this negativity about the possibility of finding the meaning results in the positive principle that the written text itself is

primary – it creates meaning with each new interaction with a
reader.

Derrida's almost methodological obsession with seeing oppositions in texts *removed* is followed up in the sphere of biblical studies
when David Jasper decries those 'deadly oppositions in Paul's
writings between law and grace, work and faith, blindness and
sight and so on',[47] and calls for the celebrative affirmation of
excess which proceeds from the disturbing power of narratives
and tropes; a sort of feeling which is, presumably, neither pleasure
nor pain (like the sexual *jouissance*). At the same time, the reader's
role is important; there is often a need in Bible reading to do
violence, to violate the text, 'to release from its textuality the
marginalized and violated victims of authoritative readings and
inscriptions'. Just as the honesty that the Watergate investigation
claimed was, according to Baudrillard, a simulacrum which the
routine dishonesty was allowed to hide, so too the ideologies of
the Bible need to be unmasked where they are most pious.[48] The
canonical process itself is most guilty for *excluding*; yet at the same
time Jasper has to admit that the canon of Scripture is a
worthwhile starting-place as long as we pay attention to the
interpretations of Scripture made through the centuries by all the
artists and writers who so often represent the marginalized.[49] Yet
this begs the question why we should be interested in Scripture at
all, if we think it needs people to correct it. The more positive
evaluation of the canonical process represented by James Sanders
(and to some extent Brevard Childs), with which Jasper takes
issue, has the beauty of admitting that the Bible allows in wisdom
from outside, but shapes it according to the understanding of who
God is as gradually gained through a painful process and eventual
progress of revelation.[50] The New Testament canon is the result
of a succession of witness-statements handed down and provid-
entially preserved.[51] However, Jasper is more concerned to make
God's 'oppressive presence' seem the result of his 'elusive
presence' leaving a vacuum for mean-spirited authors; thus his
hyper-critical spirit of challenge means he encourages little
challenge to his own position.

A less radical approach to texts, including the Bible, is offered
by Paul Ricoeur. He combines the structuralist optimism that

close reading of the text can provide illumination along with
the postmodernist idea that the reader's response to the words
makes that text alive – 'text as (orchestral) score'. However, he
has been criticized by Nicholas Wolterstorff who argues that the
words of Scripture 'exist' even when no-one is at that moment
using them.[52] And if the texts are intentional (in that as
'illocutionary' there was an effect intended), they can never really
be separated from the author's mind. Ricoeur has confused
intention as being something that has to be located in the
author's mind, when it is all too obvious from an intelligent
reading of Scripture that passages are there to effect different
things – the intention is embodied in the text. Furthermore, as
Hans Frei pointed out against Ricoeur, the narratives about Jesus
are not to be read as about 'Everyperson' but as about the
historical and particular Jesus, with Old Testament types pointing
either to him or to the God who saves, not to some idea of
model humanity.

But Ricoeur, as Vanhoozer has explained, believes that the
Christian redemption has included the renewing of the imagination. Like Kant he believes in the possibility of freedom but on a
ground that is more than just feeling; man is the intermediate
being – which goes back to the Renaissance – between the finite
and the infinite.[53] Also Ricoeur uses Saussure's distinction
between reference (the thing spoken of) and sense (that which is
meant) to privilege things external to the text. This implies that all
literature, Scripture included, is to be treated as fiction; against
structuralists the text is not a world as such, but it projects a
(common) world of imagination for readers to enter into. Ricoeur
believes in a text's ability to disclose a particular mode of being in
the world, to see the world differently and thus behave better.
Another question arises, though: is a project such as Ricoeur's,
which may be seen as an attempt to play philosophy at its own
game in order to take it captive for Christ, vitiated by doctrinal
stances such as that on sin and the fall? However, the literal
reading of Scripture in the hands of Frei and Wolterstorff
demands the priority of grace and the intervention of the meaningful from a hidden world. The four Gospels tell a story of one
individual called Jesus Christ and none other. We shall return to

Ricoeur's understanding of the implications of Christ's work for the human condition.

One of the central tenets of postmodernism is 'intertextuality', as coined by Julia Kristeva but well known to Bakhtin and Barthes[54] – the idea that every text is implicit commentary on another. 'Intertextuality' is not to be confused with *sola Scriptura*: the reader is momentarily drawn out of the flow of the text she is reading as the allusion or the archetypical biblical theme is mentioned, but the modern text acts as a commentary, a go-between for the ancient text. The book *The Postmodern Bible*, by 'The Bible and Culture Collective'[55] is an even-handed discussion of how postmodern philosophies and hermeneutics have come to grips with the Bible. Thus the first chapter, entitled 'Reader-response criticism' shows how that movement arose against the disembodied accounts of literary criticism which spoke of fictions such as 'the implied reader', for example, the work of Wolfgang Iser. His and Jauss's work has been admired by those who wish to preserve a 'then-ness' of the meaning of the ancient text – after all, reading the Bible is not like reading Salman Rushdie, no matter how exotically non-Western (and in that sense like the Bible) is some of his material (as other postmodern writers). The layout of the book suggests that the reader-response practice which has apparently prevailed is actually well out of date: it has been by-passed by (1) structuralist and then (2) poststructuralist readings. The first of these suggests that something like a collective unconscious shared by the biblical writers is what accounts for the strangeness of the biblical narratives. Akin to this is the view of narrative criticism which sees the content of Paul's theology as driven by what he wants to get – if these aims were sanctified as they should be with an apostle, so then will be his doctrine (to paraphrase J. H. Newman). Revealing Paul's motives and even 'bullying' manoeuvres need not diminish our reverence for the by-product, say the book of Romans or the letters to Philemon. Yet, according to the poststructuralist, this means that Scripture's stories contain expressions of desires which are barely civilized, let alone reconcilable. Since the work of Daniel Patte in the 1970s, psychoanalytical accounts of the formation of the Bible have, in a *post*modern bent, pointed out the darker side of the minds of the human authors, and by association, that of any divine author.

> You read not so much for the main point, in other words, the manifest meaning, the stated intentions, the conscious disclosures (thus far structuralist accounts would have agreed) ... as for what reveals itself unintentionally through slips of the tongue or pen, subtle evasions, audible silences, logical digressions and other such 'accidents' of expression.[56]

Spirituality and ethics

To call postmodernism indifferent and even passive is true to the extent that it is stamped by Heidegger's 'mysticism of being'.[57] Brian Ingraffia responds to Heidegger's view that acceptance of death is the highest virtue with the insistence that it is *faithful* not *authentic* existence which matters and which makes a difference.[58] Yet for postmodernism, there is a randomness about the acts of kindness in which loving acts are free from any plan, purpose or agenda. This is not Heideggerian in that the bleakness of his vision is denied. For Jacques Derrida, Heidegger was caught in risible modernist ontologizing (pretending to break with ontology but still believing in a sort of transcendence of stuff's hidden potential), seeing his armchair as a safe place for the 'free questioning of purely self-reliant Dasein'.[59] Postmodernists would agree with Heidegger, however, in his dislike of any notion of a representative death, since one has to take one's own responsibility. The idea of faithfulness is absent from any ethics, because that would imply someone or something to be faithful towards. Ingraffia attacks this as rebellious independence. One can agree with Ingraffia that 'Heidegger is anti-Pauline' despite his wish to preserve faith unchallenged by philosophy, and that Derrida is really anti-scriptural, for all his interest in Judaism (and by association, Christianity) and his slogan: 'the primacy of writing'. Like Heidegger, he views Being as encrypted, or tied up in everyday human discourse and thus not nameable as God. If God exists, he is beyond being. Thus the question is not so much whether God exists, but whether a God that we can speak of exists.[60] However, it is harder to believe that just because postmodernism's intellectual parents were phenomenological passivity and nihilism, then post-modernism has to be *negative* on the question of God's existence.

If postmodernism is more than a nihilism of a Nietzschean sort (and Derrida's ironic style seems similar), we have to ask what if anything positive does it offer. The overrating of humour (Jesus may have laughed, but that was not what made him different, or crucial), the tiring out of the possibilities of irony and a retreat to protest and a belief that the underdog is right, whatever the merits of any dispute. If history is 'written by the victors', then forget history![61] If modernism was based on a scientific hegemony with its logical and causal interrelations, progress and homogenization, the postmodernism is arty or artsy, sees only vague networks between things and also relegates things to a lower level of reality from the world of words in a language of 'totalizing discourse' as envisaged by Michel Foucault. So while some barriers come down, others go up. The mind and the heart are no longer strangers to each other, yet the gap between pure science and popular science grows larger. The dualisms of religion and philosophy or of Judaism and Hellenism are overcome, while *agapē* is reinterpreted as something that humans do for God by passionately loving their neighbour.[62] There is a flight from *technē*, a belief that it is better to keep science as the realm of boffins who will be so keen on research they will never want to use it, as in the case of the West's nuclear capability.[63] Thus what really makes things happen is *talk*. Foucault's famous later theory was that as experts and non-experts talked about and analysed sexuality, something happened to it – it got more divided into categories of normal and deviant and a fascination grew around it.[64] Sex is changed by discourse. Similarly, in *Listening to Prozac*, the case is made that the discussion of mental health has medicalized, or allowed to be medicalized in the interests of drug company profits, the whole issue of (un)happiness.[65] There is a lot of interest in the dark side of people. Lacan, in the wake of the Marquis de Sade, argued that (sado-) masochism was not so far removed from the religious person's need to feel oneself divided and in pain. The deepest urges must be the most profound. Freud himself spoke of humans beyond the pleasure principle (the title of a late work) as meaning that they have a strong death instinct as well as a strong life instinct; while in parallel, but on a more metaphysical plane, Nietzsche spoke of beyond good and evil, as an acceptance that, *contra* Hegel, all conflicts, whether of emotion or politics, would always be with us. All is light or dark, so there can be no shades of darkness or light, no place for distinctions – all is connected like a big chain of allusion or word-associations; nothing can be separated. The benefit is self-knowledge, and a realization that to take some things less seriously means freeing energy to fight obvious inequalities.[66] As Eagleton comments, not all injustices are addressed; there is no attempt made to grapple with the political economy. Yet postmodernism's preference to fight smaller battles may well be sensible; empowering, however, means beating the system by using its tools, and alarmingly thinks there is no such thing as the real, only that which is constructed, with alarming results for psychology and politics.[67] Foucault wrote that it is people who fascinate who will win: there is no real linguistic link between *fascinans* and facism, but the connection at the level of meaning has been noted.

Justice is perceived in anti-capitalist terms. Eagleton sees this as a sign of their negativity, that they are not interested (post-Marxism) in pretending that there is something better to offer, not a counter-system anyway. The paradigm is one of guerillas fighting a campaign for freedom against an unjust government in which there can be only moral and symbolic victory. What a critic like Eagleton fails to notice, perhaps, is the recourse to a folky, 'womanist' account of wisdom which is the collection of insights and *bon mots* out of songs, literature and the experience of the poor who are so busy with living and not, say, making money or preaching, that their conventions, the way they are, is the way things should be.[68] In all this there is much to value. But one would want to remain suspicious of certain features of the postmodern lifestyle: politicization in order to find my identity as something quite different from another group, the aestheticization of society in which tastes are what decides whether one belongs, or owes something to groupings,[69] the giving up on a search for absolute or progressively revealed truth or for 'the self' amongst a plurality of selves with a corresponding loss of focus. To write, as Middleton and Walsh do, that 'the culture of postmodernity

suffers from *something analogous* to a multiple personality disorder'
(my italics) is fair, but then to qualify it '... when we search for a
biblical analogy to multiphrenia, the demon-possessed man of
Mark 5 comes to mind', is both to overreact and to confuse the
category of cultures with that of individuals.

Postmodernism is obviously not about what lies ahead of us; it
is not the science of futurology. It is preoccupied with the present
moment. If anything it has been ahistorical, ripping styles and
theories out of their historical context, only concerned about
genealogies and traditons in order to show them as *false* indicators
of where we have come from and who in a sense we are.[70] While
'the Modern' can be said to start with the Renaissance or the
Enlightenment, or perhaps sometime between the two, it is not, as
some Christian interpreters have held, that the postmodern is a
phase or an epoque. Postmodernism is determinedly atemporal
and eschews the Hegelian myth of development; it is also
purposively non-eschatological. It is a view, perhaps from a grimy
vantage point of modernism in full career. Because things move
too fast now, there is no point in trying to keep up with them. As
in a rapid-flowing river, one can only go with the flow if one is to
remain conscious and feel at very least the exhilaration of the
process. It requires the sage, the drop-out, the fiction-writer more
than the prince, the leader, the saint. For this reason it has seemed
a bit more like the other face of modernism than a self-standing
movement. David Lyon has argued that, despite the failure of
plausibility structures to help people to live their lives when the
only thing one can be sure of is uncertainty, there is a possibility of
a hermeneutic of retrieval to get back to affirm that we are
historical creatures who view the past, not with an attitude which
values it only as markers on the road to where we are, nor with
nostalgia (postmodern), but as a place where the correlation of
words/beliefs and deeds can be pointed at.[71] We should not go on
allowing postmodern researchers and theorists to pontificate on
the present as if they were not part of it themselves, nor let them
persuade us that there is nothing one can say about the world that
bears much relation to how things are or have developed.[72]

While there is a lot in the idea that postmodernism revels in
that which is numbing, to talk of a large-scale philosophical

embracing of selfish desires at the expense of communal or global causes is only half the truth. To say there has been a mass escape from reality into hyper-reality (whatever that is – the authors, misinterpreting Baudrillard, seem to think it means satellite TV) is in danger of despising the reasons why people like their reality sweetened. *And it should be remembered that postmodernism, if it is anything, is a (admittedly not always consistent)* critique *of such things.* One thinks of the revolutionary credentials of Foucault in and beyond 1968, that Debord's *Society of the Spectacle* deplores the fact that humans are no longer defined by their 'having', let alone their 'being': we are what we passively *watch*. It is not self-evident that either modernism or postmodernism stands for individualist, predatory conquests, let alone 'ontological violence'. The proto-modernist, Pico della Mirandola insisted that to promote self-autonomy meant to promote responsibility.[73] In times of moral confusion and paralysis, Christopher Lasch is right to speak of the 'minimal self' which has contracted to a defensive core of disengagement, and a philosophy of anti-commitment. 'Such self-serving autonomy is perhaps better seen as the heroic dying breath of late modernity than as an honest postmodern confrontation with our ethical confusion.'[74] Narcissism is not to be condemned as if it were the only sin; as Lasch reminds us,[75] it is more to do with the sense of boundaries between people becoming threatened, thus with fragmentation of egos and identities rather than the puffing-up of them. Narcissism and the culture of narcissism may promote selfishness, but it is not selfishness as such.

Conclusion

What has been said is of a provisional nature. Like any new movement, so much is written on the subject that a review such as this can help by listing which books are 'key' on the grounds of profundity and clarity. I conclude this section by saying, simply, that even if postmodernism only points out areas of confusion and the church's need to do more praying, scriptural meditation and thinking, it will have been a worthwhile sparring partner. It reminds us of the fallenness of language and human beings, because each act and each statement is defined in terms of our own contexts, often unknown to our (dialogue) partner. It shows us the limits of reason alone and reminds us to seek identity in the certainties of faith – sacred history and our story – rather than in the 'eternal truths' of logic.

Contemporary evangelical responses

In their book *Truth is Stranger than it used to be*, J. R. Middleton and B. J. Walsh introduce postmodernism as being originally an architectural phenomenon. In truth, despite the occasional return to older styles and an even more pronounced eclecticism, in which jokes are made for the benefit of other architects who can tell their art deco from their art nouveau and at the expense of the general public, most architecture is material-driven, with its forms showing off to best advantage what is available, durable, affordable and functional.

> People's dreams have always been embodied in cities, buildings, and especially towers. This is as true of the tower of Babel as it is of the cathedral of Chartres, the Eiffel Tower, the pyramids at Giza, the Toronto CN tower or the World Trade Centre in New York City. Such towering accomplishments do not happen by accident. They begin with a dream of what could be, which is then progressively embodied in the concrete, historical actions of vast numbers of people.[76]

Obviously statements can be and are made, but the theory that buildings are there to express a philosophy, or its converse that they are there for the viewer and user to interpret, to project meaning on to, tend to fluctuate depending on whether one is talking to a maestro architect or to a town planner.

Part of the problem with Middleton and Walsh is their 'disaster movie' approach to semiotics and cultural history in development. They prefer biblical realism (or pessimism?) to Fukuyama's optimistic view of 'the end of history', that capitalist systems do more to keep world peace than the UN could, for example, that China needs Hong Kong too much to want to oppress it. For the world is rotten at the core, whatever the market indexes say. The next step from Derrida's view of writing as merely signifying other writing is the non-existence of values and concepts – implying that if there are no universals, since these (for example, 'human nature') are getting deconstructed in a process of denaturalization (according to L. Hutcheon), then we will eventually realize we have created the nightmare.[77] However, to blame postmodernists for this, is (1) like shooting one's wounded messenger, and (2) to deny that at least some postmodern 'fiddling while Rome burns' is actually an attempt to create some pleasant things.

Middleton and Walsh have lamented postmodernism's tendency to caricature the concept of story as a linear representation of beginnings, middles and endings. When it comes to the biblical story, is it simply there to get across a worldview that life is all about us ending up somewhere, or was it something that had to be told? After all, they argue, we need to know what we are part of in order to have consistent ethics. McIntyre had made this point in 1983 in *After Virtue*. Picking up on the arch-postmodernist Nietzsche's preference for aphorisms as also found in Buddhism, they observe: 'It is fascinating that the noncanonical Gnostic Gospels (like the Gospel of Thomas discovered at Nag Hammadi) are basically aphoristic in character, unlike the canonical Gospels which tell a definite story.'[78] This contrast is somewhat over-stated.

It is not so much ethical dissatisfaction with postmodernism than its perceived failure to consider the 'thatness' of God as the premise of our experience (and thus also of any discourse about God) that has exercised Alister McGrath.[79] He defends conservatism from the jibes of 'literalist', and contends that doctrinal affirmations such as Nicea were attempts 'to convey the experience through words'. Or for Calvin and Zwingli: '... rhetorical analogies and non-literal modes of discourse were ... a means by which a cognitive account may be given of experience'. Yet the point is, do we or can we convey *God* rather than just some ancient persons' ideas of him? J. A. T. Robinson's point, for all McGrath's caricaturing of it, was not that God in the traditional picture was an elderly man sitting in the sky, but that whatever God looked like he was thought of as dwelling 'somewhere' above the skies. McGrath himself is in danger of replacing the postliberal critique with a Romantic sort of evangelicalism which like Schleiermacher placed truth's origins in our feeling. Postliberalism as a form of theology is too ready to talk in terms of analogies with fictional narratives, linguistic grammatical coherence and 'private language'. This tends to a position where Christianity becomes a mere role-playing game, and McGrath cites Rowan Williams' astute observation that we can be too easily 'seduced to bypass the question of how it learns its own language'.[80] But is the answer to locate 'my God in my soul'? In fact, it is just this spatial understanding of God which David Wells has criticized as operative in the church. The Father's transcendence should not be understood as his remoteness, nor the Son's nearness as his chumminess – 'he lives within my heart'; both Father and Son are close and frighteningly holy, but never so close as to be thought of as 'inside' us – no, that is the place where God gives us the room to exercise faith. God is nowhere, but he knows us. One senses what Wells is getting at, but he seems all too quiet about the Holy Spirit: if *he* is not *in* us, he must be operative somewhere, somehow in the church, perhaps in quite a sporadic way. Wells' theology ends up looking 'postmodern' on account of its many gaps.[81] A similar comment can be made about D. A. Carson's book *The Gagging of God*:[82] it is good as far as it goes, but that distance is the wide cultural ocean of North America and pluralism as worked out in the spheres of religion and politics. Likewise it will not do, as Thomas Oden has done, to redefine a word such as postmodernism, so that by 'tough postmodernism' one means a refusal to allow one's agenda to be set by a modernism that is dead.

Among this brief sample of responses by evangelicals, the book *Christian Apologetics in the Postmodern World* gives a collection of essays written from and for a North American perspective, providing an up-to-date engagement. The book is well researched and richly annotated, evidencing a thorough engagement with the foe. American responses to postmodernism often have one fatal flaw; they are not so much about postmodernism at a theoretical level but are merely readings of culture tagged as 'postmodern'. Thus the Romantics' belief that mysteries could be seen through proper poetic language means that postmodernism is really Romanticism stripped of its pretensions. Just as Mark C. Taylor claimed to show how all the issues of postmodernism were already there in the Hegel-Kierkegaard debate, so Roger Lundin makes much of 'postmodernism's' being the successor of a line of romantics (Emerson–Thoreau–Stanley Fish, who saw value in nature and the manipulation of reality by the words of humans as *homo poeticus*) and pragmatists (Dewey–James–Rorty, who foster a society built on 'therapeutics'): it is important to subvert the categories of the culture which have grown up like weeds over more than a century. To try to use them, to pretend they are the flowers in our garden, is a disastrous strategy. 'The literary culture to which Hegel gave birth is one "which claims to have taken over and reshaped whatever is worth keeping in science, philosophy and religion – looking down on all from a higher standpoint" (quoting Rorty).'[83] I am not sure this is fair to Hegel or his followers – the literary culture of George Eliot (a good candidate for a Hegelian) invented the all-knowing Casaubon as a figure of *ridicule*; nor is 'omniscience' something of which Rorty would approve. Nor should postmodernism be equated simply with hedonism.

In a chapter by Nicola Creegan on 'Schleiermacher as Apologist: Reclaiming the Father of Modern Theology', there is an appeal to a pre-linguistic understanding of reality (and with it our creaturely sense of absolute dependence). I am not persuaded that Christian apologetics is well-served by trotting out one-liners as James Sire does that Rorty's 'there is no truth' is itself a truth claim, even if he can cite the example of Charles Taylor's critique of Rorty in doing so. If Christians are to do apologetics which is going to convince, they are going to have to shift the burden of proof. Rorty could easily retort: 'Well, I don't know if my ideas are true, but the strength of your belief in yours does not make them any more true.'[84] The figure of Nietzsche as the poet who does seem to have reinvented a lot and yet who is, as one on his way to insanity – which for Hans Küng vitiated much of his writing's value – a madman, is pivotal to the discussion: one senses the authors feeling their way to deal with him. Like Nietzsche, the church has stories to tell; but these are non-fictional, one hopes. Too often the dialogue partners referred to are vulnerable people such as college students searching for something, rather than the doughtier opponent at the same level of seniority as the writer. It is heartening perhaps when Philip Kenneson contends that to insist that truth is objective as a view from nowhere is no better than relativism – a view from each place.[85] However, the pragmatism which is not hedonistic is not really very satisfactory: 'the church has a word to speak to the world, not because it has a message that is objectively true, a message which could be separated from the embodied message that the church always is'. *Jesus is Lord* is not proven by anything other than discipleship, for this side of heaven, any proofs rest at the level of opinions. Wittgenstein is the obvious influence on Kenneson here.

Culture and Value[86] is a work from which the evangelical Tony Thiselton has drawn inspiration for a realist account of truth (against its postmodern sceptics). Specifically against Rorty's interpretation he argues that Wittgenstein was a realist who believed that our thoughts and beliefs corresponded to states of being (famously, we express pain when we feel it). Moreover, the process between reality and text is not just one way, but texts can actually become part of reality and influence it. The whole point of reading texts is not to find ourselves in them but, as Dilthey put it, to be brought out of ourselves: 'authentic transformation, as against mere psychological reaction, presupposes disclosure that certain states of affairs are the case'.[87] Or, as Ricoeur put it, to see one's self-narrative as part of a larger narrative, of purposes which transcend the self. However, the word 'transcend' has to be watched, and postmodernism is rightly suspicious of any totalizing vision which would subjugate our personal identity to a flow; yet Thiselton is right (in opposing Don Cupitt) that the fact of pluralism does not entail that each and every person has a different view of the world.

A trinitarian theology should do much to safeguard 'difference' without going to the extreme of believing that God has no decided will on anything. The Trinity, according to Colin Gunton, is 'an ineffable cycle of being, intelligence and communicative Life, Love and Action'.[88] The cross is a place of the power of love active in the world. Yet too often in recent theology trinity is reduced to social psychology writ large; there is too much reliance on Christology as confirming the humanity of God.

The anti-foundationalism of the New Yale theology represented by Nancy Murphy means that theological talk, drawn from
the strange world of the Bible does not have to correspond to
much that we know in the world.[89] The biblical narratives speak of
spiritual realities and refer to things beyond human ken. Yet does
that accord with the message of the incarnation – that God's
world at the very least intersects with our world – which is meant
to be the exegete's controlling hermeneutic?[90] One could argue
that the world as we see it is no reliable judge of what might pass
for true or false in revealed Christianity – not only are we fallen,
the world as it is without God's perfection of it is illusory. This
is to avoid apologetics which includes the attempt to 'translate'
everything; it is like putting off learning a foreign language with
which to communicate in order to spend more time practising the
grammar of our mother-tongue. 'Lindbeck calls a religion ontologically true if it seems to conform the adherents in the various
dimensions of their lives to what is ultimately real.'[91]

True, Christianity is about doing, but it is also about what has
been done (and is continuing here and now in an accumulation of
God's action in the world pivoted on his self-revelation in Christ).
In Kevin Hart's words:

> Christianity involves radical conversion, to be sure, but how would
> one know in what way to change one's life if it were not for some
> doctrinal content? Furthermore, if doctrine helps one to change
> one's life for the better it cannot be useless; and no doctrine is
> likely to persuade one to change one's life unless it be thought in
> some sense sound. Wittgenstein could rightly argue that there is no
> positive link between the Christian faith and *totalised* doctrines. But
> he is wrong to suggest that there is a pure form of Christianity
> untouched by doctrine and unmotivated by a will to totalise.[92]

The motto of Wittgenstein and Teresa of Avila: 'The less I
understand this, the more I believe it and the greater the devotion
it arouses in me' is not to be taken 'neat'; for Teresa it was
modified by Bernard of Clairvaux's maxim: 'love is a form of
knowledge'. And even mystical visions have content, as Stephen
Katz seems to have shown, *contra* William James.[93]

Postmodern theologies

Don Cupitt

According to Cupitt, rather than making bold claims for the human species such as our linguisticality or our rational autonomy, theologians should give up their pretences and humans surrender their pretensions. Whereas some like Eugen Drewermann want to elevate animals to the exaltation of feeling creatures,[94] Cupitt would gently let the human race down to where it can play. He has no time for the idealist spiritualization of matter. There can be meaning to our pain and no loss of so-called dignity to understand that it is part of our contribution to the natural and biological processes. Cupitt has repeated the idea that humans invented religion to keep us from fear, much as our ancestors used a campfire in a cave. The denial that there is such a thing as loss is a bit like saying that we do not have to feel the cold, while holding that religion is just to make us feel better, is a bit like thinking that because it works it cannot be true. And as Gerard Loughlin says more specifically about the Christian religion, 'Yes. But why *this* story?' The orthodox Christian concern is 'not so much with the fictionality of the (biblical) world, as with the particular world fictioned'.[95]

Yet what about the language that issues from our unconscious drives, and in that, our philosophy and theology? Cupitt responds:

> The disorder of the world and of the delirious Unconscious always comes first, but philosophy cannot deal with it. That means that our doctrine of signs ... has to be a doctrine of them as we meet them ordered in language.[96]

We are thus culturally formed through the signs which come from the unconscious, and we do not shape ourselves so much by our thinking (*contra* Descartes) but by our unreflective acceptance of signs as being 'right' or having 'fit'. Cupitt paints a very passive picture of people as caught up in games, as using a limited stock of language and ideas;[97] to use the computer metaphor, we are but screens across which flash images and phrases. It is sanity to go with the flow, since 'there's nothing structurally wrong with the human condition'.[98] The only freedom we really have is to *know* that we form ourselves so little.[99]

Cupitt's reading of the Western tradition has an odd ring about it:[100]

> When I study Western writers such as Augustine, Luther, Kierkegaard and Heidegger, I am studying a literary tradition. These writers did not look at something out there called the human condition and then make up descriptive sentences about it. What happened was that each of them first read his predecessors and then added a new text continuing the tradition.[101]

It would, however, make more sense to say, at least for the first three (and it is surely tantalizing why Cupitt completes the trajectory with Heidegger and not Barth), that each of them read his Bible in the light of their own radical experience and corrected the tradition. Ironically, Cupitt seeks to offer something much bolder than a mere reheating of old tired ideas. His aim is to 'reinvent metaphysics, at least in the very cautious sense of sketching the view of the world and the human condition which a reasonable person might hold. Somebody needs to say what it might be "to see life steadily as to see it whole" today'.[102] By being 'only human', Christians might change the world; by being artistic and creative (that is, going with the flow of one's created gifts and cutting out the problem of redemption), there is somehow salvation. According to Stephen Williams in his fine analysis, Cupitt's vision is 'primitive in a basal rejection of that which is or is suspected to be, or what is thought may be the actual case – namely that God is and God judges'.[103]

Jean-Luc Marion

The Derridean account of the world is that we have to create our own meaning; it has never been and is never given to humans. That everything outside us is reducible to a chaos which we have to push back, is, as John Milbank has observed, a sad account of transcendence. We should welcome the resistance to the 'analogy of being' with which theologians have tried to tame God, making him in our likeness, but not if it means that God beyond being is a

God who does not exist, while we look anywhere but humanity for the causes of darkness. Kevin Hart insists on the need for a negative theology to correct and supplement the penchant which theologically minded human beings have for making God in their own image. In the early pages of his book *The Trespass of the Sign*, he appears a little unsure whether there could ever have been (prelapsarian) immediate knowledge of God; the Augustinian view of a fall from a high paradise suggests so. But we need to wonder whether in fact the 'failure to observe the proper limits assigned by man to God', as taken by Hart from Dante,[104] reveals that Adam's problem was not one of idolatry: the sign was not the tree but the commandment not to eat thereof.[105] The punishment was that signs no longer mediated knowledge of God's presence wholly, but only partly; difference (to use Hegelian terminology) creeps in. Many philosophers have agreed on a fall – that the state we are in is somehow less: 'Derrida takes the thought of the fall from the primordial to the derivative to be philosophy's greatest sin.'[106] There is no presence behind – temporally, ontologically, logically – our sign-system. Like a signature on a cheque, signs indicate an absence of God in the world and do not *prove* that there is someone who could re-sign them exactly the same; for the moment of cashing the cheque he is not around. Likewise Derrida prefers to speak of texts, for books connote exclusion, finality, a unification of all apparent differences, a sense of the 'God's eye-view', any desire for totality.[107] To be trying to say something is guilty of realizing that words do not obey but run riot, as Barthes famously decreed: 'a text is not a line of words releasing a single "theological" meaning (the message of the Author-God) but a multi-dimensional space in which a variety of writings, none of them original, blend and clash'.[108]

In this context, Jean-Luc Marion (influenced by the Jewish philosopher Levinas) has written of God as linked to us by reason of causality alone – we are like him as much as we are the product of his giving; but God as the one who gives being is then outside being, despite the arguments of, for example, Charles Winquist.[109] In other words, there is no way back to God through signs in the world, the human soul or even in Scripture. 'G⊗d' (the crossed-out 'o' reminds us that we are not to think of God with all the conceptual baggage we in the West have – that is why there is so much unbelief) is identified with goodness but is not part of being. This priority of the good over the *ens* is found in Origen, Pseudo-Dionysius but not, unfortunately, in Thomas or Scotus. In fact, as Von Balthasar lamented, for the last of these, 'God' becomes swallowed up in being and is thus not personally related to us. Heidegger had the right idea in trying to separate the God of faith from the divinity of the philosophers; after all, did not Pascal, that patron saint of European Protestantism, affirm the same thing?[110] Yet the best that Marion and Heidegger can offer is a truce (an uneasy one) between the two 'orders'. The point is more than just faith's shaming philosophy into foolishness and silence – as if that were possible! – but that 'faith seeking understanding through proclamation' disarms rival accounts of Being and reshapes Being into Ontology and existence. It is in the realm of the latter (and not in the abstractions of 'ontology') that God is the particular one who reveals himself as crucified. This sounds like the Rahnerian principle that there is essentially nothing more to God than the one he has revealed himself as.[111] But to lean too heavily that way seems to make God into a role-player, and one who cannot be creator, sustainer, victim, redeemer, and much else besides at once. Marion rightly argues that the Greek fathers never claimed that *ho ōn* from Exodus 3:14 might define the essence of God as such.[112] We do have a definition at 1 John 4:8 – 'God is love' and yet that need not be confined to God's love for the world, as Marion seems to, but also surely his *agape* in and for himself.

And yet there is a sense in which postmodern theology or atheology teaches us to take theology less seriously. Marion's quest is to do this, in order that the sacramental and ethical, that is, the down-to-earth God, may speak to us, once we have been freed from our obsession with metaphysics. Marion only begins to have something constructive to say once he gets on to practical theology. In other words, as with Emmanuel Levinas, there is an attempt to de-Hellenize thinking and theology. Yet the positing of a non-metaphysical God as the Other over against 'myself' has led to Derrida's remark that this plays into the Hegelian trap: that which is other becomes the imprint of the Same, making up a totality like a mould and clay. For as we exalt and worship the Other, we are always imposing our view on them, even doing violence to them by projecting our ideals on to them.[113] Instead, God's transcendence as something which is independent of the human 'myself' should not be an embarrassment to theologians. To speak of God as other is helpful in ethics, but not in theological foundations.

John Milbank

This is not the place to attempt to critique Milbank's massive *Theology and Social Theory*;[114] not only is it difficult, it is primarily a work of social and ethical theory. Only occasionally does it deal directly with primarily theological matters, such as the tenth chapter entitled 'Ontological Violence'. Milbank resists the idea that ultimately all is chaotic as being a hopeless and ultimately fascist view of reality, a worldview for life's destroyers. Unlike Kant's view, humans do not carry around a self-correcting chip leading them to behave like gods; against this, for Nietzsche and Foucault: 'no universals are ascribed to human society save one: that it is always a field of warfare'. Against this nihilism, Milbank comments fairly enough that pagan societies were places where the strong defended the weak because that was part of their strength: morality is not necessarily an invention of the weak as Nietzsche claimed. Yet Nietzsche acknowledged that the sacrifice of the strong was understood merely as the paying off of a debt to ancestors for giving them such a privileged position. Christianity, however, gave this turn to weakness and inwardness and beyond-ness: while appearing to renounce power, it got people where they were weakest through repression and law codes, and made way for Reason as the powerful one. Christianity, however, is 'a creed which rigorously excludes all violence from its picture of the original, intended, and final state of the cosmos';[115] love need not be charity's selfish coercion (will-to-power) to make the other into the same, but can be a letting be of differences. Christian asceticism is for something, not an end in itself, but Christian spirituality means to have one's desires in the service of better ends than comfort or peace of mind. It is not handing over control to another and thus leading to a tortured soul pulled apart by external dictates, but leads to self-realization. In this we should not talk about 'depth' but about height: 'The depth that can be reported does not really arise from diving expeditions into the soul, but on the contrary, from an indefinite hermeneutic endeavour which constantly delivers new judgements upon one's external attitudes and emotions.'[116] Likewise Christian sex is about mutuality, not about bodily functions (Stoic approach). Milbank now feels the need to reinforce ethics with a medieval Augustinian-Pseudo-Dionysian ontology wherein 'the Christian equation of goodness, truth and beauty with Being itself, combined with the introduction of the relational, productive and responsive into the Godhead' leads to a view of God's eternal victory as universal and there being no heavenly perfection into which souls have to somehow escape. For our God is 'the Platonic Good, reinterpreted by Christianity as identical with being'. This sets up the 'possibility of reading reality as of itself peaceful'.[117] But does not Heidegger's pessimistic view (which one could call the intology which underpins Nietzchean ethics) have the benefit of sober realism? Even if he shockingly allowed humans to defer responsibility for their state to the way things are, the 'throwness' (*Geworfenheit*), the atmosphere of anxiety in our existence, was this any worse than Milbank's refusal to see that things are well within the realms of human possibilities at their best? When he does finally get round to dealing with Christology, it quickly collapses into ecclesiology.[118] There is also a liberal's complete lack of sympathy with any notion of divine judgment remaining over: all judgment is self-judgment, since that is what God did.[119] But if there is too much difference and no order in reality, not even a cancelling out of negatives, as Deleuze insists, then there can be only violence, flux and meaninglessness.[120] Milbank does us a service in observing this.

A recent article has symptoms of the strengths and weaknesses when it comes to the whole issue of grace and mutuality. In it Milbank has claimed that what God did in creation cannot be described as a *gift* since there was no-one around to receive what he was making.[121] However, he continues, in the incarnation, God's sending his Son *can* be called a gift – someone is there to receive it, and we can say God gives of himself, just as when we give someone something which costs us, we are giving of ourself. The gift was acceptable to the church as represented by Mary.

Yet I have problems with this: was Mary not made an offer she could not refuse? Read Luke 1. (It is analogically reminiscent of a princess of a lower class being asked by a king to accept his hand.) Also, I think one *can* argue that there was a gift in creation. God's gifts do not have to be exactly like our gifts; it could lack certain details and still be one. Thus Milbank thinks a gift does not have to have a generous intention to qualify as a gift, but it must have a recipient. Yes, perhaps in legal terms, strictly, but it is harder to distinguish a gift from a bribe when there is evidence that there was no generosity involved. And anyway we are talking of God's giving. Why need there be someone to accept the gift; why cannot the gift create the recipient? Or could we not say that in creating, God both makes us exist and adds to this all the blessings of being human as gifts? God is pure *agape*, and unlike ourselves for whom the line between moral generosity and immoral bribe or 'manipulation' is often fine. There is no necessity in God and we should not, as Milbank is in danger of doing, make him according to our image, which includes our need to have something in return. We are rather to be shaped by the perfection that he is, but admit that we are not like him. The model of the Trinity as perichoretic, in which the Persons pour themselves into each other is not so much like a fountain which pours itself into the pond of the world only to be eventually recycled. Milbank is right to say that such an all-embracing God, a totally giving good God would smother his creation. Christian love is not spontaneous but is a response to his love (1 John 4:10f.) and follows a pause and involves not the giving back of the same.[122]

North American theologies

One way out of rationalistic theology is the negative theology of the mystics.[123] The other is narrative theology. For Christian orthodoxy this involves propositions which refer back to events, unlike Islam where the words speak to the 'church' situation as commands, or Hinduism. Hans Frei lamented the fact that Christian theology accepted a dichotomy between an objective (religion looked at as a response to doctrinal statements which can be shown to be coherent, intelligible, correspondent) and an experiential (religion as articulation of each person's or each community's consciousness) approach, although that 'how to become a Christian' must be – not existentially, but theologically – subordinate to the *what* of Christianity'.[124] His solution seems to be that we should do our Bible reading in order to form our doctrine. There must be a literal reading so that the Bible speaks to us on its own terms, not on those of our allegorical interpretations built around what we think God to be – and then an application of it to our 'non-religious' lives.[125] (Frei challenges a very narrow definition of 'religious' as manifested by D. Z. Phillips' suggestion that prayer to the Virgin Mary is either superstition *or* is about admiration of the virtues she embodies.)[126]

As we have seen, Frei's colleague George Lindbeck states that doctrine is the language Christians use to shape reality, and its purpose is to remind us that there is *more* to reality than *Hamlet's* Horatio's philosophy would allow. Nancy Murphy sees this as a 'foundation hanging from the balcony'; one's epistemology depends on one's theology (presumably an epistemology which tries to correspond to the content of faith – a theological 'objectivism' which T. F. Torrance has long argued for, against Hegel's more 'postmodern' idea that what something is, depends in large measure on how we approach it).[127]

> The postmodern positions of holism in epistemology and meaning
> as use are themselves closely related. In adjusting our network of
> beliefs to fit the world, we may change particular beliefs about the
> world, but we may also adjust meanings in order to restore
> consistency.[128]

The best doctrines will be the ones which survive over time in this process of fit, with, it should be hoped, some amount of the Bible's coming to impress itself on life. There may be some sense in viewing the development of doctrine, and more particularly the acceptance of 'new' doctrines, a bit like classics of literature or music – the ones which survive continue to scratch where the majority of people itch, but just how is this to be done? Murphy (as with Lindbeck)[129] does not tell us. A church (the Roman

Catholic) known for its conservatism also wanted to recognize that the number of doctrines could be added to – the essential genius of Newman's *Essay on the Development of Doctrine* was one of adding things to cancel out the possibility of more wayward accretions becoming established.[130] Each generation sees things in Scripture that the previous one did not – with calamitous consequences perhaps – choose to see. But one would hardly call that (re-)discovering doctrines in the way that according to Newman the church has articulated the validity of heretical baptism, justification, the canon of Scripture, the sinlessness of the Virgin Mary, the Trinity, the eucharistic sacrifice.[131]

Or do we, at the end of the second millennium, find a longing to get away from theology and rest with ethics, so that we find more natural sympathy (albeit accompanied by some spiritual revulsion) with the words of Gordon Kaufman?

> The massive evils experienced in the twentieth century ... present overpowering counter-evidence to the myth of the God who cares for each person in even the tiniest details of life ... When one adds to these basic problems of credibility the growing awareness that Christianity itself, including its way of symbolizing the human and the world, may be an important root of some of the evils of modernity – western (and Christian) imperialism, certainly partly produced by the powerful sense in the Christian faith of a unique divine authorization guaranteeing the superiority of Christianity over other religions (and cultures).[132]

Kaufman removes much of God's transcendence – at best he is a symbol to focus and harmonize values and to relativize some of our principles. If God is anything, he is the creative 'humanizing' process of the cosmos.[133] In North America there is a more modish, therefore more acceptable, concept of God as lacking transcendent qualities. 'Process Theologians' (for example, David Ray Griffin) represent God and the world as needing each other to the same degree, and the followers of Tillich over-familiarize God as the Ground underneath us.

Much of North American 'postmodernist' theology streams more from Tillich than direct European influences. God is part of reality, of being, and therefore, like the rest of what is, changeable. Tillich himself is not postmodern in that he believes there are common organizing structures built into reality: these are more than just the laws of physics. 'It is the structure which makes reality a whole and therefore a potential object of knowledge. Inquiring into the nature of reality as such means inquiring into those structures, categories and concepts which are presupposed in the cognitive encounter with every realm of reality.'[134] Theology must always be ready to translate into the language of experience, since this is what the Bible does; but it must also be committed to experience the Logos who is behind the logos as the answer to matters of universal concern.[135] We cannot get to the order of being without our concepts: therefore our concepts do shape our reality.

Tillich presupposes ontological concepts (for example, individuality and universality, dynamics and form, freedom and destiny) but we can see from his list that these are only the kind of things which come before epistemological concepts (for example, the categories of time, space, causality and substance) because they have been handed down from other knowing agents' *experience*. One might feel it more fitting if the ontological and the epistemological concepts were exchanged. Unsurprisingly, Tillich concludes:

> ... it is the finitude of being which drives us to the question of God. The doctrine of man is the main entrance for ontology and the main point of reference for theology, the structure of a being which had history underlies all historical changes [to this human being].[136]

The spirit of radical Hegelianism is seen here, but it would reject Foucault's notion that the human being is too much just a figment of our imagination or scholarship. Of course, it would be too naïve to say that because humans still eat, drink, sleep, copulate and die in ways different from (other) animals, that this means the humans have got some sort of special programming that reflects God's purposes and therefore nature. Yet Tillich confidently asserts selfhood as a given, our ability to know the world that separates us from it in the glory of possible transcendence. In the

Hegelian manner we participate as we are shaped by a cosmic mind which thinks in and through history. Just as Hegel was the last philosopher of modernity, Tillich is one of the last 'modernist' theologians, and stands at the gateway to postmodern theology. Thus the step from Tillich to postmodern (a)theologies is easily taken: Mark C. Taylor summarizes: 'While the modern form of the death of God comes to its expression in humanistic atheism, the postmodern form points forward toward a posthumanistic a/theology.'[137]

> In the particular instance of the proofs of God's existence, understanding attempts to argue from contingent to necessary being, from finite to infinite design, or from the thought of God to the being of God ... What analytic understanding so sharply separates, it cannot effectively re-unite. The abyss between the defined oppositions remains so vast that it can be crossed only by a blind leap of faith.[138]

Thus it perhaps is necessary for postmodern theologians to speak of cause (*Grund*) rather than reason (*Vernunft*) for belief.[139] Our sacred existence is that ground. God-world is such a strong opposition that to cross it we need to go against the grain and deconstruct it; to make humans appear god-like by a modernist projection leads to the disappearance of the self in the light of the death of God (whereas Hegel [or Tillich?] used God as a mirror to help us see ourselves, inverting what Augustine had set up). The way to a dead God is by a dead self, by the contradiction of what is commonplace.[140]

The gap between God and humans had already been crossed in the work of Whitehead where the incarnation is a continuation of God's making the world out of himself. God may be unhappy in his creation which is part of him but that does not mean he is weak: he is still able to transform situations, according to his own processes.[141] The cross stands for something more eternal than a necessary moment in time in which God was instantly reconciled to man. God's omniscience requires his pardoning of all in advance which is one step beyond the Hegelian view that God *chose* to obligate himself to the world. As with much of Moltmann, there are more than hints of slightly sophisticated versions of 'New Age' thinking in which scientific models are made to serve anti-technological ends.

Thomas J. J. Altizer in his *Genesis and Apocalypse* denounces Tillich as one of an unholy trinity: 'witness the failure in our own time of Barth, Tillich and Rahner to incorporate the apocalyptic or eschatological ground of an original Christianity' which is defined as a thinking about totality. Altizer's vision of totality is a bit disconcerting to the postmodern reader. Although he means 'non-exclusivism', it keeps sounding like 'totalitarianism'.[142] Altizer sometimes has a 'Buddhist' ring; but it is a non-confessional preference for literature as truer theology which drives him: Joyce's 'Here Comes Everybody' character in *Finnegans Wake*. That book he regards as the continuation and (postmodernly!) the end of the modern tradition, inaugurated by Dante, of a voyage into nothingness.[143] For Altizer the boundary between art and life is very finely drawn.

It is also interesting that Dante is decontextualized, as he has often been, with his *Inferno* being decontextualized from its place in the whole *Commedia*. Altizer's vision is of an Old Testament God without the New Testament perspective – a God who pours himself out in history so that the limits between God and creature no longer exist or are shown to have never existed. In God's death history begins, for God becomes part of history as soon as he begins to pour himself out into it. From then on, there is no going back to a pure heavenly source – and this is what the cross reminds us. No, there is only an exciting ride into the ever-changing world with an ever-changing God. The crucifixion is where, as Blake suggested, and Hegel was the first to realize, God rids himself of his negativity (Altizer writes of Christ 'totally guilty in his divinity' – not just his humanity), his 'Satan'; but God will continue to do this, as he allows evil which guarantees our free choice and any meaningful selfless love. The resurrection is actually the resurrection of death, not its abolition – for that is reserved until after the judgment which is itself the peak of God's annihilation.[144] There is no eternal presence to escape into; it is our task to follow God through and into history, assured that his own dying means that our dying becomes a totalizing vision in

which all that was, is and shall be is going to be redeemed.[145] This
kind of rhetoric of ultimate triumph and universalizing seems
hardly postmodernist, until we realize that it is all about bringing
God down to the scale not of human dignity but of human death,
decay and non-being as the universal ground-reality.

Resources for a thorough response

Orthodoxy and the Roman Catholic return to the Fathers
One way of responding to the philosophical challenges of
postmodernity is to draw on the ontologies and philosophical
concepts worked out in theological argument and controversy.[146]
Thus, as Christ's natures were of a separate category from his
person, so too in all humans our person is what we have to grow
in, on top of or in spite of our nature. Then there is a liturgical
model which appropriates the jargon of semiotics but refills it with
biblico-theological content. While the theology of von Balthasar
may seem vulnerable on the grounds of conservatism of a peculiar
mix (for example, sexism),[147] hyper-intellectualism, and an
oppressively stifling Mariology, which has been associated with
anti-Semitism even in this century, nevertheless it is a case of
theology seeking to succour philosophy where its younger sibling
is too weak, notably in the realm of aesthetics. To recognize
beauty is a counter-blast to nihilism which is so prevalent. God's
salvation offers transfiguration into a spiritual, unseen but reveal-
able beauty which the created beauties give us a tantalizing
intimation of. Now this is as old as Neoplatonism, but von
Balthasar wants to show how biblical it can be, and also how
Christocentric. God is not 'other' in the sense of his being beyond
us but as the countenances of countenances is all and more of
what we could ever be; his otherness is defined by his wholly
goodness and the paradox should drive us to prayer, and keep us
inspired to be disciples.

Protestant return through Barth to the Reformation
An alternative possibility is to see theology as conceived best
where it is other to the wisdom of the world, such that, for

example, a Reformation theology is the appropriate theology for today. This can be found to a certain extent in Jüngel and yet more explicitly in Oswald Bayer.[148] For the latter, God the Word is most at home in the material, historical world and not in spiritual things, as modernist dualisms have conspired to keep him. The contribution of Pannenberg is criticized as trying to be a science of God as if God could be read as an infinite form of the finite rather than as about 'sinful humans and justifying God' on which all other doctrine, cosmological to the poltical, even Christo-logical, are predicated.[149] It must be existentially treated, never as a given but at any given minute only existentially/subjectively true. Yet at once comes Nietzsche's mocking echo: 'God is everywhere' means 'God is nowhere'.

In a similar way, Eberhard Jüngel likes to speak of God as love:

> In this respect the faith distinguishes between God and humans. It does this in support of the union of God and humans which does not destroy the distinction, a union which one had therefore better not call *mystical union*. It orientates itself then to Jesus Christ to whom the Scripture 'God is love' owes its truth. For Jesus Christ is that Human in whom God has defined himself as human. It is thus faith in the humanity of God which proves the identity of God and love ... in the death of Jesus Christ God is the end of our temporal being beyond us in that sense. Simply to go on faith is to keep God and humans too far apart.[150]

There is an ontology and thus necessarily an eschatology of love; the dead God of Nietzsche is, as with Luther, referred to the cross which is not the final, but the penultimate word. Nietzsche has forgotten that life without God is heartache and loss; the gospel of God's suffering is not, in its absurdity (so Nietzsche) a denial of pain, but an outrage and at the same time, evidence of the humanity of God.[151] Barth had already written that Heidegger and Sartre failed to reckon with the true God, but that at least they realized, unlike Leibniz or Schleiermacher, 'that nothingness is really present and at work'.[152] Barth in calling evil 'nothingness' was far from dismissive of it; it was a realization of the pervasiveness of all that is opposed to God: 'It assails us with

irresistible power as we exist, and we exist as we are propelled by it
into the world like a projectile.' The problem is that the proud *ego
cogito*, with its pretence that it can see and understand all, remains;
their viewpoint is obscured, so that Barth concludes:

> It is futile to deny that what the existentialists (and we might add,
> postmodernists or any who would give a holistic account of reality
> without reference to the biblical insights) encounter and objectively
> perceive is real nothingness. Yet it must be stated most emphatically
> that seeing they do not really see. What they see, describe and
> proclaim is not real nothingness, just as the God whom, denying or
> not denying, they ignore and replace by surrogates is not the real
> God.[153]

Jüngel, without using specific terminology, accuses Pannenberg of
coming close to what could be labelled 'modernist failings', the
wish to do theology through the history of Christian thought so
that our view of God is encyclopaedic and panoramic;[154] it is also
in danger of being Darwinian – that Christianity is the survivor of
battles with other religions. Pannenberg *could* be classified as a
modernist; or at least tends towards that classification as much as
Jüngel does to the tag 'postmodernist'. His logic sometimes seems
in danger of exploding as it tries to confront mystery. God is
Father and Jesus points to him; the Son who is eternal is only in
the sense of God the Father having so decided. 'In his extreme
humiliation, in his acceptance of death, Jesus took upon himself
the ultimate consequence of his self-distinction from the Father
and precisely in so doing showed himself to be the Son of the
Father.'[155] But if the self-distinction is just a recognition of a
distinction that is there, what choice did he have? He could have
hardly escaped the Father's will. The whole point of Gethsemane
and the possibility of angelic deliverance is that he is on a par with
the Father (Matthew 26:53). To say that the history of religions
is really a fight between God's own Being/*Sein* and his *Dasein*/
manifestations? – does this not ultimately reduce 'God' to earthly
roots, perhaps even a pantheism?

Pannenberg is right to say that the content of faith comes
before faith as act: the *fides quae creditur* before the *fides qua creditur*.

However, Jüngel instances further Pannenberg's theoretical version of Christianity as answerable to the (whims of) the natural, rational(?) religious sense of humans, and the lack of an existential dimension in which God and faith might be seen as coming close together so that a believer might find herself and her world placed in God (*lokalisiert*). Also he objects to Pannenberg's dislike of metaphorical theology, of myth and anthropomorphic tendencies such as thinking that God has a place. If Jüngel sees Christianity too much as an art (that is, painting pictures which will help us to understand at the level of emotion and will as well as cognitively), Pannenberg sees it as a science.

Pannenberg did reply that the reason he spent less time dealing with modern existential issues and more on the history of Christian doctrine was because a systematic theology is not a sermon, and because truth is only formulated through history.[156]

Pannenberg certainly talks about God's being open to the world, not in the sense that God can change or be changed, but that his eventual victory can be doubted. But is this the worst thing that can happen to God – that his eventual victory be doubted? The cross is just a fleeting set-back on the road to eventual assured victory. The Spirit acts like a safety-net for the Son of God on the cross.[157] Pannenberg's theology and its various imitations in North America need at least the critique of the more 'postmodern' theologies such as Jüngel's.

Philosophical resources

It is perhaps the most distinguishing, if not distinguished, mark of postmodern theology that its conversation partners are less likely to be other theologians or Scripture or tradition and its creeds, and so on, but great philosophers. These 'sources' are scoured for places where they opine on God or the Christian religion. Out of fifteen contributors to the recent book *Post-Secular Philosophy: Between philosophy and theology*[158] about half are teaching in religion or theology faculties, but of all the fifteen objects of their interest, only one of them (Marion) could be called a theologian. It is not necessarily a strength that for instance Barth gets 'reduced' to Hegel plus Kierkegaard with a theological dressing; nor is the fixation with names at the expense of themes. The heady stuff of

theology is reduced to metaphysics and ethics, and there seems
little place for defining orthodoxy, let alone 'biblical theology'. But
some of those working within the craft of philosophy might
indeed have useful insights for theologians to learn.

Ricoeur

A strong candidate for a Protestant who has assessed contemporary philosophy and who has taken sides (at least at times)
according to a biblically informed mind is Paul Ricoeur. His
experiment has interested and stimulated many in the theological
world, from before his collaboration with Jüngel and then with
David Tracy up to a time of being seen as a Christian philosopher
worthy of serious imitation.[159] He provides a nice corrective to
Frei's 'immanentist' obsession with the 'person' of Christ, that is,
his outward actions, as comprising the character identity of
Jesus.[160] Ricoeur insists that the Bible at once supplies a truth
which aims to stimulate a response at the level of emotions. This
means that he holds Scripture's truth as powerful; yet one
drawback of his view of divine communication is that even God
appears to be trapped inside language (of a text which takes on a
life of its own) at times.[161] To speak of 'the radical externality of
evil';[162] the self as mediated and created by the presence of evil as
a 'given' carries with it a respect for the Augustinian interpretation
of Genesis as taking sin seriously (even though Ricoeur does not
believe that the fall 'happened' one moment in time). For Ricoeur
we are therefore in need of outside aid. On the other hand, there is
freedom to reflect and choose a path: 'chance is changed into
destiny through our continuous acts of choice'.[163] The antinomy,
as Henri Blocher has recently noted, is not illuminated by
Ricoeur.[164] Yet, as Jüngel would also affirm, Ricoeur adds that
there needs to be a place for human beings to be receivers of
meaning as well as makers of it through use of their critical
faculties.

According to John Milbank, in reliance on the work of René
Girard, Christianity is defined as the fundamental opposition to
the ontology of violence. Ricoeur too concurs that Christianity has
no place for sacrifice as traditionally understood. As illustrated by
the theology of the Second Isaiah, Christ was offering a life not a

death. This is a way of avoiding seeing the cross and the incarnation as having their agenda set by evil. What Christ did was to answer a negative with a positive. Bataille, for example, had argued that Christianity is parasitical on evil: 'the very violence without which the divinity could not have torn itself away from the order of things is rejected as being something which must cease'; while, 'the divinity remains divine only through that which it condemns'.[165] But it is part of postmodern Christian theology to avoid such difficult doctrine as the traditional views of the atonement. However, something may be lost in the process.

At a more general level, on ethics which shares much common ground with the doctrine of God (his nature, being – popular in postmodern theology), Ricoeur maintains:

> It must first be said that the schema of question and answer does not hold between philosophy and biblical faith ... biblical faith adds nothing to the predicates 'good' and 'obligatory' as these are applied to action. Biblical *agape* belongs to an economy of the gift, possessing a meta-ethical character, which makes one say that there is no such thing as a Christian morality, except perhaps at the level of the history of *mentalities*, but a common morality that biblical faith places in a new perspective, in which love is tied to the 'naming of God'.[166]

Perhaps, but does not the New Testament tie God to the naming of 'good' (Matthew 19:17)? There are more than a few places where Ricoeur veers away from an orthodox understanding, presumably on the grounds that where the talk is of the human realm, there are certain things which if philosophically unsound (for example, a temporal beginning to creation and evil) or if the Christian God comes into contact with a world that has changed, he too has to operate on its terms to be credible. Thus the death of Jesus is the death of Kant's perfect man, the resurrection of Jesus is the same thing as the origin of the church, eternal life is living on in others and God's memory. It is Abelardian theory run riot. The brief statements on these matters in *La critique et la conviction* should perhaps not be taken as Ricoeur's final word on these matters, but an attempt to bring the Bible and philosophy close together without the interference of dogmatic theology, despite many valuable insights on the nature of the Bible and exegetical observations, seems to leave philosophy as mistress of all.

Habermas

Another response to postmodernism is found in theological appropriation of the work of Jürgen Habermas. His attempt to promote the possibility of rational decision-making was a recognition, during the turbulent days of the 1960s, of the necessity of reflection to resist the irrationality let loose by despair about modernity's progress. Behind this of course was the holocaust, and the reflections of the Frankfurt school, most famously Adorno's 'negative dialectics' (suspicion of all that is affirmative of the world) and Marcuse's principle of recognition of suffering as the guiding principle in all ethical debate. To this 'negative dialectics' Habermas responded with the idea that 'it is only in and through dialogue that one can achieve self-understanding. It will not happen by pure self-reflection, as important as that is.'[167] This recurs in Habermas's later critique of Foucault's irrationalism.[168] Rationality has too often sounded to our ears as something akin to rationalization which is a tool, a means to screen out the considerations which really matter (German: *Zweckrationalität*) and justify the things which do not. Instead, Habermas insists on a rationality which is 'the rationality of decisions', which 'requires the explication and inner consistency of value systems and decision maxims, as well as the correct derivation of acts of choice'.[169] Harvey Cox has commented that Habermas wants reason to be understood once again as about asking the 'why?' not just the 'how?' questions.[170]

To employ a mathematical analogy, this means showing the working as well as the results; communicative reason can be used towards systematic (political and interpersonal) rationalization, while all the time resisting any Hegelian or Utopian overcoming of differences. Rationality is not to be located within individuals as such, much less some noumenal part of them, but can be discerned in acts and projects between people. There is a strong sense of history without determinism (Hegel), of hope without romanticism

(Bloch, Moltmann) which also refutes the Nietzschean doctrine of eternal return or Heideggerian mysticization of that which is. The attempt by Arens to read the Gospel stories as describing an ethic of communicative action in the life of Jesus seems to strain the evidence, although the similarity between prophetic symbolism and action allows the other person, the onlooker to make sense (rather than it being wilfully obscure or forcing meaning upon the other).[171] What is clear, however, is that 'critical theory', as represented by Habermas, is at least as committed to 'the abolition of domination'[172] and a belief that technology and productivity providing the 'sub-systems of purposive activity' (short: multi-nationals) was not something to be accepted fatalistically. The suspicion of communitarianism whereby civic structures become politicized and thus deprived of meaning is perhaps especially relevant with regard to the church. Like Hegel, Habermas has never been interested in religion if it means a discourse which does not affect *all* people – in any case the world has changed and cannot be renewed any more on the basis of the New Testament church than of the Greek city-state.[173] Habermas also writes in praise of Daniel J. Goldhagen's *Hitler's Willing Executioners*, agreeing that leniency towards people as if they could have done no better joins historical determinism and an anthropological pessimism. Against Derrida and Foucault with the origins of the subject and what really lies 'behind' the human person comes Habermas's insistence on the 'paradigm of mutual understanding between subjects capable of speech and action'.[174] It is almost a case of 'I relate, therefore I am'. Being is not metaphysical but is about doing and explaining our action.

Kierkegaard

Although it may be crass to see both Nietzsche and Kierkegaard as polar opposites, their influence on Foucault and Barth respectively perhaps illustrates that theological contests are not fought in terms of dogmatic theology only: yet the true systematician can be the true philosopher. The second naïvety, whereby one loses original innocence only to recover it when experience loses its novelty,[175] leads to an interesting mix of irony and conviction about single issues (for example, ecology, psychology). In their

Christian readings of Wittgenstein, Rowan Williams and Fergus Kerr have both managed to oppose the modern without abandoning altogether a Christologically theistic framework.[176] The very fact of negative theology ('God is not like this or that') suggests the Christian tradition is all too aware of the risk of it appearing that Christianity is a case of humans using their language to create God. Worlds and minds create each other in a mutual process.[177] What can be stated positively is supplied by Jesus who continues (as Barth and more recently Rowan Williams have seen) 'the underlying unsettlement of our thought: the question: "What is it that is true of Jesus of Nazareth that would make some sense of the Church's commitment to new imaginings of God and humanity and of the possibility of new relation to God and humanity".' It has been a regular feature of Williams' thought, inspired by early Barth, to argue for the priority of *krisis* (that is, God's coming to judge) over *Kritik* (our cool assessment of Jesus Christ by the lights of rationality and 'reasonable scholarship').[178]

If Nietzsche and Kierkegaard can be viewed as brothers, then, in terms of the representations of philosphical types in Dostoevsky's *The Brothers Karamazov*, the latter may be viewed as the saintly/tormented son, somewhere between Aloysha and Dmitri compared with Nietzsche (a cross of Dmitri and Ivan). There is also Kierkegaard's undeniable influence on the greatest 'postmodern' theologian of the twentieth century (K. Barth) – thus he is a good 'icon' for a postmodern theology. Unfortunately Kierkegaard's statements of faltering faith in a God who is not-x (a negative theology) has been overemphasized by the likes of Taylor at the expense of works where the Dane revealed his own heart and could affirm many of the claims of credal orthodoxy (and with vehemence!). Kierkegaard's negative theology is for the non-Christian the preliminary to accepting Jesus Christ: once one has admitted no one god is better than another (since 'their works are as nothing', Isaiah 41:29), and that nothing definite can be said about him, then one is open a little more to God's own self-authentication. While then it is a start, it is not Christianity's goal to remain obscurantist and precious, denying the movement of the incarnation, but rather to set forth what we know to be the case about God.

Kierkegaard would not be much use to philosophy since he writes for an audience that took its bearings from Christianity; but for theologians today, who still do, and are about where the society of Kierkegaard's was in terms of consciousness of God, his words, from the *Sickness unto Death* are useful: sin is not an occasional thing, a deviation from the norm, but a second nature of disbelief in the possibility of forgiveness: sin is not easily brought into the continuity of growth in virtue by the way of dialectic, despite Hegel, but is a growing process on a parallel line. Sin is not a negation but a position.[179] Against the church's preaching against sin*s*, Kierkegaard posits the Pauline dictum: 'Whatever is not of faith is sin' (Romans 14:23). It is not *sins* versus *virtues*, but *sin* versus *faith*. Despair as an attitude towards sin is not humility but a resignation, a false modesty that is due to the fact that before someone falls into sin, his opinion of himself was very high. One thinks of Paul's distinction between godly and ungodly sorrow – which may not mean simply 'crocodile tears' but real despair which is absorption in the sin. Kierkegaard advocates a tough pastoral approach: '... a fool of a spiritual counsellor might be on the verge of admiring his deep soul and the powerful influence good has on him'.[180] But the good news *is* the Good News. Human beings are redeemed: this is the fundamental pivot of Christian anthropology. Of course Kierkegaard does not say whether this is ontological or ontic, nor does he enter into debates of Protestant scholasticism. It is a position because it is placed *before God*. Kierkegaard is fond of the pictorial and he interprets Luther's *coram Deo* in the sense of its occupying the space between each human and God. The thrust of his argument is that our nature is redeemed to the extent of our now having free-will whether to accept that forgiveness for sin, given that we have revelation of our position and its remedy (although not their *explanation*). Nor are we brought closer to God in our kind, or nature at any point in the proceedings: 'As a sinner, man is separated from God by the most chasmal qualitative abyss. In turn, of course, God is separated from man by the same chasmal qualitative abyss when he forgives sins.'[181] God's forgiveness only reinforces the gap. Here Kierkegaard may be too hyper-Lutheran or pre-(early)Barthian in that Jesus, in the Lord's Prayer,

POSTMODERNISM AND THEOLOGY

for example, seems to teach a correlation between divine and human forgiveness.

Derrida and Cixous?

As Kieran Flanagan has observed, in the postmodern world religious symbols seem pretty vacuous. He agrees that the work has to be done at the ethical level of virtues, to show that our religion makes sense, but this must be combined with charisma as the 'solution to disenchantment, the routinisation of grace that proffers the prospect of enchantment'.[182] Religions cannot give invisible bonds to a society which cannot understand them, and there are increasingly less social bonds already there for religion to baptize. There are behaviour codes which do tie people together – it is the church's responsibility to show how these are freeing and enchanting. Intelligible action may sound like a return to modernism's myth of progress, but rather, it is work for work's sake: 'the involvement of work/production is the essence of the human'.[183] It means, with Paul, not thinking we have arrived but continuing to be self-aware, of arriving at our ethics through a sense of failure, not in the sense of 'the withdrawal into the private cultivation of a "beautiful soul"',[184] but in setting our hearts before God. The problem that the meta-ethic of suspicion supplies is: how do you know who your God is? What about idolatry? Engagement in ethics, approving and testing is where we know God, according to a practice which looks perhaps more like Judaism than Christianity. A concomitant problem is that this content-less 'Ethics' looks at best a Talmudic *aggiornamento*, at worst an existentialist 'making it up as you go along'. In Derrida's *The Gift of Death*, he claims that ethics must be related to the claim of the *non*-universal; that which the human race would do, or society as a whole would demand is no real ethics, but simply pretending to make an ethical decision. Along that road lies ethical indifference, even the loss of love in one's life. One has to choose one's other and make it the Other, the one who really counts – you feed one cat or child, but not the host of other hungry ones. This, for Derrida is the message of Abraham's preference for God over Isaac, that there are simply some preferences which are inscrutable. We love the one nearest to us – our neighbour. But Derrida does not go on to ask the supplementary question of the Gospel: 'And who is my neighbour?'[185] There is surely in Christianity a refusal to be complacent, to acquiesce in baptizing my *eros*. To be fair to Derrida, there is irony in his prose and he by no means endorses 'inscrutable preferences'.[186] It is descriptive rather than prescriptive of the ways humans are, in an analogous way to linguistic philosophers doing philosophy from the way people use language. What is there is an admission of a lack of answers, and thus room for theologians to work.

While this essay has not knowingly strayed into the area of feminist theory, it would be wrong not to finish with some such contribution. Luce Irigaray[187] and Julia Kristeva are obvious possibilities, but I shall briefly mention something of the work of Hélène Cixous. The theologian Graham Ward sees Cixous' vision as redeemable for Christian purposes and proposes, as an answer to the question raised by her, the incarnation as providing a rescue down a ladder of meaning which is not verbal (after Derrida) but embodied.[188] She writes of a ladder of representation towards the universal, but which needs an intervening miracle: love is always in search of that to take me out of my own limited world; to give Cixous her due:

> I will talk about truth again, without which (without the word truth, without the mystery truth) there would be no writing. It is what writing wants. But it '(the truth)' is totally down below and a long way off. Paradise is down below. According to my people, writing isn't given. Giving oneself to writing means being in a position to do this work of digging, of unburying.[189]

Cixous' vision is the postmodern one of anti-eros; we don't get there by becoming better. 'Auschwitz is always there in every human being.'[190] This is akin in some respects to the doctrines of 'justification by faith' but not of *sola scriptura*. This should not surprise us. Despite the de Man case, and perhaps through it, postmodern theory can be seen as permeated by Judaism; even Cixous' guide, Kafka, and sayings like: 'We need to lose the world, to lose a world, and to discover that there is more than one world and that the world isn't what we think it is.'[191] The realm of the unclean, even the dead, is out of this world.[192] Creativity thus issues through loss, say of a loved one, although perhaps that is not everyone's experience, since loss can be numbing – Cixous presents the symbol of her young widowed mother having to find work – as a midwife! Killing someone is when we claim this as 'my ... forgetting to unceasingly (sic) recognize the other's difference'.[193] The motifs of letting go, unburying, with the Jewish overtones of the memory of the dead, and work as a relational activity, contain even a preaching quality.[194]

Yet there is despair in the original analysis, and frank admission of the strength of hatred; the references to the blackness of E. A. Poe (cf. the darkness of Lautréamont at the roots of French avant-garde and thus intellectual life). The self-effacement of the portrait painter (note Velasquez' 'joke'), 'the flesh of the dream' (which Freud's dream accounts miss but Genet's do not), the seeing truth through the emotions,[195] the attitude towards subversive reversal to undermine social hierarchy and replace it with another 'that is libidinal and imaginary'. Cixous is slightly critical of this quest for exaltation; but one can only expect that from a man. But the difference between Genet and Clarice was perhaps that the latter believed in God and in the possibility of reintegration of all in 'spirit'. Cixous and Kafka are left somewhere in the middle.[196] The whole question of 'home' which has tortured and perplexed Central Europe in the last century; the whole postmodern industry owes its existence to the transplanted French interpretation of Hegel and Nietzsche, with Americans coming in to do the sweeping up and selling back. One should not try to reduce artists and even philosophers to their tradition, nor treat them as *ersatz* saints (as is Cixous' tendency) despite the popular use of the postmodern 'genealogical' method.

Conclusion

Epistemologically ...

The arrogance of modernity is often found in evangelicalism's modernism – that is a belief in the newness yet timelessness of

our faith, that God speaks to us alone, immediately, directly. It is
healthy to be certain – but not about anything, not about me and
my friends having the right view, or even participating in the
objective view of a situation. The reproaches of postevangelicals
have unfortunately been aimed at the things that we could do with
being more certain about, for example, that the Christian God is
real and alive in and beyond our world and defined in the
particular *who is also the universal,*[197] *and who is the source of needed life
and power for new lives* (Galatians 2:20).

To evangelicals (and to many other Christians who take
orthodoxy seriously), postmodern theologies, or theology which
takes its cue from postmodern philosophies, seem to be found
wanting because they are half-baked in their commitment to the
locus of absolute truth: Jesus Christ. There is undoubtedly a lot of
insights to be gained in the destruction of our idolatrous
conceptions of God and the behaviour he requires. Yet deconstruction aims to take apart not in order to rebuild, but simply to
show that any truth-claim, any intellectual edifice is neither right
not wrong. There can be too much pride in the post-stance, of
being beyond childish things such as doctrine. If there is a calling
to live on the border between the kingdom of darkness and the
kingdom of light, of being a double agent, then tests of loyalty at
regular intervals are advisable. The problem with the dissolution
of modernity's sense of self, of having arrived, is that we are
catapulted forward, believing that what we are is to be revealed
tomorrow, or perhaps the day after. *Homo faber* or *homo ludens* – it
makes little difference.

Ecclesiologically ...
The church is called to be both the institutional and the
charismatic (to use the language of Max Weber, but also of the
nineteenth-century early church historians), and in that sense,
between the modern and the postmodern, between the church as
Christ's mystical bride and the church as his body as representative in the world (and in this 'betweenness' set under him, though
part of him), between the inexpressible and the explanation or
communication. The church's essence is not 'bishop, priest,
deacon'; the institution is an expression of the Holy Spirit and

our spirits. Catholicity, as Avery Dulles has argued, means there is mediation: not one of 'symbols of the transcendent' but of a reality which needs to be communal to survive. Theologians will work in their area of specialization in harmony with other theologians – they will not be trying to be relevant to the same fad, but will rejoice that the fragmentation of knowledge means that things can be said more deeply, with more detail, and put together as the voice of the thinking church.

Doctrinally ...

In a climate of despair, of limitation, of mistrust, of a celebration of victimization, of fragmentation, of rootlessness (and their sunnier sides of realism, humility, honesty, distinctiveness, situatedness), vague theologies of hope which aim to rule out God's intervention in favour of a realization of our responsibility and ability, but which tend at the same time to exclude God's overruling sovereignty as a factor. There is a need to recognize that hedonism does not start with postmodernism, and that narcissism does not mean an expanding self, but a self which cannot distinguish easily between what is inner and what is outer reality.[198] There is also a need to recognize that questions of truth can be so hard that the *natural* reaction is to say 'I do not know what the criteria are for choosing one religion over another.' The need is to be more theologically literate. Perhaps this means starting with the Old Testament and the theology of creation and life; the Wisdom literature and the review of human nature in the historical books, focusing not so much on 'crisis' but on the slow disappointment of expectations. It means dealing with issues presented by philosophy, the skilful reflection on experience: love, death, justice, peace and viewing these in their personal, social, political but also theological contexts. As theology it will start and end with talk about God.[199] Thus it will look at the question of why people fear death, rather than simply disliking it as putting an end to their life; often there seems something more than sadness at the prospect of love and meaning being left behind for just nothingness, although that is real too. So questions of continuation of existence and the matter of 'heaven and hell' are not so far away. And, like prophecy, the raising of disquieting questions is for *believers*, after all, is not a bit of us full of the mind-set, fixed ideas and worldviews of the world?[200]

And questions of ultimate justice, if postmodernism would lead us that way, take us to the New Testament. God does not take all evil on himself but destroys it: he is not Derrida's parent setting a bad example over against justice. There is a place for heroism in Christian ethics which should not be driven by a naturalism in which a perverse teleology persists, reminding us that by the Second Law of Thermodynamics everything is going the way of all flesh. Or the voice that urges that there can be no place for negative principles in an age where, like the global market, everyone can have ever-increasing satisfaction without anyone having to sacrifice. Christianity stands as discipleship which is caught up in a redemption that is something bigger than that often private and painful task, incorporating a shared fullness of joy.

Notes

[1] This essay is an updated version of one which originally appeared in 1998. Rather than a total rewrite I have tried to recast and update what I said four years ago. The genre remains introductory, although I would like to think there is a little more here than merely a glorified bibliography. My perception is that there is less talk about postmodernism in theological circles, as if the catch-all term sounds a bit undiscriminating and thus hardly refined enough. But if anything, the idea of doing 'pure' theology untouched by questions of meaning, discourse, power, rhetoric, etc., has become almost unthinkable. People no longer write 'Dogmatics' but 'theologies of ...' (perhaps this essay is one such, although I would argue that the cupola in 'Postmodernism and Theology' keeps the two apart).

In the interim I have had the opportunity and privilege to become more acquainted with the book by Kevin Vanhoozer, *Is there a meaning in this text?* The Radical Orthodoxy 'movement' has given rise to an eponymous book and a second editon of Graham Ward's *Theology and Critical Theory*, although the Milbank–Pickstock axis seems more interested in the definition of modernity (crucial as such questions are) than in the most recent challenges to faith and theology arising from within 'postmodernity'. I am grateful to the editors of the present volume for reissuing this 'bibliographical essay' in a slightly altered way, and to

theology students and colleagues at Nottingham and Liverpool Hope for
their interest and challenge.

2 See David Harvey, *The Condition of Postmodernity* (Oxford: Blackwell, 1990);
S. Crook, J. Pakolski, M. Waters, *Postmodernisation* (London: Sage, 1992).
For a close reading of the origins of postmodernism in the field of literary
theory, see Jonathan Culler, *Structuralist Poetics* (London: RKP, 1975); *On
Deconstruction: Theory and Criticism after Structuralism* (London: Routledge, 1982).

3 For a helpful summary of Hegel's place in 'modernism', see Jürgen
Habermas, *The Philosophical Discourse of Modernity* (ET, Oxford: Polity, 1987),
pp. 23–44. Of course Hegel's leanings towards panentheism, of a God
whose being is in his becoming (see Hans Küng, *The Incarnation of God* [ET,
Edinburgh: T. & T. Clark, 1987], pp. 184ff.) should not encourage the
view that Hegel 'postmodernly' held that all is in flux – only God or Spirit
is, because he is *free* Spirit. But as one who writes of God as, by definition,
himself as the end of the process, Hegel stands at the threshold of
postmodern theology.

4 D. Clines, *Job* 1 – 20 (Waco, TX: Word Biblical Commentary, 1989),
pp. xxx–xxxi.

5 See her *Beyond liberalism and fundamentalism: how modern and postmodern
philosophy set the theological agenda* (Philadelphia: TPI, 1996).

6 So, David Tracy, *Plurality and Ambiguity* (London: SCM, 1987); Nicholas
Lash, *Theology on the Road to Emmaus* (London: SCM, 1986).

7 This begs the question of the authoritative voice of scriptural
interpretation. This shall be dealt with only sparingly in what follows and
awaits fuller treatment. Nicholas Wolterstorff's *Divine Discourse* (Cambridge:
Cambridge University Press, 1995) is a good place to start. See also the
very worthwhile treatment by Kevin Vanhoozer, 'The Semantics of Biblical
Literature' in D. A. Carson and John D. Woodbridge (eds.), *Hermeneutics,
Authority and Canon* (Leicester: IVP, 1986), pp. 53–104.

8 T. Eagleton, *The Illusions of Postmodernism* (Oxford: Blackwell, 1996), p. vii.

9 J.-F. Lyotard, *The Postmodern Condition: a report on knowledge* (ET, Minneapolis:
University of Minnesota Press, 1984), p. xxiii.

10 A. MacIntyre, in *After Virtue* (2nd edn., London: Duckworth, 1985), p. 212,
responds to Sartre: 'And to someone who says that in life there are no
endings, or that final partings take place only in stories, one is tempted to
reply, "But have you never heard of death?" '

11 J. R. Middleton and B. J. Walsh, *Truth is Stranger than it used to be* (London:
SPCK, 1995), p. 76; their lack of insider knowledge of the movement they

claim to be critiqueing is plain at p. 79, where Derrida's notion of *pharmakon* is dealt with superficially. While 'replicants' (in the film *Bladerunner*) are surely a modernist, technological nightmare (the result of programming which did not see ahead far enough), not a postmodernist one; at least one cannot blame such scenarios on the 'flight from *techne* characteristic of *Post*modernism'.

[12] So, John Milbank, 'Problematizing the secular: the postmodern agenda', in P. Berry and A. Wernick (eds.), *Shadow of Spirit: Postmodernism and Religion* (London: Routledge, 1993), pp. 30–44.

[13] As poststructuralism is (roughly put) postmodernism in relation to literature (thus including the Bible and its traditions), the two terms will be used interchangeably.

[14] Valentine Cunningham, *In the Reading Gaol: Postmodernity, Texts and History* (Oxford: Blackwell, 1994), pp. 373f.; 384.

[15] For example, to try to define 'The Lord is my Rock' by reference to a 'strong unshakeableness' not only misses much of the point but leads one to wonder what exactly 'unshakeableness' means.

[16] Ferdinand de Saussure, *Cours de linguistique générale* (Paris: Bally-Sechehaye, Payot, 1986), p. 30: 'La langue n'est pas une fonction du sujet parlant, elle est le produit que l'individu enregistre passivment' ('Language is not the operation of the speaking subject, rather it is the product of which the individual passively takes note'). One may compare the Francophone (and more recently the Germanophone) tendency to believe in a centralized authority which conserves the language and judges what kind of usage is acceptable.

[17] In *Limited Inc.* Derrida gives the example of ou and où in French: it is in their written form that they are distinguished. Further, writing's job is to communicate to those absent. For an (often critical) introduction to Derrida, see Christopher Norris, *Derrida* (London: Fontana Masters, 1992): also his *What's Wrong with Postmodernism?* (London: Harvester, 1990), chs. 1 and 3.

[18] Kevin Mills, 'Words and Presences: the spiritual imperative' in D. Barrett, R. Pooley and L. Ryken (eds.), *The Discerning Reader* (Leicester: Apollos, 1995), p. 123; see also pp. 121–136.

[19] G. Deleuze and F. Guattari, *What is Philosophy?* (ET, London: Verso, 1994), pp. 16 and 22: 'Confusing concept and proposition produces a belief in the existence of scientific concepts ...'; rather the concept 'speaks the event of the other' (i.e. it simply recounts human experience). Only scientific

concepts which tend to have been deduced from each other to map
experience (the law of gravity, the boiling point of water', etc.) can be said
to in any sense exist; but anything (Reason, the Other, etc.) that suggests
we know absolutes or claims to bring a universally valid knowledge close
('immanent') is not. Philosophical concepts are usually the reaction to an
over-reaching of last year's bumptious concept.

20 Cf. the psychoanalytical theories of Julia Kristeva which link misogyny
with atheism, the hatred of what is 'other'.

21 Though those who would say 'Vive la différence!', and might be
considered to be *postfeminists*, such as Luce Irigaray and her supporters,
would think differently.

22 *Pace* U. Eco, 'Postmodernismus, Ironie u. Vergnügen', in Wolfgang Welsch
(ed.), *Wege aus der Moderne: Schlüsseltexte der Postmoderne-Diskussion* (Weinheim:
V.C.H., Acta Humaniora, 1988), pp. 75–78.

23 Claudius Strube, 'Postmoderne I', *Theologische Realencyclopädie*, pp. 24, 82–87.

24 J. Baudrillard, 'Simulacra and Simulations', in Mark Poster (ed.), *Jean
Baudrillard: Selected Writings* (Cambridge: Polity, 1988), p. 172; see also
pp. 166–184.

25 Although Foucault would have spoken more in terms of 'People's justice':
see David Macey, *The Lives of Michel Foucault* (London: Vintage, 1993),
ch. 12.

26 J. Culler, *On Deconstruction: Theory and Criticism after Structuralism* (London:
Routledge, 1982), p. 87.

27 J. Ellis, *Against Deconstruction* (Princeton: Princeton University Press, 1989),
ch. 1.

28 Ibid., p. 70.

29 For an informed male response to these questions, particularly with regard
to Christian hymnbooks, see Brian Wren, *Which Language Shall I Borrow?*
(London: SCM, 1989).

30 I refer to Lewis Carroll's *Alice through the Looking Glass*, famously cited in J. L.
Austin's *How to do things with words* (Oxford: Oxford University Press, 1962).
Also, T. S. Eliot, 'And so each venture / Is a shabby beginning, a raid on the
inarticulate / With shabby equipment always deteriorating / In the shabby
mess of imprecision of feeling, / Undisciplined squads of emotion.'

31 Cf. W. Ong, *Orality and Literality* (London: Methuen, 1982).

32 G. Steiner, *Real Presences* (London: Faber, 1989), p. 119: 'A semantics, a
poetics of correspondence, of decipherability and truth-values arrived at
across time and consensus, are strictly inseparable from the postulate of

theological-metaphysical transcendence. Thus the origin of the axiom of
meaning and of the God-concept is a shared one.' It all comes down to
the question of the veracity of John 1:1. However, some theologians will
wish to criticize this over-tight connection between God and meaning.
God is also *spirit*, he is 'beyond meaning'.

33 To paraphrase *Hamlet*, Act II, Scene i.

34 One of the main points of T. Thiselton's *New Horizons in Hermeneutics*
(London: HarperCollins, 1992).

35 Cited in Philip Sampson's essay 'The Rise of Postmodernity', in
P. Sampson, V. Samuel, C. Sugden (eds.), *Faith, Mission and Modernity*
(Oxford: Regnum-Lynx, 1994); one thinks of Pop Art, or the performance
of U2.

36 The old foe of Francis Schaeffer (and to a lesser degree Alistair McIntyre)
reborn.

37 In Gillian Rose, *Love's Work* (London: Virago, 1994).

38 See Lyotard, *The Postmodern Condition*.

39 H.-R. Jauss, *Towards an Aesthetic of Reception* (ET, Brighton: Harvester, 1982).

40 Yet Jauss's actual account of the process of the Bible in history speaks of
the formation of a new Christian discourse patterned on the Bible, a lowly
rhetoric that reshaped ancient standards.

41 The attempt by Graham Ward to compare a theologian with a philosopher
tends to present Barth too much in philosophical terms which were not
his own: see *Barth, Derrida and Deconstruction* (Cambridge: Cambridge
University Press, 1995).

42 See her *Spirit in Ashes* (New Haven: Yale University Press, 1985), pp. 163,
216.

43 These ideas are found in George Steiner's *Real Presences* (London: Faber &
Faber, 1989). Thus Dante's *Commedia* possibly outdoes *The Aeneid* on which
it stands. Perhaps the New Testament is *the* performance of the Old
Testament.

44 Stephen Moore, *Poststructuralism and the New Testament: Derrida and Foucault
at the foot of the Cross* (Philadelphia: Fortress, 1994). Cf. Hegel's optimism
that everything, God included, resolves into knowability.

45 Jacques Derrida, 'Edmond Jabès et la question du livre', in *L'Ecriture et la
Différence* (Paris: Seuil, 1967); (ET) *Writing and Difference* (Chicago: University
of Chicago Press, 1978).

46 I find the case of Jesus writing in the sand (in John 8:6ff.) suggestive of
the enigmatic nature of much writing.

47 David Jasper, *The Study of Literature and Religion* (Minneapolis: Augsburg-
    Fortress, 1989), p. xvii.

48 One *may* think of a film like *Forrest Gump* as an attempt to cover with an
    image of wholesomeness the after-effects of the sickness of the
    involvement in Vietnam.

49 Jasper, *The Study of Literature and Religion*, p. 25.

50 As the voices of ideolgies which debated with each other in its
    composition continue to argue through its pages – yet 'God gives the
    growth'. See James A. Sanders, *From Sacred Story to Sacred Text: Canon as
    Paradigm* (Philadelphia: Fortress, 1987); Brevard Childs, *Biblical Theology of
    the Old and New Testaments* (London: SCM, 1992). Jasper concludes: 'Why
    these [biblical] texts? My answer to that is that because these texts, the
    books of the biblical canon, have the capacity like no other collection of
    texts in the Western tradition to embrace a multitude of texts which
    celebrate their canonicity' (*The Study of Literature and Religion*, p. 141).

51 Cf. B. M. Metzger, *The Canon of the New Testament* (Oxford: Oxford
    University Press, 1987), p. 254: 'These three criteria (orthodoxy,
    apostolicity, and consensus among the churches) for ascertaining which
    books should be regarded as authoritative for the Church came to be
    generally adopted during the course of the second century and were never
    modified thereafter.' Barton's objection (John Barton, *The Spirit and the
    Letter: Studies in the Biblical Canon* [London: SPCK, 1997]), that there was a
    growth of the canon then, later, a separate process of cutting back some of
    that growth (to use a horticultural metaphor) does not alter the general
    point that *during* the first five centuries, largely through the use of Scripture
    in doctrinal debates, the shape of the canon emerged, and that by and
    large there was a fairly firm consensus as to what was holy Scripture.

52 N. Wolterstorff, *Divine Discourse* (Cambridge: Cambridge University Press,
    1995), pp. 148–152.

53 K. Vanhoozer, *Bibilical Narrative in the thought of Paul Ricoeur* (Cambridge:
    Cambridge University Press, 1991).

54 J. Kristeva, *Desire in Language: A semiotic approach to literature and art* (ET, New
    York: Columbia University Press, 1980).

55 *The Postmodern Bible* (New Haven: Yale University Press, 1994).

56 Ibid., p. 199.

57 'Dasein, man's being, is "defined" as ... that living thing whose Being is
    essentially determined by the potentiality for discourse'; the philosopher's
    task is 'to make the Being of entities stand out in full relief' (*Being and Time*

[ET, Oxford, UK and Cambridge, MA: Blackwell, 1962], p. 47) in and not despite of *Dasein*'s historicality. The truth of a thing is seeing it as a whole, not looking through or behind it to find its essence. 'Least of all can the Being of entities ever be anything such that "behind it" stands something else "which does not appear".'

58 B. Ingraffia, *Postmodern Theory and Biblical Theology* (Cambridge: Cambridge University Press, 1995), p. 154. He goes on (p. 156) to describe Heidegger's theology: 'Instead of God calling *anthropos* into relationship with him, into faithful existence, through the person of Jesus Christ (Romans 1:6), *Dasein* is called by its own (authentic) Self out of absorption in the world, out of the they-self, back to its own Self.' Some of Ingraffia's criticisms seem premised on the notion that biblical vocabulary is untranslatable into other philosophical terms; I am unconvinced that Heidegger is so far off here, or that the categories of anxiety and conscience which he employs are 'Greek, non-biblical'.

59 'Phenomenology and Theology', p. 20, cited in Ingraffia, *Postmodern Theory and Biblical Theology*, p. 164.

60 See Kevin Hart, *The Trespass of the Sign: Deconstruction, theology and philosophy* (Cambridge: Cambridge University Press, 1989), pp. 265–269.

61 As Eagleton notes (*The Illusions of Postmodernism*, pp. 34f.).

62 See Philippa Berry, 'Women and Space according to Kristeva and Irigaray', in Berry and Wernick, *Shadow of Spirit*.

63 Witnessed as early as C. P. Snow's *The Two Cultures* (2nd edn., Cambridge: Cambridge University Press, 1964), perpetuated in the Anglo-Saxon system of education; but with its roots, according to Louis Dupré (*Passage to Modernity* [New Haven: Yale University Press, 1996]), in the late middle ages.

64 See his *History of Sexuality*, 3 vols. (Harmondsworth: Penguin, 1981–90).

65 P. Kramer, *Listening to Prozac* (London: Fourth Estate, 1994), p. 37.

66 This is represented in the writings of Scott Peck but also (more theologically and academically) by Drewermann and Jaschke: the soul needs to escape 'the OT' of self-hating religion and find the freedom of the New Testament.

67 Eagleton, *The Illusions of Postmodernism*, p. 28: 'It has unleashed the power of the local, of the regional and idiosyncratic, and has helped to homogenize them across the globe … It has floated the signifier … in doing so found itself mimicking a society founded on the fiction of credit in which money spawns money as surely as signs spawn signs. It is brimful of universal

moral prescriptions – hybridity is preferable to purity, plurality to singularity, difference to self-identity – and denounces such universalism as an oppressive hangover of Enlightenment. Like any brand of epistemological anti-realism, it consistently denies the possibility of describing the way the world is, and just as consistently finds itself doing so. At once libertarian and determinist, it dreams of a human subject set free from constraint, gliding deliriously from one position to another, and holds simultaneously that the subject is the mere effect of forces which constitute it through and through.'

[68] Cf. Paolo Freire, *The Pedagogy of the Oppressed* (London: Penguin, 1996).

[69] See Zygmunt Baumann, *Postmodern Ethics* (Oxford: Blackwell, 1993), p. 56. To paraphrase, people do not live according to command anymore, but prioritize responsibilities out of a sense of commitment to *significant* others, whom we anxiously hope will continue to value us. Yet as Levinas reminds us, the Other is not the face we like, but the hidden totality of others we cannot see. See further, Simon Critchley, *The Ethics of Deconstruction: Derrida and Levinas* (Oxford: Blackwell, 1992), who writes that, for Levinas, 'The passage from ethics to politics is synonymous with the move from responsibility to questioning. God is not allowed in if that means allowing him to take the responsibility we should take for ourselves.' See E. Levinas, *Le temps et l'autre* (Paris: Quadrige/Presses Universitaires de France, 1979), p. 23: 'God appears in his texts as a decisive absence, a trace, a force that can be felt behind the ethical encounter with other people, but never a presence.'

[70] See M. Foucault, *The Order of Things* (London: Routledge, 1970).

[71] *Postmodernism* (Buckingham: Open University Press, 1994), p. 84: 'Ancient wisdom [from premodern times] is retrieved as the means of constructive critique that relativizes both modernity and postmodernity.'

[72] Cf. Eagleton, *The Illusions of Postmodernism*, pp. 36–39.

[73] Cf. Jill Kraye, 'Moral Philosophy', in C. B. Schmidt and Q. Skinner (eds.), *The Cambridge History of Renaissance Philosophy* (Cambridge: Cambridge University Press, 1988), p. 313; see also pp. 303–386.

[74] As noted in Middleton and Walsh, *Truth is Stranger than it used to be*, p. 57.

[75] C. Lasch, *The Minimal Self: Psychic Survival in Troubled Times* (New York: Norton, 1984).

[76] Middleton and Walsh, *Truth is Stranger than it used to be*, pp. 15f.

[77] Ibid., p. 37.

[78] Ibid., p. 74.

[79] *A Passion for Truth: the Intellectual Coherence of Evangelicalism* (Leicester: Apollos, 1996).

[80] Cited in ibid., p. 147. True, Foucault may have replaced 'truth' with 'honesty' (a Freudian meta-ethic surely) yet his observations on the 'will to power' as having effect in society (and thus giving 'proofs' for Nietzsche's thesis) needs a lot more respect than McGrath offers.

[81] David Wells, *No Place for Truth* (Leicester, IVP, 1993).

[82] D. A. Carson, *The Gagging of God* (Leicester: Apollos, 1996).

[83] Roger Lundin, 'The Pragmatics of Postmodernity', in Timothy R. Phillips and Dennis L. Okholm, *Christian Apologetics in the Postmodern World* (Downers' Grove, IL: IVP, 1995), p. 30, citing Richard Rorty, *Consequences of Pragmatism* (Minneapolis: University of Minnesota Press, 1982), pp. 148f.

[84] 'On being a fool for Christ and an idiot for nobody', in Phillips and Okholm, *Christian Apologetics in a Postmodern World*, p. 114, with reference to Charles Taylor, 'Rorty in the Epistemological Tradition', in A. Malachowski (ed.), *Reading Rorty* (Oxford: Blackwell, 1992), p. 258.

[85] 'There's no such thing as objective truth, and it's a good thing too', in Phillips and Okholm, *Christian Apologetics in a Postmodern World*, pp. 155–170, 162. There is the interesting comment, arguing that we should practise relativizing relativism at p. 167: 'But neither should we say that such a statement is just one opinion among others, for such a view would also require a view from nowhere.' This approach works better than Sire's attempt to put the burden of proof on the relativist (see above).

[86] T. Thiselton, *Culture and Value* (Oxford: Blackwell, 1980), esp. pp. 27 and 35. See also L. Wittgenstein, *Philosophical Investigations* (Oxford: Blackwell, 1953), pp. xi, 195ff.

[87] Quoted in A. C. Thiselton, *Interpreting God and the Postmodern Self: on meaning, manipulation and promise* (Edinburgh: T. & T. Clark, 1995), p. 66.

[88] Colin Gunton, *The One, the Three and the Many* (Cambridge: Cambridge University Press, 1993), p. 164; see also chs. 7 & 8.

[89] Nancy Murphy, *Beyond Liberalism and Fundamentalism: how modern and postmodern philosophy set the theological agenda* (Valley Forge, PA: TPI, 1996).

[90] Cf. Francis Watson, *Text, Church and World* (Edinburgh: T. & T. Clark, 1994), p. 251.

[91] N. Murphy, 'Philosophical resources for postmodern evangelical thinking', *Christian Scholars' Review* 26 (1996), pp. 184–205, 199f.

[92] Hart, *The Trespass of the Sign*, p. 100.

[93] On this see Rowan Williams, *Teresa of Avila* (London: Geoffrey Chapman, 1991), ch. 5.

[94] E. Drewermann, 'Mehr Menschlichkeit mit Tieren', *Die Zeit*, 2 August, 1996.

[95] G. Loughlin, *Telling God's Story* (Cambridge: Cambridge University Press, 1995), p. 12.

[96] Don Cupitt, *The Time Being* (London: SCM, 1992), p. 58.

[97] Don Cupitt, *The Last Philosophy* (London: SCM, 1995), p. 2.

[98] Ibid., p. 11.

[99] Cupitt, *The Time Being*, pp. 75–78.

[100] As Thiselton has observed with respect to Cupitt's interpretations of Kierkegaard and Wittgenstein; see his *Interpreting God and the Postmodern Self*.

[101] Ibid., pp. 83f.

[102] Ibid., p. 35.

[103] S. Williams, *Revelation and Reconciliation* (Cambridge: Cambridge University Press, 1995), p. 131.

[104] Hart, *The Trespass of the Sign*, p. 3. The full *terzina* (Canto 27 of the *Paradiso*): 'Or figliuol mio, non il gustar del legno/fu per sè la cagion di tanto esilio, ma solamente il trapassar del segno.'

[105] Cf. John Milton, *Paradise Lost*, IX, 'God so commanded and left that command / Sole daughter of his voice; the rest we live / Law to ourselves; our reason is our law.'

[106] Hart, *The Trespass of the Sign*, p. 18.

[107] Ibid., pp. 30–32, where Hart gives a summary compendium of Derrida's ideas.

[108] Roland Barthes, 'The Death of the author', in *Image, Music, Text* (New York: Hill and Wang, 1977), p. 146.

[109] C. Winquist, *Desiring Theology* (Chicago: University of Chicago Press, 1995) (following P. Tillich's *My search for absolutes* [New York: Simon & Schuster, 1984]), p. 82: 'the point is that Being is a hint that the framework is ontotheological – but this framework is allowed to exist by subjectivity which allows itself to be mastered – so Tillich's thought is transcendental rather than ontotheological. God is being as the aporia of thinking. There are no conceptual foundations – even above God is God; "the living God" ("God who is") is a symbol ...' (p. 74). This is a bit like Nietzsche's point about the experience of the effect being the cause.

[110] Heidegger, 'Der Glaube hat das Denken des Seins nicht nötig. Wenn er das braucht, ist er schon nicht mehr Glaube. Das hat Luther verstanden ...

Ich glaube, dass das Sein niemals als Grund und Wesen von Gott gedacht
werden kann, dass aber gleichwohl die Erfahrung Gottes und seiner
Offenbarkeit (sofern sie dem Menschen begegnet) in der Dimension des
Seins sich ereignet, was niemals besagt, das Sein könnte als mögliche
Prädikat für Gott gelten' (*Aussprache* 06/XI/1951, n. 16, p. 212): ('The
thinking about Being is not necessary for faith. If it needs it, it is no longer
faith. Luther understood this ... I believe that Being can never be thought
of as Ground and Essence of God, that nevertheless the experience of God
and his revelatory nature [inasmuch as it reaches humans] is experienced in
the dimension of being, which does not ever mean that Being could count
as a possible predicate for God').

[111] *The Trinity* (New York: Herder & Herder, 1970), p. 24: 'No adequate
distinction can be made between the doctrine of the Trinity and the
doctrine of the economy of salvation.' This motto is questioned by, for
example, Catherine Mowry Lacugna, *God for us: The Trinity and Christian Life*
(New York: HarperCollins, 1991).

[112] J.-L. Marion, *God without Being* (ET, Chicago: University of Chicago Press,
1991), p. 74.

[113] J. Derrida, *Écriture et Différence*, p. 200. Or with Wittgenstein: 'Es gibt
allerdings Unaussprechliches. Dies zeigt sich, es ist das Mystische' (*Tractatus*
[London: RKP, 1922], 6.522).

[114] J. Milbank, *Theology and Social Theory* (Oxford: Blackwell, 1989).

[115] Ibid., p. 288.

[116] Ibid., p. 291.

[117] Ibid., p. 296.

[118] Ibid., p. 397: 'Here Jesus' divinity relates to the demonstration of the
possibility of non-violence in a particular "pattern" of existence, not to the
intrusion of extra-human enabling capacities.'

[119] Ibid., p. 433.

[120] Deleuze is, none the less, aware that differences jostle and overlap ... he is
only able to perceive this intermingling as agonistic providence.

[121] J. Milbank, 'Can a gift be given? Prolegomena to a Future Trinitarian
Metaphysic', *Modern Theology* 11 (1995), pp. 119–161.

[122] Ibid., p. 150.

[123] Nietzsche had called negative theology 'a divine way of thinking', in *Will to
Power* (New York: Vintage Books, 1967), I, p. 15.

[124] Hans W. Frei, *Types of Christian Theology* (New Haven and London: Yale
University Press, 1992), p. 43.

[125] Ibid., p. 94: 'Hermeneutical silence concerning doctrine as *explicatio* and *meditatio*, and appeal to general criteria in *applicatio*.' Frei had already observed that modern criticism sought to see the text of the sign of some truth, not the truth (or even containing the truth) itself. Derrida's position concerning the absence of any authoritative meaning rests on two centuries of such criticism as recorded in Frei's *The Eclipse of Biblical Narrative* (New Haven and London: Yale University Press, 1974). Perhaps the most insightful expression of Frei's view is contained in 'The Literal Reading of biblical narrative in the Christian tradition: does it stretch or will it break?', in *Theology and Narrative* (New Haven: Yale University Press, 1994).

[126] Ibid., p. 53.

[127] And how we approach it with our philosophical epistemology: see P. C. Hodgson (ed.), *Lectures on the Philosophy of Religion* (Berkeley–Los Angeles–London: University of California Press, 1988), pp. 88f.

[128] N. Murphy, *Theology in the Age of Scientific Reasoning* (Ithaca–London: Cornell University Press, 1990), p. 202.

[129] George Lindbeck, *The Nature of Doctrine* (London: SPCK, 1984).

[130] Perhaps Newman's 'belief in historical development without also believing in liberal philosophies of development' (Owen Chadwick, *From Bossuet to Newman* [2nd edn., Cambridge: Cambridge University Press, 1987], p. 195) *is* acceptable in the majority of Catholic circles today, even though Vatican I only spoke of infallibility in the Pope's *recognition* of doctrines which originated in the apostolic church.

[131] Chadwick, *From Bossuet to Newman*, pp. 183f.

[132] G. Kaufman, *In Face of Mystery* (Cambridge, MA: Harvard University Press, 1993), p. 305.

[133] Ibid., p. 319.

[134] Paul Tillich, *Systematic Theology* (London: SCM, 1978), I, p. 18.

[135] Ibid., pp. 21–25. And thus theology should pay little attention to the natural sciences: 'Categories like quantity and quality have no direct theological significance and are not especially discussed' (ibid., p. 166).

[136] Ibid., pp. 166f.

[137] Mark C. Taylor, *Erring: A Postmodern A/Theology* (Chicago: Chicago University Press, 1987), p. 20.

[138] Mark C. Taylor, *Deconstructing Theology* (New York: Crossroad, 1982), p. 25.

[139] Winquist, *Desiring Theology*, p. 237.

[140] See especially, Taylor, *Erring: A Postmodern A/Theology*.

[141] Cf. David Ray Griffin, *God and Religion in a Post-Modern World* (Albany: State University of New York Press, 1989), with reference to the work of Hartshorne.

[142] Thomas J. J. Altizer, *Genesis and Apocalypse: A Theological Voyage towards Authentic Christianity* (Louisville, KY: Westminster/John Knox Press, 1990), p. 25: 'Nothing is a clearer sign of the advent of modernity than an ever-progressive contraction and disappearance of a theological thinking which is a comprehensive and unitary thinking.'

[143] See ibid., p. 23.

[144] Ibid., p. 65.

[145] Ibid., p. 156.

[146] See J. Zizioulas, *Being as Communion* (Crestwood, NY: St. Vladimir's Seminary Press, 1985); A. Torrance, *Persons in Communion: Trinitarian Description and Human Participation* (Edinburgh: T. & T. Clark, 1995); C. Yannaras, *Person und Eros* (Göttingen: Vandenhoeck und Ruprecht, 1982); Gunton, *The One, the Three and the Many*.

[147] Cf. D. Hampson, *Theology and Feminism* (Oxford: Blackwell, 1989), p. 110: the idea of Christ as impregnating his church on the cross (found in von Balthasar) validates abuse towards weaker members by the vicars of Christ who assume this role, however metaphorically.

[148] See his *Theologie* (Gütersloh: Gütersloher Verlagshaus, 1994). See also Gert Hummel, 'Unterwegs zur Weltlichkeit Gottes. Zu Oswald Bayers Buch: "Leibliches Wort. Reformation und Neuzeit im Konflikt"', *Theologische Beiträge*, 27 (1996), pp. 285–289.

[149] Bayer, *Theologie*, pp. 409f.

[150] E. Jüngel, *Gott als Geheimnis des Welt* (5th edn., Tübingen: J. C. Mohr, 1986), p. 469: 'Insofern unterscheidet der Glaube zwischen Gott und Mensch. Er tut es zugunsten der den Unterschied niemals verzehrenden (consummated) Vereinigung von Gott und Mensch, die man deshalb besser nicht eine *unio mystica* nennt ... Dafür beruft er sich auf Jesus Christus, dem der Satz "Gott ist Liebe" seine Wahrheit verdankt. Denn Jesus Christus ist derjenige Mensch, in dem Gott sich als menschlichers Gott definiert hat. Es ist also der Glaube an die Menschlichkeit Gottes, der die Identitat von Gott und Liebe wahrt. In Tode Jesu Christi ist Gott ... zugleich das *Ende* unsereres zeitlichen Seins' (p. 528): ('Faith distinguishes between God and Humanity. It does it in the form of the union of God and humanity, a union which never consumes the distinction between them, and which we are better not to call *unio*

mystica. So faith directs itself to Jesus Christ, to whom the phrase "God is love" owes its truth. For Jesus Christ is that human in whom God has defined himself as the human God. It thus is the faith in the humanity of God which safeguards the identity of God and love. In the death of Jesus Christ God is at the same time the end of our temporal existence.')

[151] Ibid., pp. 279–281.

[152] Barth, *Church Dogmatics*, III/3, p. 345.

[153] Ibid., p. 346. Barth had stated (p. 318) that Augustine had meant by *malum est privatio boni* that it was an assault on God's good order, and not mere privation. But I think Augustine's phrase is open to the charge of not taking evil seriously enough.

[154] The complaint, in the form of a review of Pannenberg's *Systematic Theology*, vol. 1 and the latter's response to the charges, are both found in *Zeitschrift für Theologie und Kirche*, 86 (1989). Cf. what Foucault thought of the history of ideas; D. Macey, *The Lives of Michel Foucault* (London: Vintage, 1993), p. 159.

[155] W. Pannenberg, *Systematic Theology* (ET, Edinburgh: T. & T. Clark, 1991), vol. 1, p. 314.

[156] *Zeitschrift für Theologie und Kirche*, 86 (1989), p. 357: 'Die Theologie hat es mit der Wahrheit der christlichen Lehre überhaupt und nicht speziell mit ihrem Gegenwartsbezug zu tun, so richtig es für unser geschärftes Bewußtein die Geschichtlichkeit aller Auslegung bleibt' ('In that theology has to do with the truth of Christian teaching in general and not especially with its connection with the present, it is right that the historicality of all intepretation remains for our consciousness to be sharpened').

[157] Ibid., p. 231.

[158] Philip Blond (ed.) (London: Routledge, 1997).

[159] Two remarkable surveys and interpretations by evangelicals are K. Vanhoozer, *Biblical Narrative in the Philosophy of Paul Ricoeur* (Cambridge: Cambridge University Press, 1991) and J. Fodor, *Christian Hermeneutics: Paul Ricoeur and the Re-figuring of theology* (Oxford: Oxford University Press, 1995), who writes at p. 332: 'Ricoeur's central philosophical conviction is that there is always a *being-demanding-to-be-said* that precedes our actual saying. Language and world, therefore, must be related in such a way so as not to collapse their differentiation, since conflating the two would preclude language from functioning in a properly critical and reflective manner.' Language thus has 'ontological vehemence'.

[160] As Frank Kermode saw, in his *The Genesis of Secrecy* (Cambridge, MA: Harvard University Press, 1979), the gospels do not tell us all that much about Jesus.

[161] See Nicholas Wolterstorff's critique, *Divine Discourse*, pp. 227f.

[162] In his *The Symbolism of Evil* (Boston: Beacon, 1967), p. 258.

[163] Paul Ricoeur, *La Critique et la conviction* (Paris: Calmann-Lévy, 1995), p. 221: 'Hasard transformé en destin par un choix continu', from *Soi-même comme un autre* (Paris: Seuil, 1990); (ET) *Oneself as Another*, trans. Kathleen Blarney (Chicago: Chicago University Press, 1992).

[164] Henri Blocher, *Original Sin: Illuminating the Riddle* (Leicester: Apollos, 1997), p. 59.

[165] Georges Bataille, *Theory of Religion* (ET, New York: Zone, 1989), pp. 84f.

[166] Ricoeur, *Oneself as Another*, p. 25.

[167] In Richard J. Bernstein, *Introduction to Habermas and Modernity* (Oxford: Blackwell, 1985), pp. 15–16: 'Although, certainly, Marcuse was not an affirmative thinker, he was nevertheless the most affirmative among those who praised negativity ... Marcuse did not, in contrast to Adorno, only encircle the ineffable; he made appeals to future alternatives.'

[168] In J. Habermas, *The Philosophical Discourse of Modernity* (Cambridge: Polity, 1987), pp. 238–293.

[169] In J. Habermas, *Communication and the Evolution of Society* (Boston: MIT Press, 1979), p. 117; cited in Bernstein, *Introduction to Habermas and Modernity*, p. 20.

[170] H. Cox, *Religion in the Secular City: Towards a Postmodern Theology* (New York: Touchstone, 1984).

[171] Contrast here the readings of Jesus' ministry by N. T. Wright, *Jesus and the Victory of God* (London: SPCK, 1996) and Kermode, *The Genesis of Secrecy*; Arens' view lies somewhere in between, but closer to Wright's.

[172] Cf. Rolf Wiggershaus, *The Frankfurt School* (ET, Cambridge: Polity, 1994), p. 658.

[173] See Habermas, *The Philosophical Discourse of Modernity*, pp. 25–31.

[174] Ibid., p. 295.

[175] As set out by Blake and other English Romantics.

[176] Thus R. D. Williams, 'The Suspicion of Suspicion: Wittgenstein and Bonhoeffer', in R. Bell (ed.), *The Grammar of the Heart* (San Francisco: HarperCollins, 1988), pp. 36–53, esp. p. 40: 'What Wittgenstein seeks to combat in Freudianism is the flight from particularity and the endlessness of difference (concrete detail) and the inexhaustibility of social converse,

the flight that for him represents the bondage of European thought to an epistemological problematic that remains obstinately dualist and so obstinately discontented with finitude.'

177 F. Kerr, 'What's wrong with realism anyway?', in C. Crowder (ed.), *God and Reality: Essays on Christian Non-Realism* (New York: Continuum/Mowbray, 1996), p. 142; see also pp. 128–143.

178 Rowan Williams, 'Doctrinal Criticism: Some Questions', in Sarah Coakley and David Pailin (eds.), *The Making and Remaking of Christian Doctrine: Essays in Honour of Maurice Wiles* (Oxford: Clarendon Press, 1993), pp. 260–261; see also pp. 239–264.

179 S. Kierkegaard, *The Sickness unto Death*, ed. and trans. by H. V. Hong and E. H. Hong (Princeton: Princeton University Press, 1980), pp. 96f. Hegel is one who likes to stand outside Christianity and understand it as a whole, as an object. Kierkegaard advises that theologians should stick to seeing their faith as a mystery.

180 Ibid., p. 112. Interestingly, Kierkegaard does not refer explicitly to 2 Corinthians 7:10–11 (Paul's distinction between godly and ungoldy sorrow).

181 Ibid., p. 122.

182 K. Flanagan, *The Enchantment of Sociology* (London: MacMillan, 1996), p. xi.

183 R. D. Williams, 'Between Politics and Metaphysics: Reflections in the wake of Gillian Rose', *Modern Theology* 11 (1995), 3–23, p. 7.

184 Ibid., p. 11.

185 J. Derrida, *The Gift of Death*, trans. D. Willis (Chicago: University of Chicago Press, 1995), p. 78.

186 I think that David Lehman is less than even-handed in his treatment of Derrida's response to the 'de Man case' (*Signs of the Times: Deconstruction and the Fall of Paul de Man* [London: Poseidon Press, 1991], pp. 252–258).

187 Graham Ward ('Divinity and Sexuality: Luce Irigaray and Christology', *Modern Theology* 12 [1996], pp. 221–237) comments about Irigaray that she implies that God's inner-trinitarian *agape* becomes sexualized in that it draws us erotically. Christ was singly the more able to attract men and women (or at least not to be closed off to them). And he, paraphrasing Irigaray, says something worth hearing about the person of Christ: 'Only where there is space, where there is distance, where there is difference can there be love which desires, which draws, which incorporates ... Desire is built then into the substructure of creation' (pp. 228–229). This space for others means also that Christ himself as human was not overwhelmed by

the Divine Subject (the old Chalcedonian understanding is, says Ward, very
Hegelian, in that the other gets taken over), but is set free (but that sounds
very Heideggerian!). Whether backed up by Maximus the Confessor or
anyone else with theological credentials, Ward seems to put too much of a
burden on *creation*: it is another way of saying that God draws us; it is a
natural theology which perhaps does not arrive at conversion. If the will of
people in the West at the end of the second millennium were turned
towards God anyway, that would be a helpful corrective: postmodern
theology seems a reaction to theology of decision (liberal or evangelical)
which seems hopelessly voluntaristic.

[188] G. Ward, *Theology and Contemporary Critical Theory* (London: Macmillan, 1986).

[189] Hélène Cixous, *Three Steps on the Ladder of Writing: The Wellek Lectures at the
University of California, Irvine* (Columbia, NY: Columbia University Press,
1993), p. 6. Cf. Roland Barthes' treatment of Jacob's ladder in Genesis 28
in his celebrated 'Wrestling with the angel: Textual analysis of Genesis
32:23–33', in *The Semiotic Challenge* (New York: Hill and Wang, 1988),
pp. 246–260.

[190] Cixous, *Three Steps on the Ladder of Writing*, p. 19.

[191] Ibid., p. 10. The 'postmodern' pathos in describing the passive victim that
is oneself is echoed in the recurring phrase in Franz Kafka's *Metamorphosis/
Die Verwandlung*: 'poor little legs'.

[192] Ibid., p. 116. With a play on the French *l'immonde*. These types of things
are ones which 'have never made themselves beautiful, and have stayed
just as they were when they were created' (Clarice Lispector, *The Passion
according to G.H.* [ET, Minneapolis: University of Minnesota Press, 1988),
pp. 64–65. With a logic that perhaps can be called 'rabbinic', Cixous
comments, 'The monde, the world, that is so-called clean. The world that
is on the good side of the law, that is "proper", the world of order. The
moment you cross the line the law has drawn by wording, verb(aliz)ing,
you are supposed to be out of the world. You no longer belong to the
world. Out there we shall be in the company of swans, storks and griffins
... As Clarice says, with a stroke of genius, the point for Those Bible is
that joy, jubilation, birds are forbidden because they are root.'

[193] Cixous, *Three Steps on the Ladder of Writing*, p. 130: 'Perhaps it isn't matter we
dislike, perhaps it's *anonymity*. The anonymity to which we are "destined" –
the loss of name – is what we repress at any price.'

[194] Ibid., p. 47: 'And you, what have you immured? What is your story?' Cf.
also pp. 66ff.: 'The Bible, like the dream always brings us the violent sense

of generations ... I was especially delighted by the crowd of *descending* angels ... '

'Rereading I liked the fact that God is in the dream. He is not outside the dream.' But note that Cixous' criterion for reading is that which interests her most. In one sense, that of Kafka's positive statement (culled from his correspondance of all things), that books should cut us open, is fine, but the negative implication, that that which does not *interest* or *change* us is not worth our attention, is more questionable.

[195] Ibid., p. 48: 'Meeting a dog you suddenly see the abyss of love. Such limitless love doesn't fit our economy. We cannot cope with such an open, superhuman relation.' Thus in her *Messie*, she speaks of Tobit's cat and of Abraham's donkey.

[196] See ibid., pp. 154f.

[197] As von Balthasar reminds us.

[198] See Christopher Lasch, *The Minimal Self: Psychic Survival in Troubled Times* (New York: Norton, 1984).

[199] There are hopeful signs in the form of Gerard Loughlin, *Telling God's Story* (Cambridge: Cambridge University Press, 1995); also see his 'At the end of the world: Postmodernism and Theology', in Andrew Walker (ed.), *Different Gospels* (London: SPCK, 1993), pp. 204–221. Responses in the area of Christian readings of literature can be found, notably in the work of Valentine Cunningham.

[200] Biblical references: 1 Corinthians 14:20–25; 2 Corinthians 10:5.

This edition © Mark Elliott, 2003.